The Miles Kelly Book of
QUESTIONS & ANSWERS

First published by Bardfield Press in 2006
Copyright © Miles Kelly Publishing Ltd 2006

Bardfield Press is an imprint of
Miles Kelly Publishing Ltd
Bardfield Centre, Great Bardfield, Essex, CM7 4SL

Some of this material first appeared in *Question & Answer Encyclopedia*

2 4 6 8 10 9 7 5 3 1

Editorial Director Belinda Gallagher
Art Director Jo Brewer
Editors Rosalind McGuire, Teri Putnam
Editorial Assistant Bethanie Bourne
Designers Candice Bekir, Jo Brewer, Michelle Cannatella,
John Christopher, Louisa Leitao, Debbie Meekcoms
Cover Design Jo Brewer
Picture Research Manager Liberty Newton
Picture Research Laura Faulder
Indexer Diana LeCore
Scanning and Reprographics Anthony Cambray, Mike Coupe,
Stephan Davies, Ian Paulyn

ISBN 1-84236-691-2
ISBN 978-1-84236-691-2

Printed in China

British Library Cataloguing-in-Publication Data
A catalogue record for this book is available from the British Library

ACKNOWLEDGEMENTS
All artworks are from the Miles Kelly artwork bank

The publishers wish to thank the following sources for the photographs used in this book:
Norbert Schaefer/CORBIS p221 (b/l); Sony Computer Entertainment p187 (t/r); Warren Morgan/CORBIS p232 (b/l);
Nik Wheeler/CORBIS p232 (t/r); Joel Saget/AFP/GETTY IMAGES p328 (b)

All other photographs are from:
Castrol, CMCD, Corbis, Corel, Digitalvision, John Foxx, ILN, NASA, Photoalto, PhotoDisc, STOCKBYTE

www.mileskelly.net
info@mileskelly.net

The Miles Kelly Book of

QUESTIONS & ANSWERS

BARDFIELD
PRESS

THE UNIVERSE   14

PLANET EARTH

DINOSAURS

THE NATURAL WORLD 122

SCIENCE & TECHNOLOGY 158

THE HUMAN BODY 194

AROUND THE WORLD 230

WORLD WONDERS 266

ARTS, SPORTS & ENTERTAINMENT

THE UNIVERSE

The Universe is everything that we can ever know – all of space and all of time. It is about 15 billion years old, and it is almost entirely empty, with small clusters of matter and energy. The Big Bang explosion is how scientists think the Universe began, and no one is able to explain yet what might have come before it.

Why is Mars called the red planet?

What is the biggest object in the Universe?

How does a solar eclipse happen?

The Universe is where we live – all the stars we can see, and billions more besides. Scientists think the early Universe was very small, but still contained all the matter and all the energy there is today. And, to make it more amazing, scientists also think the original Universe lasted for less time than it takes to blink your eye. Then it began to grow. They call this theory the 'Big Bang'.

When did the Universe begin?

Many scientists believe that the Universe began between 13 and 18 billion years ago but no one is quite sure exactly when. What was there before remains a mystery. Some scientists think our Universe began as a 'bubble', which split off from another universe! Others think that in the beginning, all the matter in the Universe was squeezed into a tiny, incredibly hot, incredibly massive ball. When the ball began to get bigger, like a balloon being blown up, all the matter in the Universe started to explode outwards.

What holds things in place in space?

All the matter in the Universe – stars, planets, clouds of gas, tiny particles of dust – is held together by four invisible forces. These forces are gravity, electromagnetism, and two forms of nuclear force, strong and weak, which hold the particles of every atom together. Gravity is the attraction between all matter in the Universe. It keeps the Moon in orbit around the Earth, and the Earth in orbit around the Sun. The more matter a body has, the stronger its 'pull' on other bodies.

⊙ *This is the Horsehead Nebula, one of many 'star factories' in space where new stars are born.*

What is the fastest thing in the Universe?

Nothing in the Universe travels faster than light. Light is given off by stars, such as our Sun, and it travels through space at roughly 300,000 km/sec. Yet because the Universe is so large, even at this speed, light from the Sun takes more than eight minutes to reach us on Earth.

Is the Universe getting bigger?

Yes. Scientists can tell that groups of stars, known as galaxies, appear to be moving away from us. The galaxies themselves are not moving, but the space between them is stretching. By measuring how fast this distance is increasing, scientists can work out how long it has taken for everything to get where it is now. So they have a rough idea when the Big Bang set everything off.

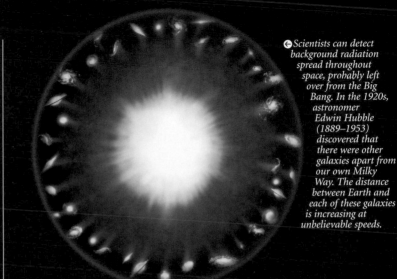

⊖ Scientists can detect background radiation spread throughout space, probably left over from the Big Bang. In the 1920s, astronomer Edwin Hubble (1889–1953) discovered that there were other galaxies apart from our own Milky Way. The distance between Earth and each of these galaxies is increasing at unbelievable speeds.

⊖ Scientists have calculated that the hot ball before the Big Bang must have swelled at a much faster rate than even the speed of light. The hot ball would have grown to the size of a galaxy within a fraction of a second!

Is space empty?

Not really. Matter was created almost as soon as the Universe began. Space is littered with stars and gas clouds, made almost entirely of two elements: the gases hydrogen and helium. There are other elements too, such as iron, carbon and oxygen, but these are rare. The space between stars and planets is full of bits of space debris, including very tiny specks of dust and larger pieces of rock. Some of this space-dust forms clouds, called nebulae. These vast clouds of matter are the 'factories' inside which new stars and planets are made.

⊕ Galaxies are giant groups of up to trillions of stars, and there may be as many as 20 trillion galaxies in the Universe.

A star is a massive ball of hot hydrogen gas. To people on Earth, a star looks like a tiny pinpoint of light in the night sky. Stars look small because they are so far away. In fact, many stars are enormous, many times bigger than our Sun – our nearest star. The Sun glows fiercely because it is a star that is still hot and active. That is why we see it shining in the sky.

Binary system with one star larger than the other

➡ *Stars are born inside vast gas clouds. Some old stars die as exploding supernovae. Others swell up and become giants, which then fade and dim.*

True binary stars orbit the same centre of gravity together

⬆ *About half the stars in our own galaxy are binary stars. They orbit around the same point, or centre of gravity.*

What are twin stars?

Some stars, like our Sun, are alone in space, but others, called binary stars, have companions or twins, which are held together by gravity. Eclipsing twin stars appear to 'dance' around each other in space. Binary stars move faster the closer together they are, but some may be so far apart that they take millions of years to orbit one another. When one star is hidden behind the other, its light is dimmed. When the star reappears, the pair of dancing stars shine brightly once more.

Where is a star born?

Stars are born inside giant dust and gas clouds called nebulae. There are nebulae in every galaxy across the Universe. Nebulae are 'star factories', as clouds of dust and gas shrink under the pull of gravity, the mass of matter becomes immensely hot and begins to give off energy as light and heat. A new star starts to shine.

1 A star is born when nuclear reactions begin

2 A star burns steadily

4 A nebula formed from cloud and dust

3 Dust swirling around a new star may form planets

Are all stars the same size?

No, they vary in size and heat. Our Sun is a medium-sized hot yellow star. The biggest stars are called supergiants and there are many supergiant stars that are hundreds of times bigger than our Sun.

⊙ *This is a globular star cluster, made up of millions of stars of different ages and sizes.*

How long do stars last?

A star's lifetime may be up to millions of years. During their lives, stars burn up energy, sending out light and heat. Some grow into blue giants and explode as supernovae. Other smaller stars swell up as their fuel starts to run out and become vast glowing red giants. They then shrink into white dwarfs, which are very small, tightly compressed stars. White dwarfs are so small that they are hard to detect in the sky. The surface of a white dwarf can reach 8,000°C.

➲ *A cluster of ancient stars, or stellar swarm, is one of 147 such clusters in our galaxy. Every star in this cluster is older than our Sun.*

Where does a star get its energy from?

A star's energy comes from nuclear fusion, in which most of the hydrogen changes to helium, but enough hydrogen is left over to produce huge amounts of energy. The light from stars streams out across space in a range of colours (blue, orange-red, yellow and white).

⊙ *A star can shine for millions of years before it swells up to become a red giant, then shrinks to a small white dwarf.*

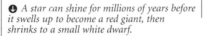

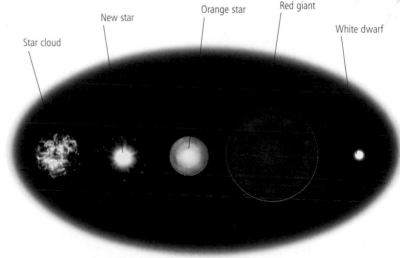

Star cloud

New star

Orange star

Red giant

White dwarf

There are 88 'star patterns' visible in the night sky. These are the constellations. When the first astronomers in ancient Babylonia, Egypt, China and Greece began looking at the stars, they saw patterns and shapes, formed by stars that appear close together in the sky. They named each constellation after an animal or a character from myth and legend – such as Taurus (the bull) and Perseus (a Greek hero). Later, more constellations were discovered and given names, such as Telescopium (the telescope).

When did people first see constellations?

Many constellations were first seen by astronomers living in China and Babylon more than 2,000 years ago. Stars fascinated early scientists, but the scientists had no telescopes, so could only name the star-groups that they could see with the unaided eye. Constellations are all different shapes and sizes, and it is not always easy to recognize the animal or object they are named after without a drawing showing an outline around the stars. Some star-groups have more than one name. The ancient Greeks, called Orion the Hunter, but the ancient Egyptians called it the god Osiris.

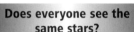

Does everyone see the same stars?

No. Different constellations can be seen in the Southern Hemisphere (south of the Equator) and in the Northern Hemisphere (north of the Equator). Many of the constellations were named before 2000 BC by astronomers in Babylonia. By AD 150, the Greek scientist Ptolemy was able to list 48. No new ones were added until European explorers sailed to the Southern Hemisphere and saw stars that are invisible to people in the Northern Hemisphere. Constellations are not easy to pick out because the night sky looks so crowded with stars. It helps to concentrate on the brightest stars.

◐ *This is Ursa Major, the Great Bear, a constellation in the Northern Hemisphere. Its other names include the Plough and the Big Dipper.*

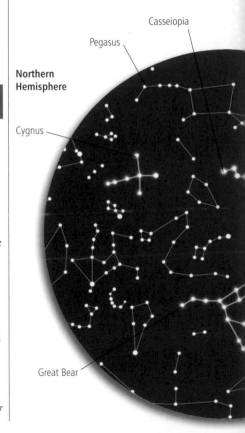

◑ ◐ *The star-groups seen in the Northern Hemisphere (below) are not the same as those seen south of the Equator, in the Southern Hemisphere (right). Stars are best seen on a clear, moonless night away from the glare of city lights.*

Northern Hemisphere

Casseiopia

Pegasus

Cygnus

Great Bear

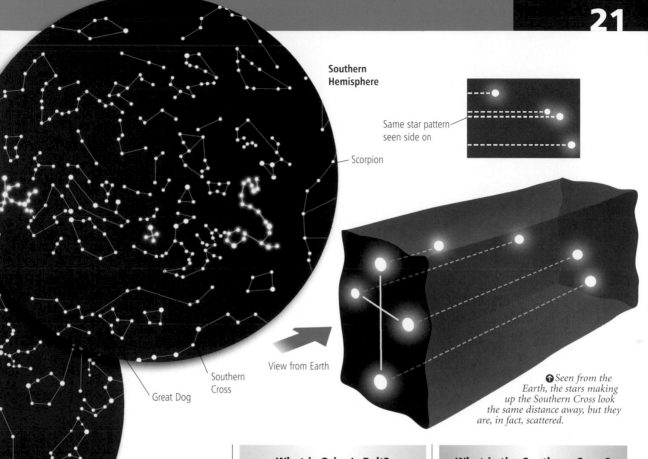

Southern Hemisphere

Same star pattern seen side on

Scorpion

Great Dog

Southern Cross

View from Earth

⊙ *Seen from the Earth, the stars making up the Southern Cross look the same distance away, but they are, in fact, scattered.*

What is Orion's Belt?

Orion's Belt is the name given to three bright stars in the constellation Orion (the Hunter). Orion can be seen from anywhere on Earth and because it is bright and easily seen, it makes a good star-guide. The Belt points in one direction to the star, Aldebaran, and in the other to the star, Sirius.

What is the Southern Cross?

The Southern Cross is the smallest of the constellations, but is well known because its stars are so bright. Some constellations contain very few bright stars and so are hard to see. Hydra, the Water Snake is the biggest constellation, but it is very dim and so incredibly difficult to spot.

A galaxy is a vast group of stars, like a stellar city, which can contain as many as a trillion stars. Galaxies are found in clusters, some with fewer than 50 galaxies, others with hundreds. There are many millions of galaxies, each of which began as a cloud of gas when the Universe was formed and new stars are still being born inside them. As the Universe expands, the galaxies fly apart.

Do all galaxies look the same?

No. The main shapes are spirals, ovals and irregular. Two kinds of galaxy look like whirling spirals with 'arms'. Spiral galaxies either have several arms of stars around a central core or, like our Milky Way galaxy, have arms that start from bars – this is a 'barred spiral'. Elliptical galaxies are oval or egg-shaped. Irregular galaxies have no set shape. Elliptical galaxies send out stars in all directions, like sparks from a huge firework.

➲ Hubble proved that the Universe was much larger than anyone had believed, by discovering that there are many other galaxies.

Who realized there is more than one galaxy?

American astronomer Edwin Hubble first realized there was more than one galaxy in 1924. Until then, people thought there was just one mass of stars – making one very big galaxy. Hubble detected a winking variable star beyond the Milky Way. He realized that the Andromeda Nebula he was studying was not a gas cloud within our Milky Way galaxy, but was in fact another galaxy. All the stars that we can see with the unaided eye belong to our galaxy, but there are millions more beyond it.

➋ The four main kinds of galaxies are spiral, irregular, elliptical and barred spiral.

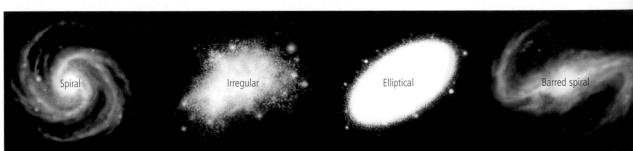

Spiral Irregular Elliptical Barred spiral

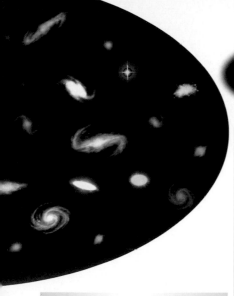

The Milky Way spins extremely quickly, moving the Sun and all the stars in it at up to 100 million km/h.

Which galaxy do we live in?

Our galaxy is the Milky Way. There are about 200,000 million stars in the Milky Way galaxy, and one of them is our Sun. The Sun is moving around the galaxy, but in the last 200 million years it has only done this once as the galaxy is so big.

What is dark matter?

Galaxies look like bright clouds of starry matter, but around them is a swirling mass of invisible 'dark matter'. Astronomers believe that nine-tenths of all the matter in the Universe is dark and know about the existence of it because its gravity pulls on stars and galaxies in the Universe. Dark matter could be the remains of ordinary matter, such as stars, which burnt out early in the life of the Universe.

This is an irregular galaxy, In ten days in 1995, the Hubble Space Telescope took photographs of almost 2,000 galaxies in one small area of sky.

How big are galaxies?

Unbelievably vast. Even travelling at light-speed, a spacecraft would take 100,000 years to cross the Milky Way. A very ordinary galaxy contains a million stars, while the super-galaxies are giants with as many as a billion stars.

Our galaxy is amazingly big: two billion stars, 100,000 light-years across. But it is just one of millions of similar galaxies. As well as stars, there are other faraway objects in space: black holes, supernovae, nebulae and quasars. No one knows how many galaxies there are, all speeding away from us. The Big Bang expansion may go on forever. Or the Universe may slow down and contract, like a deflating balloon – a theory that scientists call the 'Big Crunch'.

What is the biggest object in the Universe?

The most gigantic object detected so far is a wall of galaxies, appropriately called the Great Wall. This stretch of stars is 500 million light-years long and 16 million light-years wide. However, size does not really matter in the Universe, because there are such a lot of giants out there.

Why did scientists put a telescope into space?

The Earth's atmosphere obscures our view of the stars, so the Hubble Space Telescope was launched in 1990 from the space shuttle, to give scientists a clearer view of space. It now circles in an orbit high above the Earth, where the view is unobscured. Hubble gave scientists their first unhazy view of the stars, and even though at first the telescope did not work as planned (it had to be repaired by astronauts), the results were astounding.

The Great Wall is a vast string of galaxies, like this spiral galaxy (photographed from the Hubble Space Telescope).

The Hubble Space Telescope weighs 11 tonnes and has a mirror 2.5 m across. When first launched in 1990, the mirror was the wrong shape and a replacement had to be taken up in 1994.

⊕ *Quasars send out vast amount of energy, in the form of radiation such as light, X-rays and radio waves. Studying these objects helps astronomers discover more about the early Universe, since the radiation from a quasar probably left it billions of years ago.*

What are the most distant objects?

Quasars, which look like stars, but actually are not. A quasar is much smaller than a galaxy (a mere light-year or two across), but up to a thousand times brighter. Quasars give off radio waves and would be invisible if they were not so incredibly luminous. Quasars are at least 10–13 billion light-years away from Earth, making them the most distant objects in the Universe.

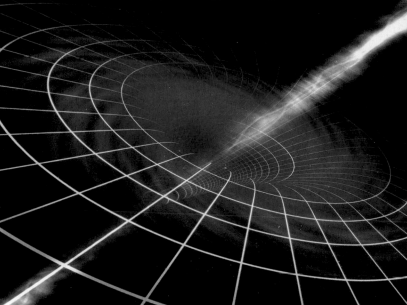

⊕ *This is an artist's impression of a black hole. Black holes suck up any type of matter. Some scientists think there may be a black hole at the heart of every galaxy.*

What is a supernova?

A supernova is a vast explosion of light, brighter than millions of suns, that happens when an old giant star collapses into itself. The collapse sets off a nuclear reaction and the explosion can be seen far across the Universe. In 1987, a supernova was visible from the Earth – a rare event.

⊙ *When a supernova explodes, star-debris is flung far out into space.*

What goes into a black hole?

Anything within reach. Nothing that goes into a black hole can come out. A black hole is all that is left of a collapsed star. It is invisible because it has such a strong gravitational pull that no matter and no light can escape from it. A black hole sucks up vast amounts of matter into an incredibly tiny space. To travel through interstellar space (between galaxies), astronauts in the future may have to use 'wormholes' – cosmic tunnels, which avoid black holes – if such tunnels exist.

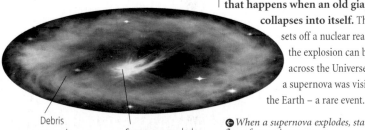

Debris expands

Supernova explodes

Space missions involve travelling vast distances, either around or away from the Earth. To send people into space costs a lot of money and effort. So far, the only way to get into space is by using a big rocket. Rockets have sent people to the Moon and probes to the planets. Astronauts live and work in space stations, which orbit the Earth. For exploring the distant planets, a robot probe is best: it needs no air, water or food – and it never gets bored!

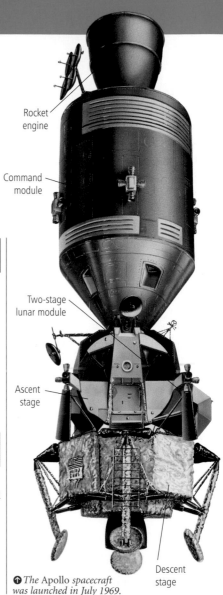

Rocket engine

Command module

Two-stage lunar module

Ascent stage

Descent stage

⊕ The Apollo *spacecraft was launched in July 1969.*

⊕ *The US Pathfinder landed on Mars with the roving vehicle* Sojourner. *The rover stopped working after three months on Mars.*

What makes rockets the best engines for space flight?

A rocket needs no air (unlike a jet engine) – indeed, air slows it down. Most rocket engines get their thrust from the reaction between a fuel, such as liquid hydrogen, and an oxidant (liquid oxygen), which allows the fuel to burn.

How many people have stood on the Moon?

Since the astronauts of *Apollo 11* first landed on the Moon in 1969, a total of 12 astronauts have stood on the Moon. From 1969 to 1972, the Americans sent seven Apollo missions to the Moon. One mission, *Apollo 13*, failed to land but returned safely after an explosion on board. The other six missions each landed two astronauts.

When did scientists land craft on the planet Mars?

Two US *Viking* spacecraft visited Mars in 1970–76. The craft orbited the planet and robot landers took samples of the soil and sent data and TV pictures back to Earth. In 1997, the US *Pathfinder* craft landed a rover called *Sojourner*, and in 2004 the US *Express Orbiter* craft sent two rovers to different sides of Mars to explore the surface.

Why do astronauts float in space?

Once in orbit, a spacecraft and the people inside it are freed from the full effects of Earth's gravity and so they feel weightless. Anything inside the spacecraft that is not fixed in place floats about. This takes a bit of getting used to, but most astronauts enjoy the experience of weightlessness. Exercises must be done to keep their muscles and bones in good shape.

An astronaut wearing a MMU (manned manoeuvring unit) can move safely about outside the spacecraft.

The Shuttle is lifted off the launch pad by the thrust of its three main engines and two booster rockets. It must reach a speed of 28,000 km/h to be able to go into orbit and not fall back down to Earth.

How is a spacecraft launched?

There are two kinds of launch systems for spacecraft: multi-stage rockets and reusable shuttles. The American space shuttle began its missions into orbit in 1981. It is launched with the aid of two solid-fuel rocket boosters, which fall off after two minutes and fall to the ground to be reused. After eight and a half minutes, the main fuel tank also drops away and the shuttle flies into orbit. On its return, the shuttle glows red-hot due to friction as it re-enters the atmosphere. It uses its wings to glide down to land.

Which spacecraft first explored the giant planets?

The US probe *Pioneer 11*, launched in 1973, flew past Jupiter and then on to Saturn in 1979 before heading out towards the edge of the Solar System. A later US space probe called *Voyager 2* flew past Jupiter in 1979, Uranus in 1986 and Neptune in 1989. The *Galileo* spacecraft visited Jupiter in 1995. Some long-range probes will probably go on travelling through space for ever, far beyond the Solar System.

The astronomers of the ancient world had no telescopes, but had to rely on their eyes to observe the stars, and on mathematics to try and make sense of what they could see. They named five of the nine planets and gave names to many stars. The use of the telescope in the 1600s revolutionized the science of star-gazing. For the first time, scientists could see details such as the craters on the Moon.

Why are telescopes put on mountain peaks?

Optical telescopes need a clear view of the night sky but the air above cities is just too 'fogged up' by air pollution, heat, gases and bright lights. Therefore telescopes are sited in observatories on high mountain peaks, where the air is thinner and clearer. Stars are best viewed from space.

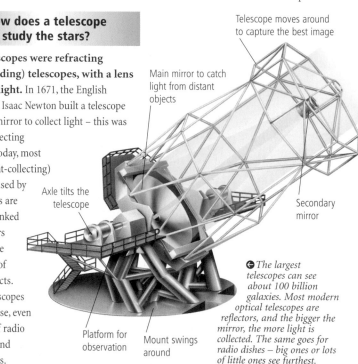

⬆ *Astronomers use large telescopes like this one, located at the Kitt Peak National Observatory in Arizona, USA, to study the night sky. With such powerful lenses, experts are able to see and study stars that are too far away for us to see with the naked eye.*

How does a telescope study the stars?

Early telescopes were refracting (light-bending) telescopes, with a lens to collect light. In 1671, the English scientist Sir Isaac Newton built a telescope that had a mirror to collect light – this was the first reflecting telescope. Today, most optical (light-collecting) telescopes used by astronomers are reflectors, linked to computers that enhance the images of distant objects. Optical telescopes are still in use, even in the era of radio telescopes and space probes.

Telescope moves around to capture the best image

Main mirror to catch light from distant objects

Axle tilts the telescope

Secondary mirror

Platform for observation

Mount swings around

⬅ *The largest telescopes can see about 100 billion galaxies. Most modern optical telescopes are reflectors, and the bigger the mirror, the more light is collected. The same goes for radio dishes – big ones or lots of little ones see furthest.*

Who made the first catalogue of the stars?

A Greek named Hipparchus, who lived over 2,000 years ago. He was the first to notice that stars change their position in the night sky (this is called the precession of the equinoxes). Hipparchus made a list of the stars, showing their brightness and position. Hipparchus' writings about astronomy were lost, but his ideas were preserved by later astronomers such as Ptolemy.

Hipparchus recorded the stars he could see with the naked eye – he had no telescope.

What do radio telescopes detect?

Radio telescopes do not collect light, but pick up different forms of radiation (rays) from stars, such as radio waves and X-rays. Such telescopes can detect these rays, invisible to the eye, which can reveal, for example, the magnetic field around a planet or allow us to see through clouds of space dust.

Radio telescopes have large dish antennae to collect rays reaching the Earth from distant space objects. Radio telescopes are linked to an array of other dishes, which together provide a clearer picture of space.

Who first looked into space through a telescope?

The first scientist to use a telescope or 'spyglass' to look at the heavens was the Italian Galileo Galilei about 1609. With a telescope he had made himself, he saw four moons circling the planet Jupiter and also got the first close-up view of the craters on the Moon.

Galileo made his own telescope. What he saw astonished scientists of the day.

The Sun is the centre of the Solar System. It is a star like the millions of other stars in the Universe. It is the 'offspring' of an older, bigger star, which, after it blew up, left clouds of gas behind. The Sun is a nuclear furnace inside, which hydrogen atoms are turned into helium – crushed by the enormous pressures. During this nuclear reaction, vast amounts of energy are created.

What makes the Sun an unusual star?

Only the fact that it is nearer to us than any other star – only 150 million km away. In all other respects, the Sun is a very ordinary star. It is middle-sized and middle-aged. But without the Sun, the Earth would be a dark, cold, lifeless world. You should never look at the Sun directly as its intense brightness could damage your eyes.

What is inside the Sun?

The Sun is not solid, but a very dense mass of gas. It has an outer surface called the photosphere and an inner layer known as the convection zone, and below that is the hottest part of the Sun – the centre or core, where the nuclear reactions take place. Energy moves from the core, through the many layers, such as the chromosphere and photosphere, to reach the surface and out into space. Without solar energy, the Earth would be lifeless.

The chromosphere is a layer of gas. Bursts of heat-light energy called spicules flame through it

The Sun's outer 'skin' is the corona, a halo-like layer of boiled-off gases

➔ *This cutaway of the Sun shows its different parts. The energy that is created inside the core takes ten million years to pass through its many layers and reach the surface.*

Giant tongues of hot gas, known as prominences, burst out from the chromosphere.

The photosphere is a mass of hot gas, radiating heat and light into space

Radiating zone

The core of the Sun reaches 15 million°C

➔ *Sunspots look darker because they are cooler than the rest of the Sun's surface.*

Why does the Sun have spots?

The photosphere or surface of the Sun is covered in dark blotches – sunspots – which are caused by changes in the Sun's magnetic field. They can be up to thousands of kilometres across. The number of sunspots we see varies from anything up to 100, over an 11-year cycle.

What are solar flares?

There are sometimes storms on the Sun, which send bursts of hot gas, called solar flares, into space. They shoot out light, heat and cosmic rays far beyond the Sun's atmosphere or chromosphere, and can break up radio communications on Earth.

What happens during a solar eclipse?

A solar eclipse occurs when the Moon blocks out light from the Sun, causing a shadow to pass across the Earth. Usually, most places on Earth see only a partial eclipse, but when the disc of the Moon blots out the Sun completely, day turns to night for about seven minutes. The Sun's corona can then be seen from Earth.

➔ *Solar flares contain vast bursts of energy and coil out 100,000 km into space.*

The Earth is the planet we know best, but the first time we got a complete view of it was in 1968, when the *Apollo 8* astronauts flew around the Moon and saw the Earth floating in space. The Earth is just one of nine planets orbiting the Sun, all held in place by the Sun's massive gravity pull. Our world is a rocky ball, not quite round, with a belt of air around it like a protective blanket.

1 Dust and gas

2 Fiery Earth cools. Surface forms a crust

3 Gases and water vapour form the atmosphere

How was the Earth formed?

Scientists believe that the Earth began as a cloud of gas and dust, whirling around a new star – the Sun – before gravity forced the gas and dust together into a red-hot ball. Over millions of years it cooled and a rocky crust began to form. An atmosphere was formed from poisonous gases, such as methane, hydrogen and ammonia, which had risen from volcanoes on the surface of the Earth. Over billions of years, water vapour fell as rain from the clouds and the oceans began to form inside basins in the Earth's crust. The remaining landmasses formed the continents.

➲ *It took about 4.5 billion years for the Earth to form as it is now.*

➲ *In the early stages of the Earth's formation lumps of rock called planetesimals formed from dust whirling around the Sun. Pulled together by their gravity, the planetesimals then formed the Earth and other planets.*

What does the Earth look like from space?

It is a beautiful blue-and-white globe, with patches of green and brown. Until about 500 years ago, most people were taught to believe that the Earth was flat. It is, in fact, round, though not a perfect sphere. It has a bulge around its centre, the Equator, and the poles are slightly flattened.

4 Oceans and landmasses are formed

North Pole

As the Earth tilts on its axis and spins around the Sun, the Sun warms different parts of the planet.

Why do we have seasons?

As the Earth moves around the Sun, different parts of the Earth get more or less light and warmth from the Sun, making the different seasons. The Earth spins on its own axis (an imaginary line through the planet from pole to pole) and is tilted 23° out of vertical. The closer one side gets to the Sun the warmer it is and is therefore summer – less warmth means winter, in-between are spring and autumn.

South Pole

Spring

Summer

Sun

Autumn

Winter

How long is a year?

A year is the time it takes the Earth to travel around the Sun once. It takes 365.24 days to travel the 938,886,400 km distance to orbit the Sun. So that is the length of a year on the Earth. Years on other planets are longer or shorter, depending on how long they each take to orbit the Sun.

What makes the Earth unique?

As far as we know, no other planet in our Solar System has life, so the Earth is unique in that life exists on it. The Sun may be an ordinary kind of star, but the third planet out from the Sun (Earth) is unique. The Earth is neither so hot that water boils nor so cold that it freezes. It has an atmosphere containing oxygen. With water and oxygen, life was able to begin and thrive.

Three-quarters of the Earth is covered by ocean. From space the Earth looks watery and blue, with swirls of cloud and the brown-green landmasses of the continents.

The Moon is the Earth's only satellite. Other planets have many more moons. Our Moon is the closest body to us in space, and has always fascinated people. Like the Sun, the Moon was thought by some ancient peoples to be a god. The Moon was probably hot when young, with volcanoes, but it has cooled down much faster than the Earth. It has also lost whatever atmosphere it may once have had.

⊙ *People once thought the flat areas of the Moon were seas or dried-up seabeds. They gave them the Latin name* mare *(sea). They are in fact plains of very old volcanic lava.*

The near side of the Moon, pock-marked with craters

How old is the Moon?

The Moon may be a little younger than the Earth, perhaps 4.5 billion years old. One theory about its birth is that a rocky mini-planet smashed into the Earth. Bits of rock from the collision were hurled into space and came together to form the Moon, which was then trapped in orbit by Earth's gravity.

⊙ *The Moon may have been formed when a smaller, newly-formed planet collided with the Earth early on in the formation of the Solar System.*

Can we see all the Moon from Earth?

No. The Moon orbits the Earth in the same time (27.3 days) as it takes for it to rotate once on its axis. This oddity keeps one side always facing away from us. Until the *Apollo 9* spacecraft flew around the Moon in 1968, no one had ever seen the far side, which actually turned out to look much the same as the near side.

What is it like on the Moon?

The Moon is very quiet and very still. It has no atmosphere, so there is no wind. It has no surface water either. The surface is dry and dusty. There are ancient craters measuring up to 1,000 km across and mountains as high as the highest mountains on Earth, such as Mount Everest, which measures 8,863 m above sea level.

⊙ *When US astronauts raised the Stars and Stripes flag on the Moon, it had to be stiffened to 'fly' because there is no air on the Moon to move it.*

Why are there New and Full Moons?

The Moon is moving around the Earth and because one side of the Moon is always in sunlight, we see different amounts of the lit half as it moves. This means that the Moon seems to change shape during each month. These changes are known as the phases of the Moon. At New Moon, we cannot see any of the lit half. After a week, we can see about half a Moon (the Moon is waxing or getting bigger), and at Full Moon, we can see the whole lit disc. Then we see less of the Moon (it is waning) until by the last quarter, we again see only half the lit part, and finally a sliver of the 'old moon'.

What made the Moon's craters?

The craters on the Moon were created by space-rocks (meteors) smashing into it. The Moon is covered with craters, as if someone had been throwing stones into a ball of soft clay. The Moon has no atmosphere to burn up incoming space debris, and no weather to wear away the craters.

⊙ *Craters on the Moon are as well-defined as when they were first made, because the Moon has no wind or rain to smooth them away.*

⊙ *The changes from New to Full Moon and back again are called the phases of the Moon. The full cycle from New to Full and back to New again takes one month.*

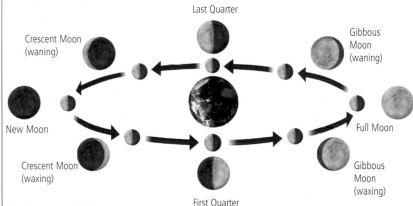

Last Quarter

Crescent Moon (waning)

Gibbous Moon (waning)

New Moon

Full Moon

Crescent Moon (waxing)

Gibbous Moon (waxing)

First Quarter

The Solar System is the name for the 'family' of planets that orbit the Sun. In addition to the planets, there are millions of much smaller bodies travelling through space around the Sun. These include minor planets or asteroids, and comets that sweep close to the Sun and then travel out far beyond the outer planets.

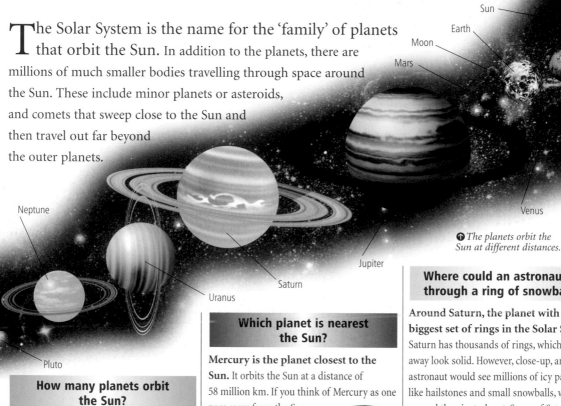

Sun

Earth

Moon

Mars

Venus

Mercury

Neptune

Jupiter

Saturn

Uranus

Pluto

⊙ *The planets orbit the Sun at different distances.*

How many planets orbit the Sun?

Nine planets orbit the Sun, including the Earth. They were formed from material which about 4,600 million years ago was spinning around the Sun. Mercury, Venus, Mars, Jupiter and Saturn can be seen with the naked eye because they shine brightly with reflected sunlight. You need a telescope to see Uranus, Neptune and tiny Pluto.

Which planet is nearest the Sun?

Mercury is the planet closest to the Sun. It orbits the Sun at a distance of 58 million km. If you think of Mercury as one pace away from the Sun, the Earth is two and a half paces away. Mercury moves very fast around the Sun. One day on Mercury is equivalent to 59 Earth days, and a year lasts only 88 Earth days.

Where could an astronaut fly through a ring of snowballs?

Around Saturn, the planet with the biggest set of rings in the Solar System. Saturn has thousands of rings, which from far away look solid. However, close-up, an astronaut would see millions of icy particles, like hailstones and small snowballs, whirling around the giant planet. Some of Saturn's smaller moons hurtle around near the edge of the rings – these have been called shepherd moons because, like sheepdogs chasing sheep, they seem to be keeping the smaller particles in their orbits.

◐ *Twice during its orbit, Mercury gets very close to the Sun and speeds up so much that the Sun seems to go backwards in the sky.*

What are the biggest planets made of?

The four biggest planets – Jupiter, Saturn, Uranus and Neptune – are vast balls of gas. There are two kinds of planet – rocky and gassy. Although the gassy planets are much bigger than the Earth, they are actually not very dense.

⊕ *The nine planets in our Solar System, in order from the Sun, are: Mercury, Venus, Earth, Mars, Jupiter, Saturn, Uranus, Neptune and Pluto.*

Do any other stars have planets?

It was once thought that the Solar System was unique, but scientists have discovered other stars with planets orbiting them. The distant star Upsilon Andromedae (44 light-years away) has three planets circling it. One of them is four times bigger than Jupiter. About 20 planets have been found orbiting other stars. But this is the only other Solar System spotted so far.

Which planets have been explored by spacecraft?

Robot spacecraft have been sent from the Earth to fly past Mercury, Jupiter, Saturn, Uranus and Neptune. Spacecraft have already landed on Mars and Venus, and mapped these planets from orbit. The 'easiest' planet to explore is Mars – at least its atmosphere does not crush or melt spacecraft landing on its surface.

The four inner planets, which include the Earth, are comparatively small. The other three are Mercury, Venus and Mars. We know more about them than we do about the outer planets, because exploration by spacecraft is possible, even though a journey to Mars takes six months – so planetary exploration is a very patient business.

What are the inner planets made of?

The four inner planets are made of rock and have hard surfaces. Each one has an outer crust enclosing a mantle of sticky-hot, semi-melted rock with, in the middle, a core of iron and nickel. They are also referred to as terrestrial (Earth-like) planets. Each of the four inner planets has some kind of atmosphere – a layer of gas – although Mercury has very little atmosphere to protect against the heat of its neighbour, the Sun. However the similarities with Earth and the inner planets end there.

⊙ *Robot landers have photographed the barren surface of Mars.*

Why is Mars called the red planet?

Mars looks reddish because its rocks contain a lot of iron dust. This dust has been oxidized by the carbon dioxide gas in the Martian atmosphere. This chemical reaction has in effect turned Mars rusty.

⊙ *Mars has seasons and what are probably water-containing ice-caps. Rivers may have flowed across Mars millions of years ago.*

Which planet looks most like the Moon?

Mercury is a small rocky ball with craters all over the surface. It has hardly any atmosphere – all gases except traces of vaporized sodium are boiled off by the blazing heat of the nearby Sun. Without an atmosphere to burn up incoming debris, any rock flying through space towards the planet is able to impact on the surface – smashing new holes in the surface.

⊙ *Mercury is the second smallest of the planets, and closest to the Sun.*

Could you see the stars from Venus?

No, because this planet has a thick atmosphere of poisonous gas clouds that blot out the Sun and stars. The sky looks red and the clouds are so thick that it is impossible to see the surface of Venus from Earth. Venus also has rainfall of acid and is altogether unwelcoming. No space probe landed there so far has kept working for more than an hour.

Which planet is the hottest?

Venus is the hottest – even hotter than Mercury. The temperature on Venus reaches 470°C, which is hot enough to melt some metals. Venus has an atmosphere of carbon dioxide, which traps the heat from the Sun like a blanket. It is like the 'greenhouse effect' on Earth, only worse.

Which planet spins strangely?

Venus spins in the opposite direction to Earth. Unlike Earth, which spins in an anti-clockwise direction, Venus spins clockwise. If it were not for the clouds, someone on Venus would see the Sun rise in the west, and set in the east. Venus also spins very slowly, only once every 243 Earth days. Venus is almost exactly the same size as Earth at 12,000 km across, but weighs one-fifth less.

⊙ *Venus is shrouded in clouds of sulphuric acid, which hide the surface.*

The outermost planets from the Sun include the four gas giants – Jupiter, Saturn, Uranus and Neptune. These planets are all much bigger than the Earth, yet apparently with no solid surfaces at all. Their rocky cores are buried within masses of liquid and slushy, frozen gas. The fifth outer planet, Pluto, with its companion moon Charon, is a ball of rock-hard ice.

⬆ *Jupiter spins so fast that a day on Jupiter lasts only just under ten hours. The Great Red Spot is a violent whirling storm on the planet.*

What is the biggest planet made of?

The biggest planet is Jupiter, but no spacecraft can land on it because there is no 'ground', it is just a whirling mass of gases, mostly hydrogen and helium. It spins faster than any other planet, so fast that the clouds in its atmosphere are whipped up into vast, swirling storms with winds of up to 500 km/h. The Great Red Spot visible on the surface of Jupiter is a huge storm, a giant gas-hurricane, which is as big as the size of two Earths.

Which planets have rings?

Jupiter, Saturn, Uranus and Neptune all have rings. Saturn's rings are the most brilliant, measuring 270,000 km from edge to edge. The rings are made of millions of blocks of ice whizzing around the planet. Saturn's rings can be seen from Earth through a telescope. When, in the 1980s, robot spacecraft flew close to Jupiter, Neptune and Uranus, their rings were seen for the first time.

➡ *Saturn's rings are one of the most spectacular sights in the Solar System.*

Which planet has the most satellites?

Uranus has at least 21 moons (satellites). Saturn and Jupiter each have more than 18 moons – new tiny ones are still being discovered. Four of Jupiter's moons are bigger than Pluto. The biggest moon in the Solar System is Jupiter's moon Ganymede, which measures 5,276 km across. Saturn's biggest moon Titan is only a bit smaller than Ganymede. The planets with the least moons are Earth and Pluto, which only have one each.

Which planet may have had a near-miss?

Uranus

Uranus is tilted on its side, perhaps because of a space collision that could have almost destroyed it. Scientists think that a giant asteroid may have smashed into Uranus and knocked it sideways. Miranda, one of Uranus's moons, looks as if it was blasted into chunks and then stuck back together again by gravity.

Which are the windiest planets?

Jupiter and Saturn are the windiest planets. Both spin so fast that all the gases in their atmosphere are whipped around at speeds of up to 500 km/h on Jupiter and even faster on Saturn, around 1,300 km/h – that is more than ten times faster than a hurricane on Earth!

Neptune

Which are the least known planets?

Hardly anything is known about Pluto and its moon-neighbour Charon. Both worlds are made mostly of ice with a thin nitrogen–methane atmosphere. Pictures taken by the Hubble Space Telescope show hazy markings and brighter areas around the poles. Pluto is the furthest planet from the Sun, and so takes 248 years to orbit the Sun, swinging out to a maximum 7.3 million-km distance away.

Like Earth, Pluto only has one moon – Charon, visible from the surface of the planet. Pluto is the smallest of the planets.

Uranus and Neptune have rings, too. Both these blue-green worlds are shrouded in clouds of poisonous methane gas above a freezing chemical slush surface.

Travelling through space across the Solar System are other bodies, including asteroids, meteors and comets. They provide brilliant light-shows in the night sky from time to time, and also give scientists clues to the origins of the Universe.

⊙ *Shooting stars flash across the night sky as meteors burn up in the atmosphere.*

➔ *Asteroids sometimes stray close to the Earth, but most stay within the so-called asteroid belt, further out from the Sun. Comets travel far out across the Solar System, occasionally passing by the Earth.*

What are asteroids?

Asteroids are mini-planets that orbit the Sun in a 'belt' between Mars and Jupiter. Most big asteroids look like rugged chunks of rock, with small craters blasted by collisions with smaller space-particles. The biggest asteroid is called Ceres, and is about 930 km across.

What is a shooting star?

'Shooting stars' are the glowing tails of meteors, which heat up as they enter the Earth's atmosphere. Millions of tiny lumps of metal or rock called meteoroids whizz through space, orbiting the Sun. As they hit the thick atmosphere around the Earth – about 90 km away from the Earth's surface – they heat up and for a second or two leave glowing trails behind them. They flash through the sky like brilliant firework displays.

Where is the biggest meteorite crater on Earth?

The biggest hole made by a meteorite is Meteor Crater in Arizona, USA – it is more than 1,700 m across and nearly 200 m deep. Occasionally meteors are big enough to hurtle through the atmosphere and smash into the ground. The charred rock that remains is a meteorite.

➔ *The biggest meteorites are massive chunks of rock, but few this big ever reach the ground.*

What are comets?

Comets are chunks of ice filled with dust and rock that orbit the Sun, just like planets. However, comets travel much farther out into distant space, often to the outer reaches of the Solar System, so comets can take up to thousands of years to make one orbit of the Sun. As a comet nears the Sun's heat, the ice core warms up and throws out a glowing tail that can be millions of kilometres long. It is a spectacular sight.

⊕ *Small asteroids are burnt up by the Earth's atmosphere every day. The chances of a big one colliding with us and destroying the Earth, like in this illustration, are remote.*

⊕ *Comets are Solar System wanderers, which return on schedule. This photograph of Halley's Comet was taken when it last came close to Earth in 1986. The comet comes back close to Earth, within visible range, roughly every 77 years.*

What happened when an asteroid struck the Earth?

Many scientists believe that the effects of an asteroid collison about 65 million years ago may have been responsible for wiping out the dinosaurs. An impact crater, called the Chixulub Basin in Mexico, lies partly beneath the sea and is 300 km across. It must have been made by a very large object, such as an asteroid, smashing into the Earth. Such a collision would have caused great changes to the climate, and so altered conditions for life on Earth. Every 50 million years, an asteroid measuring more than 10 km across hits the Earth.

1 How long ago is the Big Bang thought to have taken place?

2 Galaxies moved away from each other during the Big Bang. Do they still move today?

3 In which century did astronomers realize what galaxies consist of?

4 Did galaxies begin to form 3 million years, 30 million years or 300 million years after the Big Bang?

5 Stars are balls of hydrogen and which other gas?

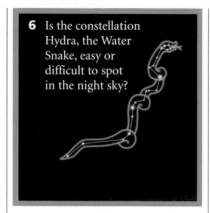

6 Is the constellation Hydra, the Water Snake, easy or difficult to spot in the night sky?

7 What kind of alphabet do astronomers use to list constellations?

8 Why do stars twinkle?

9 What do stars generate other than light?

10 How many constellations is the sky divided into?

11 Which telescopes can detect matter further away from the Earth: light telescopes or radio telescopes?

12 Are there links between stars in constellations?

13 What is the name of the galaxy that Earth is in?

FACTFILE

Light years and **parsecs**

Earth distances are measured in miles or kilometres, but these units are too small to be useful in space. Scientists measure the Universe in light-years and parsecs. Light is the fastest thing in the Universe, so by measuring in light-years scientists are able to get a better idea of such great distances. A light-year is the distance that light travels in one year – about ten million million km. A light-year is roughly 3.25 parsecs. Light from even the closest stars takes years to reach us.

The nearest star is over four light-years away, so this means that when astronomers look at it through a telescope, they are actually looking back into the past – seeing the star as it was four years ago. Light from the most distant galaxies takes about 10,000 million years to reach us.

➲ *The Universe may go on expanding for ever. Or it may eventually stop and begin collapsing in on itself to possibly start all over again.*

14 How long does it take light from the Sun to reach us on Earth?

15 If a star is 1,800 light years away do we see it as it was at 20 BC, AD 20 or AD 200?

16 Why don't astronauts float around in the spacecraft when they are asleep?

17 What did the first astronauts to land on the Moon bring back with them?

18 Who was the first astronomer to try to work out how far away the Sun is?

19 What shape is the Milky Way?

Developments in **astronomy**

Early astronomers could only see stars visible with the unaided eye. Today, scientists use light-collecting telescopes and radio dishes that pick up radio and other waves to scan and photograph the most distant objects in outer space. Scientists depend mostly on these photographs to study space.

➲ *With the help of his sister Caroline, William Herschel (1738–1822) discovered Uranus in 1781. He later identified two of the moons of Uranus and Saturn.*

➲ *Johannes Kepler (1571–1630) became the great Danish astronomer Tycho Brahe's assistant and took over his work when Brahe died.*

Amazing **Universe**

• In the first micro-seconds of the Universe, matter did not exist. There was just very hot space.

• Anti-matter is equal and opposite to matter: when the two collide, they eliminate one another.

• Hydrogen is the the most common element found in the Universe.

• Some scientists think there may be lots of 'parallel' universes, like a pack of cards – each 'card' separated by a fraction of time.

20 What earthly force acts against spacecrafts on take-off, and means that they must be equipped with rockets?

21 How many times bigger is the Sun than the Earth: ten times, 100 times or 1,000 times?

22 What is the temperature of the Sun's surface?

23 Why are observatories often built on mountain-tops?

24 Are sunspots hotter or cooler than the rest of the Sun's surface?

25 As comets orbit the Sun, they can form tails of up to how long: 100,000 km, 10 million km or 100 million km?

FACTFILE

Clouds of **dust and gas**

Nebulae are huge clouds of dust and gas, made mostly of hydrogen and helium, in which new stars are made. It is intensely cold inside a big nebula – the Boomerang Nebula, 5,000 light years from Earth, is the coldest region in the Universe. Clumps of gas are pulled together by gravity, and the more the atoms are squeezed, the warmer they become. It is possible to see some nebulae through telescopes, some because they glow faintly and others because they reflect light from stars. There are also some nebulae that are dark, veiling the stars being born inside them.

➲ *The word nebula was originally used to describe any patch of light in the night sky, but now refers to the luminous mass of a star cluster.*

26 How many planets away from the Sun is the Earth?

27 Has the Earth been formed over the last 4.5 million or 4.5 billion years?

28 Did volcanoes help to create the Earth's atmosphere?

29 Approximately how long does it take the Moon to orbit the Earth: a day, a month or a year?

30 If a moon waxes, can we see more or less of it?

31 What are comets made of?

32 Is the gravity on the surface of the Moon more or less than on Earth?

33 How many planets are in our Solar System?

34 Which planet is the smallest in our Solar System?

35 Which planet is nearest the Sun?

36 'The Evening Star' is another name for which planet?

37 Who predicted that a comet would return in 1758, 16 years after his death?

38 What was the first spacecraft to leave the Solar System?

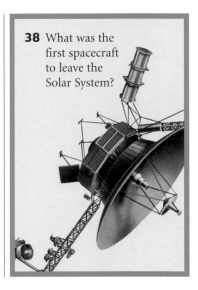

Neutron **stars**

Neutron stars are the smallest known stars. They form when a big star uses up its fuel and collapses under its own gravity. Its matter is squashed together, and the star then explodes as a supernova leaving only a spinning core, called a neutron star. Neutron stars were first spotted as fast-spinning 'pulsars' in 1967.

A photo of the Horsehead Nebula, taken with a telescope on Earth. This nebula is in the constellaton Orion.

A neutron star only 20 km across contains more matter than the Sun.

39 What passes directly in front of the Sun to create a solar eclipse?

40 How many moons does Mars have?

41 Which is hotter: Venus or Mercury?

42 Which planet is the biggest in our Solar System?

43 How long does Saturn take to travel around the Sun: two years, 20 years or 29 years?

44 Who was the first person to see Saturn's rings?

45 Which star do most asteroids orbit?

FACTFILE

Countless **stars**

Stars are made of 75 per cent hydrogen, 22 per cent helium and traces of other elements. The Sun is more than 100 times bigger than the Earth. Even huge stars look tiny in space because they are such vast distances away from us. The biggest stars are 700 times larger than our Sun.

→ Scientists estimate that there are about 10 billion trillion stars in the Universe.

→ The biggest, most powerful telescopes enable us to see about 100 billion galaxies. A galaxy can have up to 100 billion stars in it. Astronomers call this galaxy NGC 4214, and it is about 13 million light-years from us.

Answers

1 15 billion years ago
2 Yes
3 20th century
4 300 million years
5 Helium
6 Difficult, because it is very dim
7 Greek
8 Because we see them through the Earth's atmosphere
9 Heat
10 88
11 Radio telescopes
12 No, they are simply patterns

13 Milky Way
14 Eight minutes
15 AD 200
16 They are held in place by special stirrups
17 Moon rock
18 Hipparchus
19 Spiral shaped
20 Gravity
21 100 times
22 6,000°C
23 So city lights cannot interfere with the astronomers' vision
24 Cooler

25 100 million km
26 Three
27 4.5 billion years
28 Yes
29 A month
30 More
31 Ice
32 Less
33 Nine
34 Pluto
35 Mercury
36 Venus
37 Halley
38 *Voyager I*
39 The Moon

40 Two
41 Venus
42 Jupiter
43 29 years
44 Galileo
45 The Sun

Amazing **Universe**

Brightest star: Sirius in the constellation Caris Majoris. **Smallest stars:** Neutron stars are only 20 km across. **Nearest star (excluding the Sun):** Proxima Centauri, 4.22 light-years away.

Types of stars	Temperature (°C)
Blue	up to 40,000
Blue-white	11,000
White	7,500
Yellow	6,000
Orange	5,000
Red	3,500

PLANET EARTH

The story of the Earth began about 4.6 billion years ago when dust whirling around the newborn Sun formed lumps of rock called planetesimals. These slowly clumped together to form the Earth and the other planets. As the Earth formed, the pieces rushed together with such force that the young planet turned into a fiery ball. It slowly cooled down, and the continents and oceans formed.

Can a river flow backwards?

What is it like on the ocean floor?

How does an avalanche start?

There is no other planet like our Earth – so far as we know. The Earth is unique in the Solar System because it is the only planet with life. The Earth has a vast array of environments, from scorching deserts to misty rainforests, in which living things have thrived for millions of years. The Earth is still changing, reshaped by natural forces and, increasingly, by human activity.

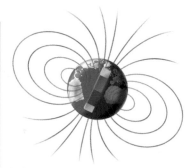

◐ *The Earth's magnetic field stretches out invisibly into space.*

◐ *The distance around the Earth at the Poles is slightly less than the distance around the Earth's middle, the Equator. Although the planet looks round, it has a bulge just south of the Equator.*

How big is the Earth?

The Earth is the fifth biggest of the Sun's planets, with a circumference of 40,075 km and weighing about 6000 million million million tonnes. It is a ball of rock, mostly covered by water, wrapped in a thin, protective layer of gases – the air. Yet the Earth is tiny compared with the planet Jupiter, which is more than 300 times bigger.

When was the Earth formed?

The Sun and its nine planets formed at around the same time, about 4,600 million years ago. The Earth grew from a whirling cloud of gas and dust in space, which became squashed together by gravity. Most of the material in the cloud came together in the middle to make the Sun. The debris left over formed gas balls and rocky lumps: the planets. One of those lumps was the Earth.

◐ *The young Earth was a violent planet, shaped by storms and volcanoes.*

How is the Earth like a magnet?

The Earth's magnetism is made by the Earth's electrical currents, generated by movements inside the planet. It has a magnetic field stretching far out into space. Like all magnets, the Earth has north and south poles where the magnetism is strongest.

⊕ *Seen from space, the Earth is a planet of oceans.*
Only about 29 per cent is land.

Why is the Earth a watery world?

Earth is a watery world because about 71 per cent of it is water. The water on the planet is in the oceans, as ice at the poles and on mountain tops, in lakes and rivers, and in water vapour in the atmosphere, which falls as rain. The rainiest places on Earth are near the Equator on the coast or on islands. In parts of West Africa and the Amazon region of Brazil it rains almost every day.

Pacific Ocean

➡ *Oceans contain 97 per cent of the Earth's water and the three biggest (Pacific, Atlantic and Indian) together cover an area of 350 million sq km.*

Atlantic Ocean

Indian Ocean

How is the Earth moving?

The Earth moves in three ways: on its own axis, through space and as part of the Solar System. Firstly, it spins on its own axis – an imaginary line from pole to pole. Secondly, it races through space as it orbits the Sun, held in position by the Sun's gravity. Thirdly, it is part of the Solar System, and moves through space as the Milky Way galaxy, which contains the Earth, rotates at about 250 km/sec.

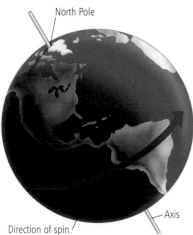

North Pole

Direction of spin

Axis

⊕ *The Earth spins on its axis – an imaginary line between the Poles.*

The Earth is made of rocks. Geologists (scientists who study the Earth's rock history) can uncover the prehistory of the Earth by studying the rocks, which are laid down in layers rather like a gigantic sandwich. Rocks provide us with useful materials, such as coal for fuel and limestone to make cement. They also contain clues to life long ago in the form of fossils – the hardened remains of long-dead animals and plants.

What is the Earth's crust?

The Earth's rocky skin is the crust, which is thickest (up to 40 km) beneath 'young' mountain ranges. The crust beneath the oceans is much thinner, between 5 and 11 km. The rocks of the continents are much older than the rocks under the oceans.

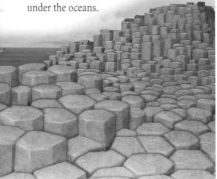

🔾 *The Giant's Causeway in Ireland is a formation of basalt, the most common volcanic rock in the Earth's crust.*

What is inside the Earth?

The Earth's crust rests on a layer of hot, partly molten rock called the mantle, which in turn surrounds the two cores. The core or centre of the Earth is a solid ball of very hot rock, about 6,400 km beneath the surface and under enormous pressure. The core is too hot and solid for us to drill down to. The deeper down, the hotter it gets – more than 4,000°C at the Earth's core.

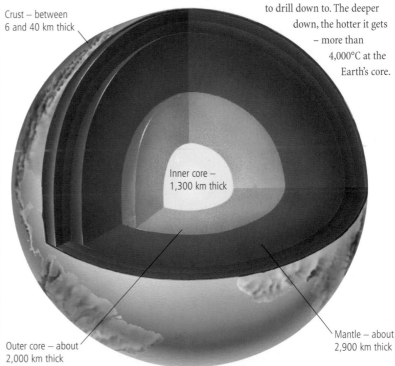

Crust – between 6 and 40 km thick

Inner core – 1,300 km thick

Outer core – about 2,000 km thick

Mantle – about 2,900 km thick

What are fossils?

Fossils are the hardened remains of dead animals and plants. They are found in rocks that were once soft sand or mud, such as sandstone, often when ancient rocks are exposed by wind or rain weathering, or by quarrying and mining. Shells, bones and teeth are most likely to end up as fossils rather than soft parts, which decay. Sometimes scientists find a whole skeleton, which can be removed bone by bone and carefully reconstructed.

This ancient trilobite, a shellfish, would have died millions of years ago. Over time only its bones and shell remain, buried by minerals in the seawater to become a fossil.

1 Animal dies

2 Body buried in mud

3 Mud becomes rock

4 Body parts fossilize

5 Rock wears away to reveal fossil

This fossil ammonite is a mollusc that swam in prehistoric seas. The soft body parts decayed millions of years ago but the impression of the animal's shell is preserved.

Fossil of a Tyrannosaurus rex *skull, a dinosaur that lived on Earth about 65–70 million years ago.*

What are rocks made of?

Rocks are made of minerals. Most rocks are what geologists call aggregates – that is, combinations of several minerals. There are three kinds of rocks, made in different ways. The most common kind are sedimentary rocks.

Chalk is a form of limestone, made from the shells of tiny single-celled sea animals called foraminiferans. Limestone is a type of sedimentary rock.

Which is the most common element?

The most common element in the Universe is hydrogen, but on Earth it's oxygen, which accounts for about 47 per cent of the planet's mass. Elements are substances that are made of only one kind of atom. All matter in the Universe is made of elements.

Continents are landmasses with water all around them, or almost all around them. The continents contain landscape – such as mountains, rivers, lakes, deserts, grassy plains, forests and cities. The continents are made of very old rocks, dating back some 3,800 million years. Yet, although they are so massive, they are not fixed in place but are drifting very slowly.

➲ *This is what Pangaea, the original super-continent, may have looked like. Scientists believe the present continents have reached their shape and position by a process of fracture and drift over millions of years.*

Have the continents always looked the same?

No, all the continents once formed one huge landmass, which scientists call Pangaea. This was 280 million years ago. Over time, the super-continent broke up into two smaller but still huge continents – Laurasia and Gondwanaland. Laurasia included North America, Europe and part of Asia and Gondwanaland contained South America, Africa, Australia, Antarctica and India. Later, these fractured and the pieces drifted apart to form the continents as we know them today.

How many continents are there?

There are seven continents: Africa, Antarctica, Asia, Europe, Oceania, North America and South America. Each of the continents encompasses various countries and bodies of water. From the map (right), you can see how the outlines of South America and Africa look as if they might fit together – suggesting that they were once joined together.

➲ *The seven continents include Antarctica, which has land beneath its thick ice, but not the Arctic, which is mostly frozen ocean.*

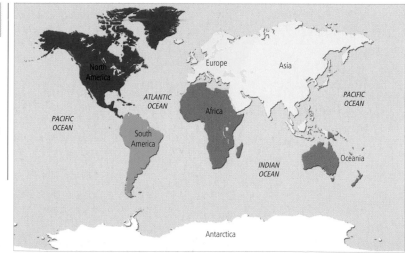

Which is the biggest continent?

Asia is by far the biggest continent. The total land area of Asia is 44 million sq km, which is four times bigger than Europe and nearly twice as big as North America. Asia includes the biggest country by land area (Russia) and the two biggest by population (China and India).

How can continents move?

The Earth's crust is made of curved rocky plates, which float like pieces of gigantic jigsaw on the molten layer of hot rocks in the mantle. There are seven large plates and some 20 smaller ones, and they move very slowly (between 1 and 10 cm a year) on currents circulating within the mantle. Over millions of years, the continents that rest on top of these plates move, too.

⬆ *Ocean plates can be pushed down beneath other plates, producing unstable movements beneath continents. Rocks are folded by pressure and magma is forced up through volcanoes.*

Why do we have time zones?

Time is not the same all around the Earth because the Earth turns once on its axis in just under 24 hours. When one spot on the Earth is in sunlight and so has day, another place on the far side is in shadow and has night. The world has 24 different time zones, and the clock time in each zone differs by one hour from that in the next. The United States and Canada are such big countries that they encompass six time zones.

Asia

PACIFIC OCEAN

INDIAN OCEAN

⬅ *This view of the globe shows Asia, which extends into Europe and is the biggest of the continents.*

⬇ *When the time is 12 noon in London, UK, it is 7 a.m. in New York, USA (five hours earlier) and 11 p.m. in Wellington, New Zealand (11 hours later).*

7 a.m. in the USA

Noon in England

11 p.m. in New Zealand

Geographers (scientists who study the Earth and its features) rely on maps. The word 'geography' comes from a Greek word meaning 'description of the Earth'. A map is a small picture of a large area, and is drawn to scale (for example 1 cm on the map might represent 1,000 km of land on the ground). Most maps are flat, but a globe is spherical, like the Earth. Modern maps are very accurate, made with the aid of computers and photographs that have been taken from aircraft and satellites in space.

❶ *The first reasonably accurate maps of the world were made in Europe in the 1500s. Lines of latitude and longitude are marked in degrees. On a map, 1° is one-360th of a circle.*

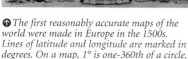

Who made the first maps?

About 5,000 years ago people in Egypt and Babylonia made drawings to show who owned which bit of land and where rivers were. The oldest map in existence is a clay tablet found in Iraq, which has what may be a river valley scratched on it. The first maps to show lines of latitude and longitude, to fix a position, were made by the ancient Greeks about 2,000 years ago.

Where are the tropics?

The tropics are the regions of the Earth that lie immediately north and south of the Equator, an imaginary line around the middle of the Earth. The northern region is the Tropic of Cancer, the southern region is the Tropic of Capricorn. Each tropic is about 2,600 km wide and here the Sun shines almost directly overhead at noon. The tropics are each approximately 2,570 km from the Equator. On a map, the tropics lie at a latitude of 23° north and south of the Equator.

❷ *The Equator is an imaginary line around the middle of the Earth, with the tropics north and south of it.*

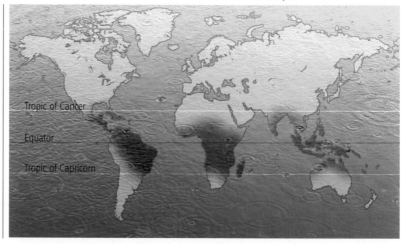

Tropic of Cancer

Equator

Tropic of Capricorn

What are latitude and longitude?

A network of lines across a map, forming a grid. Lines of longitude are drawn from north to south, while lines of latitude are drawn from east to west. The lines make it easier to locate any spot on the map. The Equator is the line of 0° latitude. The line of 0° longitude runs through Greenwich in London, England and is known as the prime meridian.

⊙ *Early navigators used a sextant to measure the height of the Sun above the horizon to help them work out latitude. Finding longitude become possible in the 1750s with the invention of accurate clocks for use at sea.*

⊙ *Cook's voyage (shown in blue) and Magellan's voyage (shown in green) sailed around the Oceanic islands for the first time.*

Why do people need never get lost today?

Global positioning system (GPS) satellites in orbit around the Earth can inform travellers where they are, to within a few metres. The satellites send out radio signals that are picked up by a computer on an aeroplane, ship or car; three or more 'fixes' give a precise position. Satellite navigation began in 1960 with the US Transit satellite. The more advanced Global positioning system became operational in 1995.

Why is Australia not shown on early maps?

Because until the 1600s no one in the Northern Hemisphere knew it was there. Chinese and Indonesian sailors may have been the first outsiders to visit Australia, after the aboriginal people settled there some 40,000 years ago. European sailors discovered Australia by accident when straying off course on voyages to Asia. The discovery of the islands that make up the continent of Oceania was only made from the 1500s onwards when sailors such as Ferdinand Magellan and Captain James Cook sailed the Southern Hemisphere. However, the islands were already inhabited by this time by the Polynesians, Melanesians and Micronesians, who had settled there after arriving from Asia more than 1,000 years before.

⊙ *Navigation satellites now encircle the Earth, providing data for travellers to be able to find where they are at any given moment.*

The surface of the Earth looks solid, but underground in some places there are holes or caves. Most were hollowed out of soft rock by water trickling down from the surface. Some are as big as soccer pitches! Others contain unusual mineral formations. People who explore caves are known as cavers, potholers or (in the USA) spelunkers.

Where are the world's longest caves?

The world's longest caves are the Mammoth Caves of Kentucky in the United States, first explored in 1799. This cave system has 560 km of caves and passages, with underground lakes and rivers.

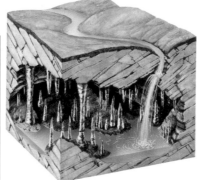

❶ Stalactites and stalagmites are made by the slow build-up of minerals in dripping water. They turn a cavern into a subterranean wonderland, full of interesting shapes.

How can you tell a stalactite from a stalagmite?

Stalactites are mineral formations that look like giant icicles as they hang down from the roof of a cave. A stalactite more than 12 m long was measured in a cave in Brazil. Stalagmites grow up from the floor of a cave, as water drips down from the cave roof. A stalagmite more than 30 m high was measured inside a cave in Slovakia.

❶ Some cave systems contain huge caverns, large enough for people to stand in. Others are cramped and narrow, and can only be crawled through by cave explorers.

Which caves have the oldest paintings?

Prehistoric people lived in caves, for protection against the weather and wild animals. Some caves contain pictures of animals made by these cave-dwellers, and the best-known are those at Lascaux in France and Altamira in Spain. Similar paintings were found in 2003 at Creswell Crags in Nottinghamshire, England. A few large caves were home to many generations of prehistoric people.

❶ Stone Age people drew the cave paintings, such as this bison, at Lascaux in France more than 13,000 years ago.

Stream flows underground

Underground waterfall

Stalactites

Stalagmites

Limestone rock worn away to form cavern

Water emerges into a lake

⊕ *Limestone caverns and cave systems are eroded (worn away) by chemical weathering.*

What caves are made by chemistry?

The soft rock in limestone caves is worn away by 'chemical weathering'. Calcium carbonate in the limestone reacts with rainwater to form a weak acid, which gradually dissolves the rock. Water seeping down the rock forms cracks and potholes, which open up into caverns. The chemical 'drips' can create growths, and formations of stalactites and stalagmites. Underground waterfalls, rivers and lakes form, and water often flows into an open-air lake or river.

Do any animals live in caves?

Caves provide shelter for a number of animals, including bats and birds, such as cave swiftlets of Asia and Caribbean oilbirds. These animals roost in the cave by day (bats) or at night (birds) and come out to hunt for food. Cave swiftlets are hunted by the racer snakes who also inhabit the caves. Many insects also live in caves, and underground lakes are home to various species of fish. Many cave species are blind and so rely on smell, touch or echolocation (using echoes from sound to judge distances and obstacles) to find their way around in the darkness.

⊕ *Birds such as swifts build their nests in caves.*

In parts of the world violent upheavals shake the ground and send fire and smoke into the sky, causing terrible damage and loss of life. These are volcanoes and earthquakes, and they often occur in the same regions. Volcanoes belch smoke, fire, ash and molten rock. Earthquakes shake the ground with an energy many times greater than that of an atomic bomb.

⬆ *Erupting volcanoes throw smoke, ash and rocks into the sky.*

What makes a volcano erupt?

A volcano erupts when molten rock (called magma) is pushed up from deep inside the Earth and is forced out through the mouth of the volcano. When the magma reaches the air it becomes lava, flowing down the sides of the volcano. Some volcanoes explode violently, hurling rocks, lava and ash into the air.

What made the loudest ever bang?

The biggest volcanic explosion was in 1883, when Krakatoa Island in Indonesia blew up. The noise was heard four hours later almost 5,000 km away! The tidal wave Krakatoa produced killed 36,000 people. However, after the Tambora volcano (which struck Indonesia in 1815) 90,000 people were killed by the volcano, the tidal wave or the famine that occurred afterwards.

Why are some volcanoes not dangerous?

Not all volcanoes erupt. Extinct volcanoes can no longer erupt. Dormant volcanoes do so only occasionally. Some just 'grumble', trickling out lava and steam. However, active volcanoes erupt often. The most famous is Mount Vesuvius, above the Italian city of Naples. It destroyed the Roman city of Pompeii in AD 79, and will almost certainly erupt in the 21st century.

⬇ *Mount Fuji is Japan's biggest mountain – the result of many eruptions of ash and lava. It is now extinct, and last erupted in 1707.*

🔾 *During an earthquake, the rocks shift along a fault line in the crust. Here, part of a road has fallen away during a quake.*

🔾 *Tsunamis are large and potentially devastating waves that are caused by undersea earthquakes.*

🔾 *During an earthquake, pressure waves ripple out from the epicentre. Earthquakes are caused as two blocks of rock crust move along a fault line (shown by the arrows) in opposite directions.*

What sets off an earthquake?

Like volcanoes, earthquakes occur where the rocks of the Earth's crust are put under tremendous pressure by movements of the plates on which the continents rest. Seismologists (scientists who study earthquakes) measure the strength of the shock waves with a seismometer. The earthquake is then graded using the Richter scale, which starts at 1 (slight tremor) and rises above 9 (devastating quake). The world's worst earthquake of modern times was in 1976, when a quake in China measuring 8.2 on the Richter scale led to the deaths of at least 250,000 people.

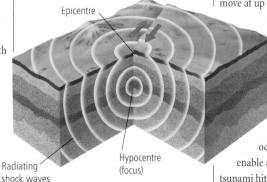

Epicentre

Radiating shock waves

Hypocentre (focus)

What is a tsunami?

Undersea earthquakes can produce huge waves, called tsunamis. These waves move at up to 800 km/h but may not be noticed in the open sea. In shallow waters however, the wave builds into a colossal wall of water up to 30 m high, which rushes inland drowning everything in its path. A warning system was developed in 1948 in the Pacific Basin, where most tsunamis occur. Several hours warning can enable areas to be evacuated before the tsunami hits, to minimize casualties.

Mountains are made by movements of the Earth's rocky crust. The highest mountains are the youngest and are still growing, pushed up by enormous pressure deep inside the Earth. For example, the Himalayas have been built-up over the last 40 million years, whereas the Adirondacks in New York, which are over one billion years old, have been worn flat, or reduced to mere hills.

Rivers meander through the landscape to flow into open water, such as lakes, seas or oceans, shaping the land as they run.

What is the highest mountain on land?

Mount Everest, which rises to 8,863 m in the Himalayan range of Asia. The Himalayan range has the world's 20 highest mountains, all more than 8,000 m high. An even higher peak, Mauna Kea in Hawaii, rises out of the Pacific Ocean. It rises 10,203 m from the ocean floor to its summit, but only 4,205 m of this is above water.

How do rivers shape the land?

Over thousands of years a river carves out a course through the rocks and soil, as it flows towards the sea or into lakes. These river courses create valleys and canyons, and where they wind slowly through flat country, they move in snaky curves called meanders. They wear away the bank on one side and pile up silt on the other.

The highest mountains in each continent.

Jayakusuma
Oceania
5,030 m

Elbrus
Europe
5,642 m

Kilimanjaro
Africa
5,895 m

McKinley
North America
6,194 m

Aconcagua
South America
6,960 m

Everest
Asia
8,863 m

➊ *The biggest canyon on Earth is the Grand Canyon in the USA – in places it is 1.6 km deep.*

What is the world's biggest canyon?

The Grand Canyon is a huge gorge in the Earth's surface, which has been cut by the Colorado River in Arizona, USA. The process of cutting the canyon, 350 km long and in places more than 20 km across, has taken millions of years. In some parts of the canyon, rocks of up to two billion years old have been uncovered.

What starts an avalanche?

Avalanches can be started by strong winds, melting snow, loud noises or even by people skiing on loose snow. An avalanche is an enormous mass of snow that slips down a mountainside. Millions of tonnes of snow fall at speeds of up to 400 km/h. The biggest avalanches occur in the world's highest mountain range – the Himalayas.

How can weather change a landscape?

The Earth's landscape is changing all the time because of erosion, which is the wearing away of rocks and soil by 'scouring' forces such as wind, water, ice and frost. In winter, water trapped in cracks in rock freezes, expands and causes chunks of rock to split off. Heavy rain can quickly wash soil down a slope, especially if there are no trees on the slope to 'bind' the soil with their roots.

➋ *The landscape is shaped by the weather often into formations like this rock arch.*

➊ *The fastest avalanches are masses of dry snow. Wet snow moves at a more sluggish pace.*

Water from the oceans is drawn up into the air as water vapour by the warmth of the Sun. It is blown over land by winds, cools to become water droplets and falls as rain. Rainwater fills up lakes and rivers, and eventually finds its way back to the oceans. All the water on Earth is recycled, over and over again.

4 Rivers flow into ocean

◑ *In the water cycle, water is drawn up from the oceans by evaporation and later falls as rain over the land. This is known as precipitation. The rainwater then flows back to the ocean in rivers.*

3 Water vapour falls as rain and snow

2 Moisture from ground evaporates

1 Ocean water evaporates

Which is the deepest lake?

Baikal in Siberia, Russia, is 1,637 m deep, roughly four times deeper than Lake Superior in North America. Baikal is a very ancient lake, about 25 million years old, and is unique in being home to the world's only freshwater seal. Lake Tanganyika in Africa is the next deepest lake but is only two million years old.

Why are the Great Lakes so named?

Canada and the United States share the five Great Lakes, so named because they are the biggest group of freshwater lakes in the world. They are: Lake Superior (the world's biggest freshwater lake), Lake Huron (the 5th largest lake in the world), Lake Michigan (the 6th largest lake), Lake Erie and Lake Ontario. Canada has the most fresh water (by area) – twice as much as any other country.

Which river has the largest volume of water?

The Amazon River carries more water than any other. It pours 770 billion l of water into the Atlantic Ocean every hour. The Amazon also has the most tributaries (rivers that flow into it). Second to the Amazon in volume of water-flow is China's Huang He, which is the muddiest river. Another name for Huang He is the Yellow River, so-called because of the colour of the silt washed into it.

◔ *The Amazon River winds in and out of lush rainforest that grows on either side.*

Lake Superior

Lake Huron

Lake Michigan

Lake Ontario

Lake Erie

◔ *Only Lake Michigan is situated entirely in the USA. The other four cross the border between the USA and Canada.*

Where would you find a delta?

Where rivers meet the sea, they can form v-shaped deltas. The river flows slowly and piles up silt into sandbanks, through which the river flows into the sea. The biggest delta is in Bangladesh, where the Ganges and Brahmaputra rivers create a delta almost as big as England. The Mississippi River delta in the United States extends over 300 km into the Gulf of Mexico.

● *The River Nile empties its waters into the Mediterranean sea through a great delta.*

Can a river flow backwards?

An incoming push of seawater, as the tide flows in, can make a wave that rushes upstream – so making a river flow backwards. This wave is called a tidal bore, and there is a famous one on the Severn River in England, which moves upstream at about 20 km an hour. A bore more than 7 m high rushes up the Qiantang River in China. Normally, rivers flow from their source (often on a mountain) downhill to the sea, drawn by the pull of gravity.

● *The highest falls are the Angel Falls in Venezuela, South America, with one drop of 807 m, and a total drop of 979 m, more than twice as high as the Empire State Building! This diagram compares the largest waterfalls in each continent.*

● *Victoria Falls are on the Zambezi River, on the border between Zambia and Zimbabwe in central Africa. Waterfalls with such immense flows of water produce huge clouds of spray and a thunderous noise.*

What makes a waterfall?

Waterfalls occur when a river flows over a band of hard rock, and then over softer rock which is more quickly worn away by the water. The hard rock forms a step over which the river pours, creating a waterfall. Famous waterfalls include Niagara in North America, Angel Falls in South America and Victoria Falls in Africa.

Angel Falls	Giessbach Falls	Sutherland Falls	Ribbon Falls	Jog Falls	Victoria Falls
South America	Europe	Oceania	North America	Asia	Africa
979 m	604 m	579 m	491 m	253 m	108 m

Viewed from space, the Earth looks like a planet of blue ocean – more than 70 per cent is water. About 97 per cent of all the Earth's water is in the oceans, which cover more than 360 million sq km of the planet. The oceans can be more than 10 km deep in places.

What causes tides?

Tides rise and fall twice every 24 hours, as the gravity of the Sun and Moon pull on the waters of the Earth – drawing the ocean towards them. The oceans move in different ways. Currents are streams of warm and cool water, some pushed by winds, others by the tides. The land is pulled too, but water moves more easily, causing a vast wave, which moves around the globe and forms the tides.

Spring tides (high)

As the tide rises, the sea flows upwards and inland

Neap tides (low)

As the tide drops, the sea ebbs, retreating from the shore

How many oceans are there?

There are five oceans, which all connect to make one vast body of water. The three biggest oceans are the Pacific, Atlantic and Indian Oceans. They meet around Antarctica, in the Southern or Antarctic Ocean. The Pacific and the Atlantic also meet in the smaller Arctic Ocean. Seas, such as the Baltic Sea are smaller areas of saltwater, but most seas are joined to an ocean, such as the Mediterranean Sea, which is linked to the Red Sea by the Suez Canal, and to the Atlantic Ocean at the Strait of Gibraltar.

◒ *There are two high and two low tides every 24 hours. The very high spring tides occur when the gravity from the Sun and the Moon combines to tug at the oceans.*

Which is the biggest ocean?

The Pacific Ocean is the biggest of the Earth's oceans. About 45 per cent of all the seawater on the Earth is in the Pacific Ocean. It has a surface area of 181 million sq km, which is equivalent to one-third of the Earth. The Pacific Ocean is larger than the second and third biggest oceans (Atlantic Ocean at 94 million sq km, and Indian Ocean at 74 million sq km) combined.

◔ *Some maps name the North and South Pacific, and the North and South Atlantic separately, but the Pacific and the Atlantic are each one ocean.*

NORTH PACIFIC

NORTH ATLANTIC

SOUTH ATLANTIC

What is it like on the ocean floor?

The ocean floor is a varied seascape of mountain ranges, deep trenches, hot springs and mud oozing for hundreds of metres. At the coast, the land slopes gradually to a depth of about 180 m – this is the continental shelf. At the edge of the shelf, the ocean floor drops away in the continental slope, leading to the deepest part of the ocean floor, the cold and sunless abyss. On the ocean floor, hot springs reach temperatures above boiling point (100°C) in places.

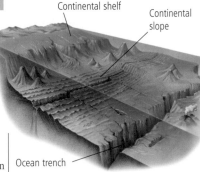

The ocean floor has features, just like dry land, with ridges, canyons and mountains.

Continental shelf

Continental slope

Ocean trench

Why is the Dead Sea so salty?

The saltiest sea is the Dead Sea, which is enclosed by hot desert where the fierce heat evaporates so much water that what is left becomes very salty. Seawater tastes salty because it contains minerals washed into the oceans by rivers. The most common mineral in seawater is common salt (sodium chloride).

SOUTH PACIFIC

INDIAN OCEAN

Could you drink a melted iceberg?

Yes, because although icebergs drift on the ocean, they are made of fresh water. Icebergs break off the ends of glaciers – slow-moving rivers of ice – that move down mountain slopes in the polar regions. Icebergs also break off from the edges of ice sheets.

Only about 11 per cent of a tall iceberg shows above water; the rest is submerged.

The water of the Dead Sea is so salty that it is more buoyant than ordinary seawater.

Dry desert, where the land gets less than 250 mm of rainfall in a year, covers almost one-eighth of the Earth's surface. The driest place on Earth is the Atacama Desert in Chile, South America, where many years pass without a single drop of rain. Not all deserts are hot though. The hottest ones are near the Equator, but even there it can be chilly at night.

◑ *People and animals have adapted to desert life. Arabian camels are still used as baggage carriers by desert nomads, who traditionally travelled from oasis to oasis, living in tents that provided shade by day and warmth by night (when it gets cold in the desert).*

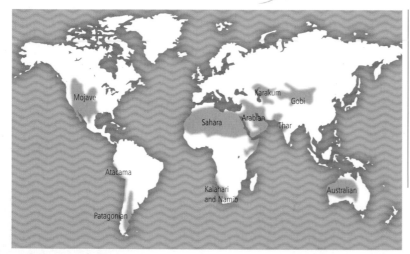

Which is the biggest desert?

The biggest desert is the Sahara in North Africa, which is 5,000 km across, bigger than Australia. It has the world's largest sand dunes, some of them more than 400 m high. Cave paintings found near the region, drawn by ancient people, depict grassland animals. This shows that thousands of years ago the Sahara was actually wetter, with lakes and plains.

◐ *Dry deserts occur in warm areas where cool air sinks, warms up and then absorbs moisture from the land. The map shows the world's biggest deserts.*

Are all deserts sandy?

Only about 20 per cent of the Earth's deserts are sandy. The rest are rocky, stony, covered by scrub and bush, or ice-covered. In the Arabian Desert is the world's biggest area of sand dunes – the Rub' al-Khali, which means 'Empty Quarter' in Arabic.

⊙ Underground water allows people to cultivate palms and vegetables in a desert oasis. Some oases support small towns.

⊙ Sand dunes can travel across the desert, like waves across an ocean.

Can sand dunes move?

Loose sand is blown by the wind and piles up in wave-shaped formations called dunes. Sand is made up of tiny mineral grains, less than 2 mm across. Like waves of water, sand is blown up, rolls over the crest of the wave and down the steeper far side. Dunes rolls across the desert in this way.

What is an oasis?

An oasis is a green 'island' in the desert, a haven for thirsty travellers. Plants can grow there by tapping water from a well or underground spring. Even beneath the Sahara Desert a lot of water is trapped deep in the rock strata (layers).

⊙ Many desert creatures, such as insects, scorpions, lizards and snakes feed at night, when it is cooler.

How do desert animals and plants survive?

Desert animals are able to go for days without water, getting most of the moisture they need from their food. These animals include mammals such as antelope, camels, foxes and rodents, as well as birds and insects. Other animals, such as desert frogs, go into a state of suspended animation in burrows until the next rain.

Many trees covering an area of land create a forest. A wood is a smaller area of trees. Some forests in cooler regions of the Earth have only two or three species of trees growing in them, but other forests have a tremendous variety of trees and other plants. The first forests grew in prehistoric swamps over 350 million years ago, but these were forests of tall ferns and moss-like plants, not trees.

Are there different types of forest?

There are different types of forest around the world, depending on the climate in the world's vegetation zones. In the warm tropics there are rainforests and seasonal forests (where trees lose their leaves during the dry season) and savanna (warm grassland) forests. Rainforests also grow in cooler zones, where there is a lot of rainfall. In cooler zones, there are forests of mixed deciduous trees (which shed their leaves before winter), and of evergreen conifers, such as fir and pine. Boreal forest or taiga is found in cold sub-polar lands.

Which is the world's biggest rainforest?

The Amazon rainforest of South America, which stretches from the foothills of the Andes Mountains in the west to the Atlantic Ocean in the east.

⬆ About 40 per cent of the the world's plants are found in rainforests.

There are other rainforests in west Africa, Southeast Asia and northeastern Australia. Rainforests are abundant with wildlife. There are more species of animals and plants in the Amazon than anywhere else on Earth.

What starts a forest fire?

Forest fires can begin naturally, when the vegetation is very dry after months without any rain. Often humans are responsible for starting the fires by carelessly lighting campfires or sometimes even by deliberate arson. Many forest trees and other plants regenerate quickly after a fire, but wildlife can be seriously affected.

⬇ Forest fires can spread rapidly. Firefighters often cut trees to create a strip of open ground, called a firebreak, to stop the flames spreading.

🔾 *There are 450 different species of oak trees, most of which belong to the* Quercus *group, which grow mostly in the northern parts of the world. Oak trees can live for more than 1,000 years and some of the oldest trees in Europe are oaks. Wood from the oak tree is very strong and has been used in the building of houses and ships over the past centuries.*

Why do some forest trees shed their leaves?

Trees in a deciduous forest shed their leaves to save water, because their roots cannot soak up water very well from cold soil.

Deciduous forests grow in countries with warm summers and cool winters. The trees in these forests include oak, beech, maple, ash and chestnut, and as summer gives way to autumn, the leaves of the trees change colour and begin to fall.

What is meant by a sustainable forest?

Forests provide people with many products, including timber, foods, cosmetics and drugs. Coniferous forests of pine, spruce and fir are felled for timber or newspaper pulp. In a well-managed sustainable forest, new trees are planted to replace those that are felled. Sadly, many tropical rainforests are being destroyed not just for timber, but also to clear the land for farming and ranching. Felled trees are not replaced, leaving a stump-littered wasteland.

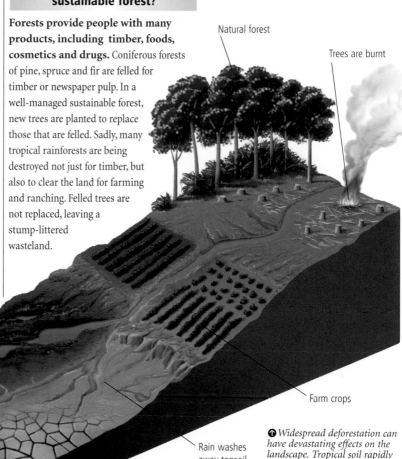

Natural forest

Trees are burnt

Farm crops

Rain washes away topsoil

Soil becomes useless

🔾 *Widespread deforestation can have devastating effects on the landscape. Tropical soil rapidly loses fertility. Rain washes off the topsoil, and once-lush forest becomes scrubland or desert.*

The atmosphere is the layer of gases that surround the Earth. It is held in place by the Earth's gravity, which keeps most of the gases in the atmosphere close to the ground. Most of the atmospheric gases are packed into the lowest layer of the atmosphere, starting at ground level, which is called the troposphere.

Exosphere 500–800 km

Thermosphere 80–500 km

Mesosphere 50–80 km

Stratosphere 10–50 km

Ozone layer

Troposphere 0–10 km

◑ We live in the lowest layer of the atmosphere. Planes cruise in the layer called the stratosphere. Phenomena such as the auroras – Borealis of the Northern Hemisphere and Australis in the Southern Hemisphere – occur in the thermosphere. Above that lies space.

How does the atmosphere protect us?

In the upper levels of the atmosphere is a layer of ozone (a form of oxygen), which forms a protective layer blocking out harmful ultraviolet rays from the Sun. On the fringes of the atmosphere are two doughnut-shaped radiation belts, known as the Van Allen Belts, which shield us from cosmic rays coming from space.

◑ The atmosphere is a protective belt, burning up meteorites and shielding life on Earth from harmful cosmic radiation.

How many layers are there in the atmosphere?

There are five main layers in the atmosphere. The lowest is the troposphere, up to 10 km high. Next is the stratosphere, about 50 km high, and above that is the mesosphere, to about 80 km. The upper layer is called the thermosphere. The higher you go, the thinner the atmosphere, and above 800 km there is no atmosphere left and the exosphere (a very thin fifth layer) gives way to the airless near-emptiness of space.

Why does the sky look blue?

Light from the Sun passes through the atmosphere and is scattered by tiny particles of dust and moisture in the air. This has the effect of breaking up the white sunlight into its rainbow colours, just like a spectrum does. The blue rays scatter most, and reach our eyes from all angles. The result is that we see blue more than the other colours in sunlight, so the sky looks blue.

⊙ *The Northern Lights, or Aurora Borealis, makes the sky glow and streak in a beautiful display of colours ranging from purple to golden-green.*

⊙ *Clouds change shape all the time. Some are big billowing masses, others are feathery traces. The wind changes the shape of clouds, which often obscure the blue sky above.*

What causes the Northern and Southern Lights?

The Northern and Southern Lights are caused by the solar wind (radiation from the Sun) hitting the atmosphere. Most of the incoming energized particles are absorbed by the Van Allen Belts, but at the poles, where the belts are thinnest, the particles impact on the atmosphere, producing a spectacular light show in the sky. The Aurora Borealis (Northern Lights) makes the night sky glow green, gold, red or purple. The aurora seen in the Southern Hemisphere is the Aurora Australis (Southern Lights).

Where is the air coldest?

Anyone who climbs a mountain soon realizes that it gets colder the higher you climb. The temperature falls by about 5°C for every 100 m altitude. However, in the atmosphere high above ground level, it is a different story. The outer layer of the atmosphere can be warmer than the layers closer to the surface. Within the layer called the troposphere it gets coldest when the air rises highest, which is over the Equator. It is actually warmer over the North Pole, where the air does not rise as high.

egular weather charts have been kept for only about the last 250 years, and accurate temperature readings date from the 1800s. But people have always been interested in the weather. Historic Chinese weather records show that 903 BC was a very bad winter in China, and the Romans recorded that the weather was poor when they landed in Britain in 55 BC.

The different types of cloud in the sky form at different heights. Clouds are made of tiny droplets of water or ice.

What are the highest clouds in the sky?

The highest clouds are the rare 'mother of pearl' nacreous clouds, which can be found at 24,000 m. Cumulonimbus clouds can tower as high in the sky as 19,000 m. The more common cirrus clouds form at around 8,000 m. The lowest clouds are stratus clouds, from 1,100 m to ground level.

How deep can snow be?

The most snow to fall in 24 hours was 1.93 m – enough to cover a tall man. This snowfall buried Silver Lake in Colorado, USA between 14 and 15 April 1921. The deepest snow covering ever measured was 11.46 m in California in 1911 – enough snow to cover a small house to the roof!

Snowfall tends to be heaviest in mountainous regions, such as the Rocky Mountains and Sierra Nevada ranges of North America. People who live in these regions have learned to cope with blizzards (heavy snowfall) that half-bury cars and houses.

Snowflakes are made up of snow crystals, that can be seen under a microscope. Each has six sides but every snowflake is different.

Where is the thickest ice?

The ice covering Greenland is about 1.5 km thick, but the ice in Antarctica is three times thicker, up to 4.8 km thick! Antarctic icebergs are flatter than Arctic ones. The biggest iceberg was spotted in the Antarctic in 1956. It was 335 km long and 97 km across. A country the size of Belgium would have fitted on top of it.

What is a hurricane?

The most destructive storms are hurricanes, known as cyclones in the Indian Ocean and typhoons in the Pacific Ocean. In a hurricane, winds spiral at speeds of more than 400 km/h, yet at the centre is a calm area, known as the 'eye' of the hurricane. A hurricane does most damage when it hits the land.

⬆ Lightning flashes between clouds, or from cloud to ground, heating the air around it to more than 33,000°C. This is five times hotter than the surface of the Sun.

What causes lightning?

A lightning flash is a giant electric spark, caused by electrical charges that build up inside clouds and on the ground. Lightning is incredibly hot and so can seriously injure and even kill people. An American park ranger named Roy Sullivan was struck by lightning seven times (and survived) between 1942 and 1977.

⬅ Hurricanes can be photographed from high above, in space. The 'eye' can be seen quite clearly on the photographs. Satellites in space track hurricanes over the ocean.

➡ Each colour in the white sunlight is bent to a different extent. The light is split into the spectrum colours: red, orange, yellow, green, blue, indigo and violet, to form the rainbow.

When might you see a rainbow?

You might see a rainbow – an arc of up to seven colours in the sky – during a rainfall. A rainbow is caused by light being refracted (bent) by the raindrops. To see a rainbow, the Sun must be behind you. If the Sun is high in the sky, no rainbow will appear.

The Earth has many natural resources, which sustain life. The planet has air, water, forests, minerals and a range of environments that living things can use. Some of these resources, such as the Sun's energy, are limitless. Others are renewable, such as plants, which means that they can be regrown. But some, like coal and oil, are non-renewable resources. Once used, they are gone for ever.

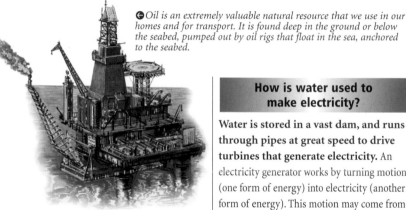

◐ Oil is an extremely valuable natural resource that we use in our homes and for transport. It is found deep in the ground or below the seabed, pumped out by oil rigs that float in the sea, anchored to the seabed.

⬆ Diamond is the hardest known substance.

How is water used to make electricity?

Water is stored in a vast dam, and runs through pipes at great speed to drive turbines that generate electricity. An electricity generator works by turning motion (one form of energy) into electricity (another form of energy). This motion may come from a turbine that is driven by steam or water.

Why is a diamond like a lump of coal?

Diamond and coal are both forms of carbon. About 95 per cent of all compounds (substances made of two or more elements) contain carbon, which is the key element in substance-building because it has atoms that form chains, rings and other structures, making them stronger and more durable.

⬇ A hydro-electric power station uses water to drive its turbines.

What are raw materials?

They are the Earth's resources that make our lives more comfortable. We cut trees for timber to make homes and furniture. We mine minerals, such as copper, to make the electrical wire in our buildings. We mine coal to burn as a fuel. All of these materials are non-renewable, which means we cannot make more of them.

What is coal?

Coal was formed over 250 million years ago, from dead and decaying plants in prehistoric swamp-forests. Over that vast length of time, the plant matter got squashed so tightly that it changed and became a soft black-brown rock. Coal is found in seams or layers, with other rocks on top and beneath. It is extracted either by digging deep mine shafts and tunnels, or by 'stripping' coal seams near the surface, known as opencast mining.

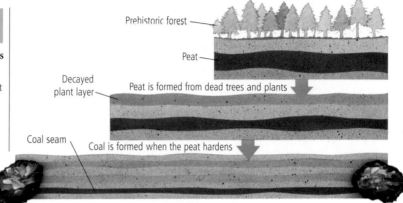

Prehistoric forest

Peat

Decayed plant layer

Peat is formed from dead trees and plants

Coal seam

Coal is formed when the peat hardens

Where is the world's richest gold-field?

The mines of the Witwatersrand in South Africa yield about 50 per cent of the world's annual gold production, making them the richest gold-mines in the world. Several times in history gold-miners have rushed to find gold in various parts of the world. The most famous gold-rush was in California in 1849. There was another in South Africa in the 1880s.

What is the 'greenhouse' effect?

Gases, such as carbon dioxide, act like the glass in a greenhouse, letting through the Sun's rays, but trapping some heat that would otherwise filter back into space. Since the 1800s, human activity (especially factories, vehicles and power stations) has caused an increase in the amount of carbon dioxide and other gases in the atmosphere. The trapped warmth that is created raises the Earth's temperature and many scientists believe this is bringing about climate change.

◆ *Few gold-rush prospectors ever made the fortune they dreamed about, by finding nuggets of gold.*

◐ *This diagram shows how coal seams are formed over millions of years. Much of the coal lies deep beneath rock layers, called strata. The pressure of the topmost layer squeezes the layers below, turning sand and mud into hard rock, and plant remains from peat into coal.*

◑ *Gases that have risen into the atmosphere trap the heat from the Sun, causing what scientists call the 'greenhouse' effect.*

Sun

'Greenhouse' gases

1 Is there more land or water making up the Earth's surface?

2 How long does it take for the Earth to revolve around the Sun?

3 Is the diameter of the Earth 1,270 km, 12,700 km or 127,000 km?

4 Do longitude lines run horizontally or vertically around the Earth?

5 What type of rock was marble before it was changed under great pressure?

6 What type of scientists study fossils, such as this ammonite?

7 What source does Geothermal energy come from?

8 Is chalk a type of limestone or granite rock?

9 Which continent has the highest population?

10 What are the remote areas of Australia's interior known as?

11 On which continent would the Rhine River be found?

12 At what degree latitude is the Equator: 0°, 45° or 90°?

FACTFILE

In the **Earth**

The three main kinds of rocks are igneous, sedimentary and metamorphic rocks. Igneous rocks are made deep inside the Earth from rock called magma, which is so hot (over 1,000°C) that it is molten. It is also crushed by enormous pressure. When magma gets pushed to the surface by volcanic action it cools to form igneous rocks.

➡ *Rock materials are continually recycled to make new rocks.*

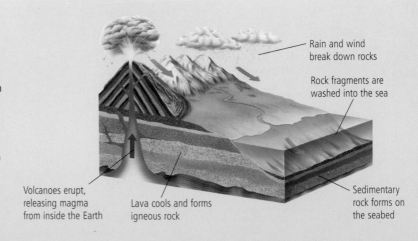

Rain and wind break down rocks

Rock fragments are washed into the sea

Volcanoes erupt, releasing magma from inside the Earth

Lava cools and forms igneous rock

Sedimentary rock forms on the seabed

13 The inner core of the Earth acts like a huge magnet: true or false?

14 The world's deepest mine can be found in which country?

15 Is the mantle below Earth's crust, mainly solid or molten rock?

16 The three most active volcanoes in South America are found in which country?

17 Is a plain a flat or hilly area?

18 What rock formed by volcanoes can be so light it will float on water?

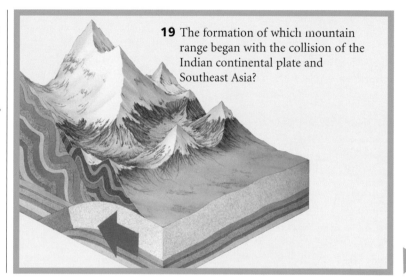

19 The formation of which mountain range began with the collision of the Indian continental plate and Southeast Asia?

Types of **rock**

Sedimentary rocks are made by the action of wind and water, which grind other rocks into sand and mud, carried by rivers until they are deposited as sediments. Sediment piles up in layers, and is squeezed by the pressure of layers on top, until it becomes rock.

Metamorphic rocks are rocks that have been changed by chemical action, heat or pressure into another form of rock. This can happen when magma pushes through them or when the Earth's crust moves beneath mountain ranges. Limestone, for instance, becomes marble when subjected to these kinds of changes: a sedimentary rock becomes a metamorphic rock.

Igneous rocks form from molten material deep in the Earth's crust. They can be distinguished from other kinds of rocks because they are made of a mosaic of mineral crystals.

➲ *Scientists study the Earth's history to understand how it has developed, as natural forces reshape the landscape.*

20 What is the name given to a small warning shock delivered by an earthquake?

21 Is four-fifths of all farmland used to feed people or animals?

22 The Grand Canyon is found in which country?

23 The Thames River flows through which British city?

24 In which continent would you find the Amazon River?

25 On which river are the Victoria Falls?

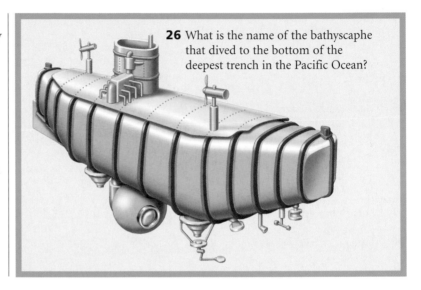

26 What is the name of the bathyscaphe that dived to the bottom of the deepest trench in the Pacific Ocean?

Underground

Caves are holes in the ground, often hollowed out by water wearing away rock. But many 'potholes' are so narrow that explorers have to crawl on hands and knees, or even swim through flooded sections, using flashlights to penetrate the gloom. The world's biggest cave chamber is called the Sarawak Chamber, in a cave system in Sarawak, Malaysia. It is 700 m long, has an average width of 300 m and is about 70 m above the cave floor.

⊙ *An explorer inside a cave that has been made from lava from a volcano.*

The deepest **caves**

Krubera, Georgia, Asia	**1,710 m**
Reseu Jean Bernard, France	**1,602 m**
Shakta Pantujhina, Georgia	**1,508 m**
Sistema Huautla, Mexico	**1,475 m**
Sistema del Trava, Spain	**1,441 m**
Vercors, southeast France	**1,271 m**
Gunung Mulu, Borneo	**470 m**
Carlsbad Cavern, USA	**316 m**

27 What ocean separates Europe from North and South America?

28 What is the world's largest ocean?

29 Which ocean is larger: the Indian or the Atlantic?

30 What is the largest desert in Africa?

31 The Gobi Desert can be found on which continent?

32 Where is the Great Victoria Desert?

33 Are pine trees hard or softwoods?

34 In which continent is the world's largest rainforest?

35 Rubber can be made from the sap of certain trees: true or false?

36 What is the second most common element in the air?

37 What is mixed with fog to make smog?

38 In which layer of the atmosphere do aeroplanes cruise?

39 Evangelista Torricelli studied under Galileo and was the first to make what type of meteorological instrument?

Formation of a **cave**

⊙ *These diagrams show how limestone caves are formed by the action of water.*

1 Streams enter from the surface and water trickles down through cracks in the stone

2 As the water dissolves the limestone, it hollows out tunnels and caverns

3 In time, part of the cavern roof may collapse, and the stream becomes a subterranean river

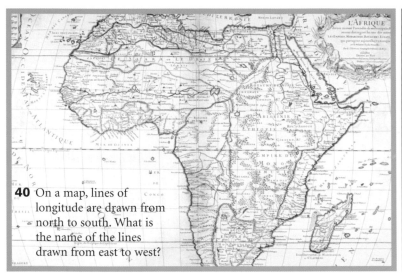

40 On a map, lines of longitude are drawn from north to south. What is the name of the lines drawn from east to west?

41 What simple device can show the direction of the wind?

42 If you were in the Northern Hemisphere in October, what season would you be in?

43 Meteorology is the study of what feature of Earth?

44 Is amber a mineral or a metal?

45 Is oil a fossil fuel?

46 Tenant Creek and Weipa in Australia are famous mining areas for which precious metal?

FACTFILE

Forming **mountains**

Mountains can be made in three ways. Volcanic mountains are pushed up by volcanoes. Fold mountains are made when layers of rock fold like wrinkles on a blanket. Fault block mountains are made when a section of rock tilts or is pushed up during an earth tremor. This happens along faults or breaks in the Earth's crust.

Volcanic mountain   Fold mountain   Fault block mountain

Answers

1 More water	16 Chile	31 Asia	46 Gold
2 One year	17 Flat	32 Australia	
3 12,700 km	18 Pumice	33 Softwoods	
4 Vertically	19 The Himalayas	34 South America	
5 Limestone	20 Foreshock	35 True	
6 Geologists	21 Animals	36 Oxygen	
7 Heat from the Earth's rocks	22 USA	37 Pollution	
8 Limestone	23 London	38 Stratosphere	
9 Asia	24 South America	39 Barometer	
10 The outback	25 Zambezi	40 Latitude	
11 Europe	26 Trieste	41 Wind vane	
12 0°	27 Atlantic	42 Autumn	
13 True	28 Pacific	43 Its atmosphere and weather	
14 South Africa	29 Atlantic	44 Mineral	
15 Mainly solid	30 Sahara	45 Yes	

Highest **mountains**

The five highest peaks in the world are all in the Himalayan range in Asia:

Everest	**8,863 m**
K2	**8,610 m**
Kanchenjunga	**8,598 m**
Lhotse	**8,511 m**
Makalu	**8,481 m**

Other **famous peaks**

Cotopaxi (Mexico)	**5,897 m**
Ararat (Turkey)	**5,185 m**
Mont Blanc (France/ Italy/ Switzerland)	**4,807 m**
Jungfrau (Switzerland)	**4,518 m**
Matterhorn (Switzerland/Italy)	**4,478 m**
Fuji (Japan)	**3,776 m**
Olympus (Greece)	**2,917 m**

➔ *Mount Everest was first climbed in 1953 by Sherpa Tenzing Norgay and New Zealander Edmund Hillary, supported by a British Commonwealth team of climbers.*

DINOSAURS

For about 160 million years dinosaurs were the most successful animals on Earth. Some dinosaurs were giants, much bigger than elephants. Others were as as small as pet cats. Dinosaurs lived from about 225 million to 65 million years ago. This period is known as the Age of the Dinosaurs or the Mesozoic Era.

Which was the first dinosaur?

How did dinosaurs care for their young?

Did dinosaurs hunt in packs?

Dinosaurs lived on Earth many millions of years ago and none survive today. We know about dinosaurs because their bones have been preserved as fossils in rocks. Scientists have excavated thousands of dinosaur fossils and studied them with great care. By examining the fossils, scientists can tell what the dinosaurs looked like and how they lived. The scientists who study dinosaur and other ancient animal and plant fossils are called palaeontologists.

Where can I meet a dinosaur?

In a museum of natural history. Many museums have complete skeletons of dinosaurs mounted so that they are in lifelike poses. These show how large the dinosaurs were when they were alive and the sorts of actions they could make. Some dinosaurs could run very quickly, or even leap in the air. Others were able to walk only very slowly.

What is a fossil?

An object from millions of years ago that has been preserved in rock. Most fossils are of bones or teeth because these hard objects are preserved more easily than soft skin or muscles. Over millions of years the original objects rot away and are replaced by minerals from the surrounding rocks. The fossils can be very heavy and are often fragile as well. Sometimes rare fossils of skin or muscles are found.

⬆ Fossils are preserved in rock and are often displayed as they were found.

⬆ Some fossils are extracted from the rock and mounted as they would have been in life.

An excavation in the field. Each fossil must be carefully recorded, together with the precise place where it was found.

Where are dinosaur fossils found?

In Mesozoic rocks. These date to the time of the dinosaurs – 230 to 65 million years ago. When a dinosaur died its bones might have become covered by sand or sunk into mud. This might then have become buried and turned to stone. When these rocks are lifted to the surface by earthquakes or erosion the fossils can be found and excavated.

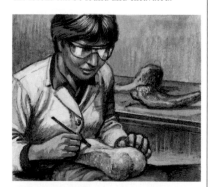

Fossils are cleaned to ensure that even the smallest details can be seen.

In the laboratory specialists carefully remove the fossils from the rock.

How are fossils prepared for study?

By cleaning them. The palaeontologist must remove the fossil from the surrounding rocks, called the matrix. Some types of rock can be dissolved away with chemicals, but most need to be scraped away with metal hooks and chisels. Some palaeontologists like to use a dentist's drill to remove final traces of rock. The fossils are then often soaked in chemicals to make them less fragile. Finally they are photographed and drawn in detail.

How do scientists study fossils?

By comparing them to the bones of other animals. Palaeontologists search for animals that have teeth of a similar shape to those of the fossil. If the two animals have similar teeth, they probably ate similar foods. The marks left on bones by muscles show how strong the dinosaur was and in which direction it could move its legs, neck and other parts of its body.

Which are the most fragile fossils?

The most delicate dinosaur fossils are coprolites, the remains of dinosaur droppings. Fossilized droppings are known as coprolites and can reveal to scientists what the dinosaur had been eating, and how much food it consumed. In some areas dinosaur footprints have been preserved as fossils.

Thousands of coprolites have been found at fossil sites all over the world.

The name 'dinosaur' means 'terrible lizard'. This name was given to this group of animals in 1842 by the scientist Richard Owen. The dinosaurs were a group of reptiles closely related to the crocodiles, that held their legs underneath their bodies, like modern mammals.They are recognizable because some features of their skull bones are unlike those of any other type of reptile. It is thought that birds are probably descended from one type of dinosaur.

How many types of dinosaur were there?

Hundreds of different types of dinosaur have been named by scientists, but nobody is certain how many there are. Some different types of dinosaur are very similar, so some scientists think they should be put together as just one type of dinosaur. Other scientists believe that different fossils that are said to belong to only one type, should belong to several.There are thousands of dinosaur fossils that remain buried and have not yet been discovered.

Why are dinosaur hips important?

All dinosaurs belong to one of two groups, which are divided by the shape of their hip bones. The saurischian dinosaurs had hip bones shaped like those of modern reptiles – the name 'saurischian' means 'reptile-hip'. The ornithischian dinosaurs had hip bones that resemble those of modern birds – 'ornithischian' means 'bird-hip'. These two groups are divided into smaller groups known as orders, within which are families of similar dinosaurs.

⬇A scene from the late Cretaceous Period (around 75–65 million years ago). Success stories included the hadrosaurs or duckbilled dinosaurs, whose fossils have been found by the thousands.

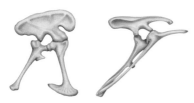

⬆The saurischian (left) had hips like modern reptiles. The ornithischian (right) had hips more like those of modern birds.

Were all dinosaurs large?

No, a number of types of dinosaur were quite small. The hunting dinosaur *Compsognathus* was the smallest. It was about the same size as a modern chicken and weighed around 2.5 kg. *Compsognathus* had a long tail and neck, so it may have reached over one metre in length, but would have stood only about 40 cm tall. *Compsognathus* was a speedy hunter of little creatures such as insects, worms and small lizards.

How large were dinosaur eggs?

Different dinosaurs laid eggs of varying sizes, depending on how large the adult dinosaur was. The smallest dinosaurs laid eggs that were about 4 cm long, or perhaps even smaller. The largest dinosaurs laid the largest eggs that have ever existed. They were about 40 cm across, or as large as a football, and were probably laid by sauropod dinosaurs.

◑ *Dinosaur eggs varied greatly in size and in shape with some being smaller than a modern hen's egg.*

◑ *The remains of embryonic dinosaurs have been found within a few fossilized eggs.*

How did dinosaurs have their young?

They laid eggs, which hatched into baby dinosaurs. Because eggs are fragile, they do not often become fossils. However, scientists have found a few fossilized eggs. These show that dinosaur eggs were shaped rather like modern crocodile eggs. Most were long and oval in shape, but the eggs of giant sauropod dinosaurs may have been round.

◑ *Hunting dinosaurs were able to track other creatures, so they were probably about as intelligent as modern wild dogs.*

Were dinosaurs stupid?

Some dinosaurs had very small brains and were probably unintelligent, but others had fairly large brains and were quite bright. The hunter *Deinonychus* from North America was an intelligent dinosaur that could even co-operate with other dinosaurs when it was hunting.

◑ *The fastest dinosaurs could easily have kept up with the fastest modern animals.*

How fast could dinosaurs run?

One family of dinosaurs were able to run very fast, perhaps at over 80 km/h. These ornithomimids looked similar to ostriches, and could run just as fast. They had lightweight bones and slim bodies, but very long, powerful rear legs. One genus, *Struthiomimus*, was about 3.4 m long and had longer legs than any other ornithomimid. It was probably the fastest dinosaur of all.

Dinosaurs were not the first animals to exist on Earth. Creatures had been living and evolving for millions of years before the dinosaurs existed. Animals first appeared in the water, but they later evolved so that they could survive on dry land. The reptiles began to dominate life on land soon after they evolved. There were lots of different types of reptile all competing against each other to survive. The scene was set for the dinosaurs to emerge.

What were the ancestors of land animals?

The Coelacanth fish, which first appeared about 390 million years ago. It had fins that were very strong and muscular. These are known as lobe-finned fish, or Coelacanth, and would eventually evolve into land animals. It was originally thought that the Ceolacanth died out around 70 million years ago, but in 1933 one was caught off Madagascar. At the time it was thought that the Coelacanth must be extremely rare, but the local fishermen said they had been catching the creature for many years without realizing that it was anything special. It is now known that these fish can be found in deep waters of the Indian Ocean, although they are endangered and so their numbers are not huge.

⊕ The Coelacanth fish was for many years known only from ancient fossils, but scientists now know that it has survived in deep ocean waters to the present day.

When did fish first evolve?

Around 450 million years ago. The first fish had skeletons of cartilage instead of bone, and lacked jaws. They probably fed on microscopic plants or animals. By 430 million years ago, fish had both bony skeletons and jaws. This made them better swimmers and allowed them to hunt larger creatures for food. All later vertebrates are descended from these early fish. The possession of two eyes and limbs arranged in pairs originated with these earliest creatures.

○ *The therapsid reptiles were covered with fur or hair and would have looked very much like modern mammals, though under the skin they remained very much ancient reptiles. Their descendants later became mammals.*

○ *The ammonites were one of the most successful groups of sea creatures. They survived for millions of years, but are now completely extinct.*

What were other sea animals like?

They were of many different shapes and sizes. Among the most common were the ammonites, which are closely related to modern squids and octopus. Ammonites first appeared around 330 million years ago. They had long, coiled shells filled with air that helped them to float, while tentacles helped them to catch small animals. Some later ammonites had straight or curved shells. All the ammonites died about about 65 million years ago, at the same time as the dinosaurs.

○ *Reptiles had hard skin covered in scales that is impervious to water, and four limbs, though some forms walked on their hind legs only and used their front limbs as arms.*

When did the first reptiles live?

About 310 million years ago. Reptiles evolved from amphibians to become more suited to life on land. They laid hard-shelled eggs that could protect their young on land and had tough skin that prevented their bodies from drying out. *Dimetrodon* lived about 270 million years ago in North America. This reptile was about 3 m long and hunted other reptiles. It had a large sail of skin along its back that helped it to heat up its body in warm sunshine. Several other reptiles have evolved a similar sail of skin to help regulate their temperatures, including the dinosaur *Spinosaurus*.

What were the ancestors of mammals?

The therapsid mammals that appeared on Earth around 260 million years ago. These reptiles evolved into many different forms over the next 120 million years. Some therapsids were plant eaters, others hunted other animals. They gradually evolved features such as hair and specialized jaw muscles. Some time before 200 million years ago one group of small therapsids evolved into mammals. These creatures survived through the age of the dinosaurs, then spread rapidly and evolved into a wide variety of forms.

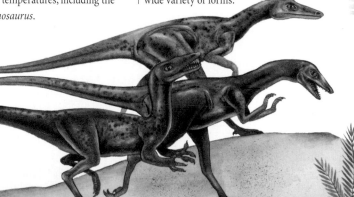

The dinosaurs first appeared on Earth, around 230 million years ago in South America. At this time, they were just one of many types of reptile. They quickly spread across the world and evolved into a large number of different species. By 190 million years ago, the dinosaurs were the dominant animals on Earth, and they remained so for over 120 million years.

What was the first dinosaur?

One of the oldest known dinosaurs was *Herrerasaurus*, which lived in South America about 230 million years ago. It was about 4 m long and hunted other animals. It had jaws filled with sharp teeth, that curved backwards. These would have been able to grip struggling prey and stop them from wriggling free. The jaws were powered by extremely strong muscles that would have been able to inflict a strong bite on any creature unfortunate enough to be caught by this predator. *Herrerasaurus* may have been the ancestor of the later sauropod dinosaurs, or of the theropods. There were also other dinosaurs living at about this time – scientists have found the fossils of a smaller predator, *Eoraptor*.

➔ Herrerasaurus *belonged to a group of large, powerful hunting reptiles. The first dinosaurs may have evolved from this group.*

What were the ancestors of dinosaurs like?

Dinosaurs belong to a group of reptiles known as the archosaurs, which means 'ruling reptiles'. This group includes crocodiles and several types of reptiles that are now extinct. *Ornithosuchus* was an early archosaur that may have been related to the ancestors of the dinosaurs. It was about 4 m long and was a hunter with powerful muscles.

Which was the first numerous dinosaur?

***Coelophysis* is a dinosaur that has been found in vast numbers.** Hundreds of fossilized *Coelophysis* have been excavated in North America. The most dramatic find came in 1947 at the Ghost Ranch in New Mexico. Scientists found the fossils of an entire pack of these animals, almost 100 strong. The pack included *Coelophysis* of different ages from young to adult. The adults were about 3 m long with powerful hind legs and shorter front legs equipped with sharp claws. It is thought the pack was killed by a sandstorm.

⬆ *Scientists have found* Coelophysis *skeletons in large groups so it is likely that these animals lived in groups and hunted together.*

Was there a link between crocodiles and dinosaurs?

The very earliest archosaur reptiles would have been the ancestors of both crocodiles and dinosaurs. *Erythrosuchus* lived about 250 million years ago in southern Africa. It grew to be about 4.5 m long and was able to run fairly quickly when hunting other reptiles. The jaws were filled with dozens of sharp, conical teeth that were used to attack other animals. *Erythrosuchus* and similar animals already had the longer hind legs that were to become characteristic of almost all the later dinosaurs and crocodiles.

⬇Coelophysis *was one of the most agile of the early dinosaurs. It used its speed to hunt lizards and other small animals, which it then tore apart with its teeth and claws before eating them.*

How did Coelophysis live?

Coelophysis **hunted plant-eating dinosaurs and other animals.** It was able to run fast, while its long tail helped to balance the body as it changed direction at speed. *Coelophysis* may have also hunted smaller animals such as lizards. One fossilized *Coelophysis* was found with a baby *Coelophysis* in its stomach, so this dinosaur must have eaten its own kind. This is known as cannibalism and is extremely rare in animals. It is not clear if *Coelophysis* ate others of its own kind as part of its usual diet or if this was strange behaviour. The fossil was found in what was then a desert, so the adult animal may have eaten the younger only because there was a shortage of food. Not until scientists find more evidence will we be sure of the truth.

The largest dinosaurs of all were the sauropods, which were also the largest land animals that have ever lived. All sauropods were saurischian dinosaurs and had a similar body structure. They had large bodies supported by four pillar-shaped legs. A small head was set on the end of a long neck, while a long tail was held out behind. Strong tendons ran between the neck and tail to help lift both clear of the ground.

Which was the longest dinosaur?

Seismosaurus **was up to 45 m long and was probably the longest dinosaur of all.** The name *Seismosaurus* means 'earthquake lizard' – it was given to this animal because the scientist who discovered it thought that the ground would shake as it walked. *Seismosaurus* was similar to *Diplodocus*. These diplodocid dinosaurs lived worldwide in the Jurassic Period but later lived only in eastern Asia.

◑ *Sauropods such as the* Argentinosaurus *were the largest of all the dinosaurs, and the largest land animals that ever lived.*

Which was the biggest dinosaur?

The most massive dinosaur was probably *Argentinosaurus*, which lived in South America about 100 million years ago. Although scientists have found only parts of the skeleton, they think that the complete animal was about 40 m long and may have weighed up to 90 tonnes. This would make *Argentinosaurus* one of the largest animals that has ever lived.

How did sauropods live?

Scientists believe that the sauropods lived in herds of up to 30 animals. Fossilized footprints have been found that show numbers of sauropods all moving together in the same direction. The smaller, younger animals were in the middle of the

◑ Seismosaurus *had an extremely long, thin neck and and an even longer tail. This made it the longest animal ever to walk on the Earth.*

group so that they could be protected from hunting dinosaurs. When no danger was near, the herd of sauropods would have spread out to find food, though they would have needed to remain alert for danger.

Why are the names of some dinosaurs changed?

Scientists can sometime make mistakes when describing fossils, so the names of dinosaurs sometimes have to be changed. For instance, in 1985 an American scientist discovered the remains of a huge sauropod that he named *Ultrasaurus*. Before he could register the name, a Korean scientist used it for a different dinosaur, so the American registered the name

Ultrasauros instead. A few years later he realized that his *Ultrasauros* was really just a large *Brachiosaurus*, so the name was dropped completely.

Decisions about what name can be used to describe a dinosaur are made by a scientific body called the International Commission on Zoological Nomenclature, usually known as ICZN. The 25 members of the ICZN are elected by respected zoologists from countries across the world.

◐ *The gigantic* Brachiosaurus *was one of the heaviest dinosaurs that ever lived. Several different sorts of this dinosaur have been found by scientists, and there has been much confusion over the names that should be used to describe them.*

Are sauropod remains still being found?

Yes, the sauropods *Jobaria* and *Janenschia* were discovered in Africa during the 1990s. Only parts of the skeletons of these huge dinosaurs were found, so scientists have had to reconstruct these animals by comparing them to other sauropods. *Jobaria* was about 21 m long and weighed around 18 tonnes. *Janenschia* was slightly smaller. What may be another new type of sauropod was found in America in 2004, but it has not yet been properly studied.

What did sauropods eat?

The teeth of sauropods are fairly small and usually blunt, which shows that they must have eaten plants. Sauropods would have needed to eat vast amounts of plant food to gain enough energy for their huge bodies. These dinosaurs became much rarer after about 100 million years ago, so perhaps the plants that they ate began to disappear. Scientists know that flowering plants began to appear at this time, so ferns became rarer than they had been.

Dinosaurs have left behind them large numbers of fossils of their teeth and bones, but very few of the muscles, organs and other features have been preserved. Scientists have tried to work out what the soft parts of dinosaurs were like by comparing the skeletons with those of animals that are alive today. We now have a fairly complete idea of what the insides of a dinosaur would have looked like.

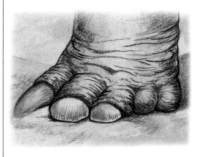

● Footprints are left behind in mud or sand, but soon disappear. They are fossilized under only the rarest of conditions.

● The astonishingly long necks of sauropod dinosaurs evolved to help these creatures find and eat the large quantities of food needed to keep their massive bodies going.

How did sauropods eat?

Sauropods had to eat vast amounts of plant food, but their teeth were quite small and their jaw muscles were weak. The teeth of *Apatosaurus* were long and narrow – like pencils. Experts think *Apatosaurus* may have used its teeth like rakes, grabbing a mouthful of leaves, then pulling its head backwards to remove the leaves from the tree or bush.

Why did sauropods have such long necks?

The long neck allowed sauropods to reach the plant food that they ate. The neck of *Mamenchisaurus* was the longest of any dinosaur. It was about 11 m long and made up of just 19 bones. Scientists think that sauropods may have stood still and used their necks to enable them to gather food from a large area before moving forward to the centre of a new grazing patch. This would have meant the animal did not need to walk about much and so would have saved energy.

How are footprints fossilized?

Footprints are fossilized only if they are buried in sediment almost as soon as they are made. If a dinosaur made footprints in wet sand on a beach, they might be buried beneath fresh sediments by the incoming tide. Or a flood might lay mud down on top of footprints made on a river bank. Only if the new sediments were different from those in which the footprints were made would the prints become fossilized. This means that fossilized footprints are extremely rare, and also fragile. If the fossils are not excavated within a few weeks and taken to a museum for storage they are likely to be broken up by frost or washed away by water. Many fossil footprints are lost before they can be studied.

How did sauropods digest their food?

The teeth and jaws of sauropods were too weak to chew up the vast amounts of food the animals ate. Instead, the food was swallowed whole. In the stomach the plants were mashed to a paste by stones, called gastroliths, swallowed by the dinosaur. The bacteria in the stomach broke down the nutrients in the plants so that the dinosaur could digest them. This method of digesting food is used by several modern animals. Some birds keep gravel in their digestive systems to grind up seeds or tough plants, while crocodiles swallow stones to help pound bones to pieces.

◑ *The skulls of diplodocid sauropods had only a few short teeth at the front of their mouths, so they were unable to chew their food properly.*

◑ *The feet of sauropod dinosaurs were large and wide so that they could carry heavy weights. Smaller dinosaurs had narrow feet better suited to fast running.*

Were sauropod feet special?

Sauropods were enormously heavy, but had to support their weight on their four feet. Each foot was made up of toes that pointed down and outwards from the ankle, leaving an empty space between them. It is thought that this space was filled by strong, soft tissue similar to tendons. This would have cushioned the foot when it was put down, and helped support the great weight of the animal.

◑ *The neck bones of sauropod dinosaurs were hollowed out to make them as light as possible so that the animal did not need to use up huge amounts of energy just lifting its head.*

Have any complete skeletons been found?

It is very rare that a complete dinosaur skeleton is found. For bones to be fossilized they need to be buried in mud or sand quickly, which doesn't often happen. It would be extremely rare to find an entire sauropod skeleton. Most dinosaur fossils consist of just a few bones, though the whole skeletons of some smaller types have been found. This means that many types of dinosaur are known from only part of the skeleton. Scientists have to reconstruct the whole animal when they have direct evidence for only part of it. They do this by looking for a similar dinosaur for which the missing parts have been found. They then adapt the known features to match the missing parts and produce a composite reconstruction.

The Jurassic Period lasted from about 200 to 135 million years ago. During the Jurassic Period the world's climate was much warmer and wetter than at other times. There were no flowering plants at this time, but the land was covered by lush growth of ferns and other plants. The largest animals were the sauropod dinosaurs, but there were many different types of dinosaurs and other animals as well.

Ichthyosaurs were reptiles that were adapted to life in the sea.

Which were the first large ornithischian dinosaurs?

For millions of years the ornithischian dinosaurs remained small and fairly rare. Then, about 160 million years ago, a new family of ornithischians appeared. These were the stegosaurids and they spread across the world in large numbers. After around 50 million years of success the stegosaurids died out and were replaced by other types of dinosaur. The largest was *Stegosaurus*, which grew to be about 7 m long and lived in North America.

Stegosaurus was a massive creature armed with sharp spikes on its tail. It was a plant eater that used its weapons for defence.

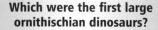

What animals lived in Jurassic seas?

During the Jurassic Period there were many different sorts of fish, but the largest animals were reptiles. Large areas of what is now land were flooded in Jurassic times by warm, shallow seas. Among the reptiles that lived here were turtles up to 4 m long. Plesiosaurs had long necks so they could snap up fish in their jaws. Ichthyosaurs were reptiles that swam like fish.

❶ *The crests of* Dilophosaurus *are a mystery.*

Why did hunting dinosaurs have crests?

Scientists are not certain why several of the large, meat-eating dinosaurs had crests or horns of bone growing from their skulls. The most likely explanation is that the crests were used to signal to other dinosaurs of the same type, but they may have helped the dinosaur sight on prey or contained special glands of some kind.

Which animals lived in the early Jurassic Period?

The early part of the Jurassic Period saw a group of dinosaurs called prosauropods roam the Earth. Prosauropods all died out about 160 million years ago, though one group then evolved into sauropod dinosaurs. The largest prosauropods were about 8 m long. They ate plants and most could run on their hind legs for short bursts.

Why did Stegosaurus have back plates?

The large plates of bone that grew from the back of *Stegosaurus* and other stegosaurid dinosaurs may have had more than one purpose. The skin covering the plates was filled with large blood vessels. If *Stegosaurus* was too hot, it could fill these with blood to cool down. Or it could stand in the sun and soak up warmth if it were too cold. The skin may also have been able to change colour, like that of some modern reptiles, allowing *Stegosaurus* to signal to others of its kind.

Was Stegosaurus stupid?

The brain of *Stegosaurus* was tiny – it had the smallest brain for its size of any dinosaur. The brain was only about 6 cm long while the complete animal was over 7 m. This may indicate that *Stegosaurus* was not very clever, but it was obviously clever enough as it managed to survive for several million years. There was a large mass of nerves located in the hips, which some scientists believe may have controlled the movements of the legs and tail, so the brain did not have to do this job.

❶ Riojasaurus *was a prosauropod that lived in South America right at the start of the Jurassic Period.*

The skies above the dinosaurs were filled with flying animals, but they were very different from modern birds. First to take to the air were the pterosaurs, or winged reptiles. These creatures were archosaurs, and therefore related to the dinosaurs, evolving into hundreds of different types. Later, the birds appeared, probably having evolved from a small type of dinosaur about 170 million years ago.

❶ *The flying reptiles, or pterosaurs, dominated the skies for tens of millions of years. They evolved into a wide variety of forms in all shapes and sizes.*

Which animal was the first to fly?

Several different sorts of reptile were able to glide from tree to tree, but the first vertebrate able to fly properly was a pterosaur, or winged reptile. One of the earliest pterosaurs was *Rhamphorhynchus*, which had a wingspan of about 1.5 m and lived 180 million years ago in Europe. Like all early pterosaurs it had a long tail with a small flap of skin at the end. This may have acted like the rudder on an aircraft, enabling the animal to change direction in flight.

Which was the largest pterosaur?

***Quetzalcoatlus* of North America was the largest pterosaur and also the largest flying animal ever known.** *Quetzalcoatlus* had a wingspan of about 12 m and weighed an amazing 100 kg. As far as is known, it probably flew slowly, soaring on air currents while looking for food. The animal is named after *Quetzalcoatl*, a god of the Aztec people of Mexico. The god was said to have had the appearance of a snake and was covered in feathers.

Were all pterosaurs alike?

No, because over the millions of years that pterosaurs existed they gradually changed and evolved dramatically. The earliest pterosaurs lived about 220 million years ago. They were small, agile flyers with long bony tails. The latest pterosaurs lived 65 million years ago and were huge, soaring creatures. However, the wings of all the pterosaurs were composed of leathery flaps of skin supported by fourth fingers, which had evolved to be extremely long.

Which was the first bird?

***Archaeopteryx* was the earliest known bird – its name meant 'ancient wing'.** It lived in Europe about 150 million years ago, and had feathers that were laid out exactly as in modern birds. *Archaeopteryx* was probably able to fly short distances. It was about 45 cm long and may have hunted insects and small creatures in a forested area. Because it lacked strong muscles attached to its wings, it was probably not a very good flyer.

❷ *Archaeopteryx swoops down from a branch to catch an insect. With feathered wings, this creature was better suited than a pterosaur to flying among trees in a forest with its easily damaged wings of skin.*

What did the ancestor of birds look like?

Most scientists think that birds are descended from a small hunting dinosaur of some kind. This little creature probably looked like the *Protoarchaeopteryx*, which was about the size of a modern turkey and was covered in feathers. The front legs of *Protoarchaeopteryx* were not strong enough to be used as wings, but were longer than those of most small hunting dinosaurs.

➲ *Sinosauropteryx was a hunting dinosaur that was covered in feathers. The name means 'Chinese lizard wing'.*

Did only birds have feathers?

No, several different types of small dinosaur were also covered in feathers. The first dinosaur to be found which had fossilized feathers was *Sinosauropteryx*, which lived about 125 million years ago in China. This small hunter was 1.3 m long and was covered in small feathers. It probably used the feathers to help it keep warm.

How did the birds evolve?

After the time of *Archaeopteryx*, birds evolved slowly, but by about 80 million years ago birds were the most numerous flying vertebrates. The pterosaurs were becoming much rarer than they had been. *Ichthyornis* was a small seabird that was a good flier and probably hunted fish in the open ocean.

➲ *Ichthyornis looked like a modern seagull and lived in the Cretaceous Period.*

About 85 million years ago a new type of dinosaur evolved – the ceratopsids, or horned dinosaurs. At first these animals were quite small, around 1.8 m long, but they rapidly evolved to become larger. The largest ceratopsid was *Triceratops*, which grew to over 9 m in length. By 65 million years ago these were among the most numerous of all dinosaurs.

Triceratops

Styracosaurus

Euoplocephalus

Protoceratops

⬆ *Armoured and horned dinosaurs became more common in the Cretaceous Period.*

How many types of horned dinosaur were there?

Scientists have identified about 30 types of horned dinosaur, but there were probably many others, have not yet been found. The earliest were quite small and had no horns, such as *Protoceratops*, which lived in Asia about 85 million years ago. Later ones were larger and had several horns, such as *Styracosaurus* from North America 80 million years ago. Dinosaurs that had armour, such as *Euoplocephalus*, lived at the same time.

Why were the horned dinosaurs so successful?

The horned dinosaurs became numerous and widespread because of their teeth and jaws. The large frills at the back of the skull allowed for powerful muscles to work the jaws, which were filled with dozens of sharp, slicing teeth. Ceratopsids were able to slice up and swallow large quantities of tough plant food that other dinosaurs could not eat.

How large were the eggs?

The eggs of *Protoceratops* were about 20 cm long and were oval in shape. Most of the eggs were laid in nests that had been scooped out of the ground. The eggs were laid in circles lining the nest and were sometimes piled up on top of each other. Each nest contained between 12 and 18 eggs.

⬇ *Protoceratops eggs were shaped like long ovals. This may have stopped them rolling off the edges of the nest.*

⬇ *Like other horned dinosaurs, Protoceratops had a beak at the front of its jaws to nip leaves from plants and teeth at the rear to chew food.*

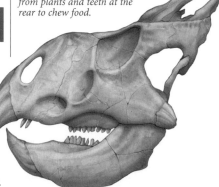

Which was one of the most famous fossil discoveries?

In 1922 an American expedition travelled to the Gobi Desert in central Asia to search for fossils of ancient humans. Instead they found hundreds of dinosaur fossils. One of these was a complete nest, together with eggs and mother. The dinosaur was *Protoceratops* and this proved for the first time that dinosaurs laid eggs and that the mother looked after the nest. It took the expedition months to excavate the find and carry news to the outside world. When the fossils reached America, they caused a sensation. Soon, other expeditions were sent to the Gobi Desert to look for more nests, but only a few were found.

⊕ *Protoceratops guards its nest of eggs. The eggs would probably have been buried under piles of leaves. As the leaves rotted they gave off heat that kept the eggs warm. The discovery of fossilized nests caused a sensation.*

Did dinosaurs migrate?

It is likely that at least some dinosaurs moved from one area to another as the seasons changed, just as modern birds and mammals do. If plants grew well in one place during the summer, but in another during the winter, the horned dinosaurs that fed on them would have moved to feed. Horned dinosaurs such as *Centrosaurus* lived in herds and would have migrated in search of food. So far there is little direct evidence that dinosaurs behaved in this way, though fossils of the forest dinosaur *Plateosaurus* have been found in what was then a desert. It may very well have been migrating between forests when it died.

⊕ *Triceratops uses its horns to fight off an attack by* Tyrannosaurus. *The long, sharp horns would have been able to inflict a serious injury on the hunter, but the flanks and tail of* Triceratops *were vulnerable to attack and would have been easy targets.*

Were the horns good weapons?

Horned dinosaurs had long, sharp horns that grew from their skulls and were used as powerful weapons. *Triceratops* had three extremely sharp horns, which may have been used to fight off attacks from hunting dinosaurs, such as *Tyrannosaurus*. They may also have been used to settle disputes between rival horned dinosaurs fighting over feeding grounds or to see who would lead the herd.

Around 100 million years ago a new group of dinosaurs evolved in Asia. Hadrosaurs were all large, plant-eating dinosaurs, which could walk on all four legs or on just two. Hadrosaurs were closely related to *Iguanodon*, but had webbed feet and slightly different sorts of teeth. Scientists have so far found over 40 types of hadrosaur, all of which lived between 100 and 65 million years ago in Asia, North America and South America.

🔾 *Faint marks on the jaws of hadrosaurs show that these animal had cheek muscles.*

Why were hadrosaurs special?

The jaws of hadrosaurs contained hundreds of teeth, which were packed very tightly together. When a hadrosaur closed its mouth, the upper jaws slid outwards over the lower jaws. As the teeth ground past each other they would have reduced any plant food to a mushy pulp. This made the food easy to digest and allowed hadrosaurs to feed on plants that other dinosaurs could not eat.

Did all hadrosaurs have crests?

Many species of hadrosaur did not have crests of any sort on top of their heads. *Anatosaurus* was over 10 m long and weighed around 3 tonnes. Like other hadrosaurs it had strong muscles attached to its tail, which it may have used for swimming.

Which was the oddest hadrosaur?

The hadrosaur dinosaurs are famous for having strange bony crests, but the largest crest by far was that on *Parasaurolophus*, which was over 1 m long. Scientists believe the crests were covered with colourful skin and were used as a way of signalling to other dinosaurs of the same species. They may have been used to frighten off rivals or to attract mates.

🔾 *Hadrosaurs were probably able to swim well and it is thought that they may have plunged into deep water to escape from packs of hunting dinosaurs.*

Anatosaurus

Velociraptors

⊕ *Many scientists think that hadrosaurs such as* Parasaurolophus *lived close to water for most of their lives. They probably ate both water plants and plants that grew on land.*

How did hadrosaurs care for their young?

Adult hadrosaurs brought food to the nests for their young. The fossils show that young hadrosaurs stayed in the nest for several months after hatching. This allowed the adults to feed them and also to protect them from danger.

How did hadrosaurs build their nests?

Hadrosaurs built nests by digging earth into a round mound. In 1978, a colony of fossilized hadrosaur nests, belonging to the dinosaur *Maiasaura*, was found in Montana, USA. This showed that hadrosaurs built their nests close together.

⊖ *This* Maiasaura *egg is pointed so that it fitted closely with other eggs in the nest.*

⊕ *Young dinosaurs such as* Maiasaura *probably stayed in or close to the nest for a few weeks after hatching.*

Why are hadrosaurs called 'duck-bills'?

The front of the mouth of hadrosaur dinosaurs was wide and flat, like that of a modern duck, so some people call these the 'duck-bill dinosaurs'. However, the beaks of the hadrosaurs were strong, sharp and worked by powerful muscles, unlike the soft, weak bills on ducks.

Among the rarest dinosaur fossils are those of the armoured dinosaurs. Very few of these fossils have been found, and usually only part of the dinosaur is preserved as a fossil. The armoured dinosaurs existed from 180 million years ago until 65 million years ago and are found on most continents, so they were a successful group. Perhaps they lived in areas where fossils did not form very easily, such as in mountainous regions.

Which dinosaur had the most armour?

The most heavily armoured dinosaur was *Ankylosaurus*, which lived in North America about 70 million years ago. The entire back of the body was covered by plates of solid bone, while spikes and knobs stuck out at odd angles. The head was covered by thick sheets of bone and even the eyelid had a covering of bone armour.

What was the Ankylosaurus like?

The armoured *Ankylosaurus* was a large plant-eating dinosaur that grew to be over 11 m long and stood almost 3 m tall. The legs were strong, but solid, so the animal probably walked quite slowly. Its teeth were adapted to eating plants, but the jaw muscles were weak so *Ankylosaurus* must have eaten quite soft plants.

◑ *A* Spinosaurus *attacks an* Ankylosaur. *The armoured dinosaur is fighting back with the heavy club on the end of its tail.*

How did Ankylosaurus defend itself?

The *Ankylosaurus*'s main defence against attack was the armour that covered its body, but it had a more impressive weapon it could use. At the end of its tail was a huge mass of solid bone. *Ankylosaurus* may have used its powerful tail muscles to swing this heavy weight at an attacker. The tail club used like this could have seriously injured even the largest hunting dinosaur.

⬆ *The club on the end of* Ankylosauru's *tail contained several large bones fused together.*

What were the bone-head dinosaurs?

Bone-head dinosaurs are properly called pachycephalosaurs, and were dinosaurs with skulls that were topped by massively thick layers of solid bone. *Stegoceras* lived in North America about 70 million years ago and was 2 m long. Like other pachycephalosaurs, it ate plants and walked on its two hind legs.

Which was the smallest bone-head dinosaur?

The smallest of the pachycephalosaurs so far known to scientists was *Wannanosaurus*, which lived in China about 70 million years ago.

Wannanosaurus was only 60 cm long. The largest of the pachycephalosaurs was *Pachycephalosaurus* which grew to be over 8 m long. The size of most other forms of bone-head is unclear as the bodies are rarely fossilized intact. Only the thick bone of the skull is found.

⬆ *A pair of large* Pachycephalosaurus *strike each other during a conflict. These were the largest of the bone-head dinosaurs measuring 8 m in length.*

Why did bone-heads have such thick skulls?

The pachycephalosaurs used their heads to fight with. When two *Stegoceras* fought, they would lower their heads and charge straight at each other. When the two animals collided, their heads would crash into each other with great force, but the thick bones stopped them from being seriously injured. Eventually, the weaker animal would give up and lose the fight.

⬆ *The butting could be very fierce, but after several clashes the weaker bone-head dinosaur would give up the fight and retreat.*

The Cretaceous Period saw more different types of dinosaur than any other time in history. Among the most impressive were the hunting dinosaurs, which preyed on the plant-eaters of the time. All these hunters were saurischian dinosaurs that had replaced earlier *Coelophysis*, *Dilophosaurus* and similar creatures. They varied greatly in size from barely 2 m long to giants that were the largest carnivores ever to walk the Earth.

❶ *Troodon was a fast, agile hunter that used its superior brain power to track down or ambush prey.*

Which was the brainiest dinosaur?

The dinosaur that had the largest brain in relation to its body size was *Troodon*. This small, agile hunter lived in North America about 75 million years ago and may have been about as intelligent as a modern parrot. The parts of the brain related to sight were particularly large, so it probably had very keen eyesight.

❶ *This fossilized skull of Troodon shows the large area towards the rear of the skull where its brain was located.*

Did dinosaurs hunt in packs?

Some of the smaller hunters, such as *Deinonychus*, probably worked together to kill larger plant-eaters that a single hunter could not tackle alone. *Tenontosaurus* was a plant-eater that grew to about 6 m long. A single *Deinonychus* could

❶ *A pack of* Deinonychus *attacks a plant-eating* Tenontosaurus. *Only by acting together could hunters bring down prey larger than themselves.*

not bring it down, but several hunters attacking at the same time could overwhelm an animal of this size. Such co-operation required larger brains so that they could understand what the others were doing.

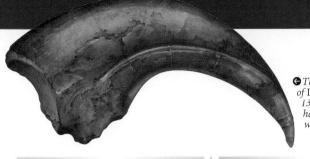

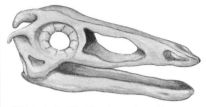

⊙ *The fiercely curved claw of* Deinonychus *measured 13 cm long, but would have been even longer with its horny covering.*

⊙ *This skull of* Ornithomimus *shows that it had no teeth in its jaws.*

Which dinosaur ate fish?

The dinosaur *Baryonyx* probably ate fish, not other dinosaurs. The mouth of *Baryonyx* was filled with a large number of small, sharp teeth. These were ideal for gripping slippery objects, such as fish. The front legs of the dinosaur were equipped with curved claws to hook fish from the water. The shoulders of this dinosaur were unusually powerful, so it could use its very large thumb claw to capture large creatures. *Baryonyx* lived in Britain about 120 million years ago and grew to be 11 m long.

Which dinosaur is called the 'Mystery Killer'?

In 1970 scientists from Poland found two mysterious fossilized dinosaur arms in the Gobi Desert, which they called *Deinocheirus* meaning 'Terrible Hand'. The arms were over 2 m long and carried razor sharp claws about 28 cm long. Nobody knows what the rest of the dinosaur looked like as only the arms have been found – so it is a mystery killer.

What was the 'Terrible Claw'?

The name of the dinosaur *Deinonychus* means 'Terrible Claw'. It got its name from the ferocious, hooked claw on its hind legs. Located on the second toe, the claw could be flicked back and forward very quickly. These claws were vicious weapons of attack and could cause terrible injuries.

⊙ *A pair of racing* Ornithomimus. *Scientists are unsure of the lifestyle of this dinosaur.*

Which hunters had no teeth?

The ornithomimids – a group of hunting dinosaurs. *Ornithomimus* was about 3 m long, but weighed only 150 kg. It was very light for its size, with long legs that made it a fast runner. This dinosaur may have eaten insects, eggs or other food that did not require teeth for feeding.

One of the most famous dinosaurs is *Tyrannosaurus rex*, a huge meat-eating creature from the very end of the Cretaceous Period about 65 million years ago. Some scientists think that *Tyrannosaurus* was powerful enough to hunt and kill the largest plant-eating dinosaurs of the time. Other scientists think that it was too slow to catch prey and that it fed on dinosaurs that had died a natural death instead.

What did Tyrannosaurus rex look like?

Tyrannosaurus rex walked on its hind legs only, with its powerful tail balancing the weight of its body and head. It was a muscular animal that had a large mouth filled with long, sharp teeth and a jaw so wide it made a formidable predator.

◑ Tyrannosaurus *had large eyes, so it probably hunted by sight.*

◐ *Fossilized footprints can show scientists how fast the dinosaur was moving.*

How fast could Tyrannosaurus move?

Scientists think that *Tyrannosaurus* was a fairly active dinosaur. It had stout, muscular legs that could not move quickly, but they were long enough to cover quite a distance with each step. It may have been able to reach 30 km/h, but only for short bursts of time. More usually it would have walked at about 5 km/h.

What dinosaurs did Tyrannosaurus rex eat?

At the time that *Tyrannosaurus* lived in North America there were large numbers of plant-eating dinosaurs called hadrosaurs, on which *Tyrannosaurus* probably preyed. *Tyrannosaurus* may also have fed on horned dinosaurs, which also existed at this time, though their horns may have made them more difficult to kill. It would certainly have fed on large plant-eaters so that it got enough to eat at each meal.

◐ *A* Tyrannosaurus *towers over a young* Parasaurolophus. *Many scientists think the hunter ambushed its prey rather than chasing it for long distances.*

Why were their arms so small?

The arms of *Tyrannosaurus* might have been used to help it stand up.
Tyrannosaurus had tiny arms, barely one metre long compared to its overall length of 13 m. It is thought that *Tyrannosaurus* lay on its stomach when resting because very strong bones have been found along the chest and the stomach that may have helped support it when it was lying down. When standing up it could have braced itself, fusing its small front legs, and heave itself up using its powerful leg muscles.

Why was its skull so strong?

The skull of *Tyrannosaurus* may have been so strong because of the hunting technique it used. *Tyrannosaurus* had a skull that was reinforced by strong pieces of bone at the main pressure points. Some scientists think it may have attacked prey by running at them with its jaws wide open. This would inflict a terrible blow on the victim, but *Tyrannosaurus* would have been protected from injury by its strong skull.

➊ *Tyrannosaurus may have lived in forests and hunted in packs.*

Was Tyrannosaurus the biggest hunter dinosaur?

No, the largest meat-eating dinosaur so far found by scientists was *Giganotosaurus*. This dinosaur was about 14.5 m long and may have weighed up to 8 tonnes, more than 2 tonnes heavier than *Tyrannosaurus*. It is thought that *Giganotosaurus* may have hunted the sauropod dinosaurs that survived in South America longer than elsewhere. Only a few fossils of *Giganotosaurus* have been found, so it is not as well-known as *Tyrannosaurus*.

Some time around 65 million years ago the dinosaurs disappeared. Rocks older than this date are filled with the fossils of different types of dinosaurs, but younger rocks contain no dinosaurs. The reason why a group of animals that had dominated the world for 140 million years should vanish so completely has puzzled scientists ever since the dinosaurs were first discovered. There have been many different theories to explain the event.

➊ *The collision of a gigantic meteorite would have killed all dinosaurs near the impact immediately, but all life on Earth would have been affected within a few weeks.*

➊ *Vast volcanic eruptions are known to have taken place about the time the dinosaurs died out.*

What was the world like just before the extinction?

About 66 million years ago the world was dominated by dinosaurs. In Asia and North America there was a wide variety of armoured dinosaurs, horned dinosaurs, hadrosaurs and hunting dinosaurs. Elsewhere, there were sauropods, stegosaurs and various meat-eaters. Some of these animals existed in large numbers, and all of them seemed to be thriving. There was no sign that a disaster was about to happen.

Did the dinosaurs die out all at once?

Scientists who study the extinction of the dinosaurs are not certain if the event happened in a single year or over a period of several thousand years. The rocks that contain the fossils cannot be dated accurately enough to give this information. However, we do know that dinosaurs all over the planet died out at the same time. Whatever caused the extinction affected every part of the world.

Could a meteor have killed the dinosaurs?

It is thought that if a large meteorite hit the planet it would throw up a dense cloud of dust and water that would block sunlight from the Earth's surface for several months. This would cause plants to die off, which in turn would cause the death of most types of animal, which could have included dinosaurs.

Could mammals have wiped out the dinosaurs?

One theory that nobody takes seriously any longer is that the mammals may have wiped out the dinosaurs. It was said that the small mammals of the late Cretaceous Period were adapted for eating eggs. If they ate enough dinosaur eggs, they would have wiped out the dinosaurs by stopping them producing any young. However, there do not seem to have been enough mammals to have achieved this. In any case, if the egg-eating mammals ate all the dinosaur eggs then they would have destroyed their own source of food, which means they would have died out themselves.

What happened after the dinosaurs?

After the dinosaurs vanished from the Earth, the world still had many kinds of animals. The creatures that survived included mammals, birds, insects, lizards and other small creatures. It would be many years before these animals evolved to become larger and more powerful. However, as time passed, the mammals began to inhabit and thrive in the world once governed by the dinosaurs. Today, the world is dominated by mammals in much the same way that it was once dominated by dinosaurs. Nonetheless, there is no modern land animal that is as large as the largest dinosaur would have been.

Within a few million years of the death of the dinosaurs the world was filled with new types of animals such as crocodiles, snakes and birds.

Did volcanoes have an effect?

About 65 million years ago, volcanic eruptions were taking place that may have caused the death of the dinosaurs. These eruptions were larger than any today, covering thousands of square kilometres of land with lava. Gas and dust thrown up would have affected the climate, which may have been enough to wipe out the dinosaurs.

1 In what period did *Eustreptospondylus* live?

2 What are scientists who study dinosaurs called?

3 Which two parts of a dinosaur are most often found as fossils?

4 What are coprolites?

5 What does the word 'dinosaur' mean?

6 What are the two groups into which all dinosaurs are classified?

7 Did dinosaurs lay eggs?

8 What did the sauropods eat?

FACTFILE

10 famous **fossil finds**

1822 Dr Gideon Mantell discovers the first dinosaur fossils in Sussex, England. They belong to *Iguanodon*.

1858 Joseph Leidy discovers the first dinosaur skeleton in New Jersey, USA. It is a *Hadrosaurus*.

1878 Coal miners at Bernissart in Belgium discover 40 complete *Iguanodon* skeletons.

1909 Earl Douglass discovers the largest known find of fossils in the world, in Utah. It is now Dinosaur National Monument and is still being excavated.

1925 Dinosaur nests and eggs are discovered for the first time by Roy Andrews digging in the Gobi Desert in central Asia.

1969 Fossils of *Deinonychus* are found by John Ostrom showing that some dinosaurs were fast, agile creatures.

1974 Hundreds of fossils are found in a remote area of Xigong Province, China. Most belong to previously unknown types of dinosaur.

1993 The largest dinosaur, and largest land animal, *Argentinosaurus* is discovered.

1995 Discovery of fossils of the 14.3 m long *Giganotosaurus*, the largest meat-eating animal ever to walk the earth.

1998 The discovery of *Caudipteryx* in Liaoning, China, shows that some smaller dinosaurs were covered with feathers.

9 Did the first fish have skeletons made of bone or cartilage?

10 Where does the coelacanth fish live today?

11 To which modern animal is the extinct ammonite related?

12 When did the first dinosaurs live?

13 Where did the first dinosaurs live?

14 Do dinosaurs usually have longer hind legs or fore legs?

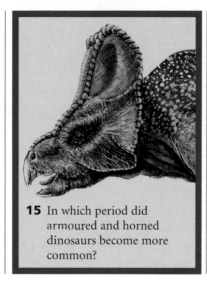

15 In which period did armoured and horned dinosaurs become more common?

16 How long was *Seismosaurus*?

17 Where were the fossils of the dinosaur *Jobaria* found?

18 What is a gastrolith?

19 Which dinosaur had the longest neck?

20 Did sauropods live only in swamps?

21 Which reptiles looked like fish and lived in the sea?

22 Where did *Stegosaurus* have a large mass of nerves?

Key **dates**

1676 Robert Plot of Oxford publishes a book containing pictures of strange giant bones found in England.

1824 The first dinosaur to be named in scientific literature, *Megalosaurus* by Dr William Buckland.

1842 British scientist Dr Richard Owen uses the word 'dinosaur' for the first time to describe three different large ancient reptiles.

1854 Concrete model dinosaurs are erected at London's Hyde Park – they are now in Crystal Palace.

1933 The Hollywood movie *King Kong* shows humans and dinosaurs together, although all dinosaurs died long before humans evolved.

Naming **dinosaurs**

All dinosaurs have two names – a genus name and a specific name. The genus name is used most often.

If scientists discover a new type of dinosaur they can name it after anything they like, except themselves.

Many dinosaur names include the ancient Greek word 'saurus', meaning 'reptile' or 'lizard'.

➲ *Iguanodon hands could grip plants or act as a foot.*

23 How large was *Lesothosaurus*?

24 Did *Rhamphorhynchus* have a long tail?

25 Which was the earliest known bird?

26 How large was the wingspan of *Pteranodon*?

27 Where were the fossilized nests of *Protoceratops* discovered?

28 Which dinosaur had the largest skull?

29 Did *Psittacosaurus* have horns?

30 When did hadrosaurs first appear on Earth?

31 How long was the crest of *Parasaurolophus*?

32 Did hadrosaurs store air in their crests when diving underwater?

33 Where did *Ankylosaurus* live?

34 What did the bone-head dinosaurs eat?

35 Which dinosaur was named from a single bone?

36 How long was *Tenontosaurus*?

37 Where did *Baryonyx* live?

38 Which is the only part of the dinosaur *Deinocheirus* to have been found?

39 Did *Tyrannosaurus* eat hadrosaurs?

40 How long were the arms of *Tyrannosaurus*?

41 Which relative of *Tyrannosaurus* grew to about 9 m long and weighed 3 tonnes?

42 When did the dinosaurs die out?

Amazing **facts**

• The oldest known rocks are about 3,900 million years old.

• Frogs have lived on Earth for 240 million years.

• The tuatara of New Zealand is the only survivor of the Rhynchosaur group of reptiles that evolved about 240 million years ago.

• Sharks appeared 400 million years ago and have changed little since.

• Sharks survived the huge mass extinction 65 million years ago, which wiped out the dinosaurs.

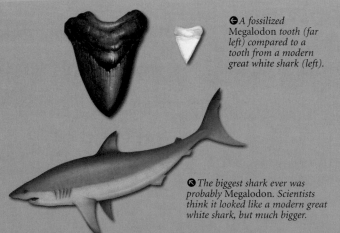

↺ *A fossilized* Megalodon *tooth (far left) compared to a tooth from a modern great white shark (left).*

↺ *The biggest shark ever was probably* Megalodon. *Scientists think it looked like a modern great white shark, but much bigger.*

Answers

1 Jurassic
2 Palaeontologists
3 Bones and teeth
4 Fossilized dung
5 Terrible Lizard
6 Saurischian and Ornithischian
7 Yes
8 Plants
9 Cartilage
10 In the Indian Ocean
11 Squid and octopus
12 About 230 million years ago
13 South America
14 Hind legs
15 Cretaceous Period

16 About 50 m
17 Africa
18 A stone swallowed by an animal to help it digest food
19 *Mamenchisaurus*
20 No
21 Ichthyosaurs
22 In its hips
23 About one metre long
24 Yes
25 *Archaeopteryx*
26 About 9 m
27 Mongolia
28 *Torosaurus*
29 No

30 About 100 million years ago
31 About one metre
32 No
33 North America
34 Plants
35 *Cryptodraco*
36 About 6 m
37 Britain
38 Its arms
39 Yes
40 About one metre
41 *Daspletosaurus*
42 About 65 million years ago

43 Cretaceous
44 Triassic
45 India
46 Thick-headed reptile

Small **dinosaurs**

- *Heterodontosaurus* was named for the three different types of tooth in its mouth. It ate plants in Africa about 180 million years ago.
- *Lesothosaurus* was one metre long and ate plants. It lived in southern Africa 190 million years ago.
- The planteater *Othnielia* came from North America 140 million years ago and was just 1.4 m long.
- *Compsognathus* was a tiny hunter from Europe 140 million years ago. It was just 90 cm long.

➲ Compsognathus *was one of the smallest dinosaurs – about as tall as a modern chicken. It hunted tiny creatures such as insects and worms.*

THE NATURAL WORLD

The natural world is all around us. For most of the time we are not aware of the plant and animal kingdoms growing, reproducing and changing before our eyes. Animals fly through the air, inhabit the ocean's depths and roam the land, while plants grow in the most inhospitable landscapes. The Earth provides unique habitats for all kinds of life.

What are living things made of?

Why do some animals hibernate?

Which plants have no flowers?

Life on Earth began over 3.5 billion years ago. How? Perhaps by chemical processes within the primeval 'soup' of elements; maybe by a haphazard collision of lifeless molecules; possibly by the impact of 'seeds' of life-bearing dust from outer space. Life began in the oceans and the oldest known forms of life are fossils of bacteria and algae. Today, there are at least two million species of living organisms on Earth.

How are living things unique?

Only living things can reproduce to make identical copies of themselves. The first living cell, bobbing in the ocean millions of years ago, was unlike anything else on the planet. It used chemical energy in seawater to feed and was able to reproduce.

⊙ The gorilla is a primate, one of the most advanced of all animals. Yet it is made up of cells, just like the simplest forms of life.

⊙ The prehistory of the Earth is divided into very long periods of time called eras, and shorter ones called periods. This is a scene from the Jurassic Period, when plants and animals were very different from those today.

What are the main groups of living things?

The two main groups of living things are animals and plants. There are five groups, or biological kingdoms. The other three groups are monera, protists (both microscopic one-celled organisms) and fungi. All living things are given names to identify them.

What are living things made of?

All living things are made of cells, which are like tiny chemical factories. Most cells can be seen only through a microscope. Our bodies, and those of every animal and plant, are made of many cells. The simplest plants and animals, such as diatoms, have just one cell, whilst plants, such as trees, or mammals, such as whales and humans, consist of many millions of cells.

⊙ Diatoms are very simple life-forms, with just one cell. Most are less than 1 mm in size. They float in the oceans, trapping energy from sunlight by a process called photosynthesis.

⊙ An amoeba is a single-celled organism that reproduces by dividing, to create two new cells. There are many kinds of amoeba. Some live in water; others are parasites, living inside the bodies of animals.

What is an animal's most important activity?

For most animals, finding food is the most important activity. Unlike plants, which use energy in sunlight to make their food, animals have to seek out food to provide their bodies with the energy they need. Animals eat different types of food. Herbivores eat only plant food, carnivores eat other animals and omnivores eat both plants and meat.

🔽 *Male mandrills have colourful red and blue markings on their face as a display to attract females, whilst females have more muted coloured markings.*
The mandrill spends much of its time looking for food, such as fruits, seeds, eggs and small animals.

🔼 *There are only three species of elephants alive today: the African elephant (left), the recently discovered African forest elephant, and the smaller Asian elephant (right). Other species of elephant existed in earlier times.*

What is a species?

A species is one kind of living thing. Male and female of the same species (two African elephants, for example) can breed. Individuals of different species (an African and an Asian elephant) cannot reproduce. Scientists use classification, in terms of species and genus, to group living things by appearance and relationship. So, for example,

all red foxes belong to the same species and would be able to reproduce with one another. The red, grey, Arctic and all other foxes are then placed among the fox genus (with the Latin name *Vulpes*). The fox genus is then part of the larger dog family (*Canidae*).

For about 160 million years (from 225 million years ago to 65 million years ago) dinosaurs were the most successful animals on Earth. The giant dinosaurs were the biggest reptiles of all time, and were much bigger than elephants. Flying prehistoric reptiles were the biggest animals ever to take to the air. As well as land giants, there were also reptile monsters in the oceans.

Like many dinosaurs, Herrerasaurus *had flaps of skin on its neck, back and tail. Early fossil studies missed these faint impressions.*

Why did the dinosaurs die out?

The most likely explanation for the extinction of the dinosaurs is that a comet, asteroid or meteorite hit the Earth. There have been other extinctions in Earth's history, but the disappearance of the dinosaurs around 65 million years ago was a cataclysmic event. Dust-clouds flung up by the impact caused climate change: plants died, eggs failed to hatch and mature animals died of starvation or cold.

A Maiasaura mother watches over her eggs as the young hatch.

Which prehistoric animals could fly?

Insects and some reptiles. There were dragonflies as big as pigeons in prehistoric swamp-forests. Flying reptiles, called *Pterosaurs*, flew with bat-like wings of skin stretched between bony fingers. The flying reptile *Quetzalcoatlus* was as big as a small plane with a wingspan of 15 m. The bird-like reptile *Archaeopteryx* had feathers, but scientists believe that it would not have been able to fly very well.

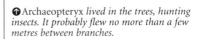

Archaeopteryx lived in the trees, hunting insects. It probably flew no more than a few metres between branches.

What were baby dinosaurs like?

Like mini-versions of their parents. Being reptiles, dinosaurs laid eggs. Some dinosaurs, such as *Maiasaura*, were careful parents. They made nests, guarded their eggs against predators and stayed with the young until they were able to fend for themselves.

Which were the most awesome dinosaurs?

The most frightening of all the dinosaurs that lived were the giant meat-eaters. *Tyrannosaurus rex* was up to 13 m long, 6 m in height and 6 tonnes in weight. *Tyrannosaurus'* mouth opened so wide it could have swallowed a 10-year-old child with ease. A second giant, *Allosaurus*, was up to 12 m long, weighed up to 6 tonnes, and had

enormous jaws that were lined with incredibly sharp teeth. But just as awesome and savagely fierce were the smaller killers, which included the vicious 'slashing claw' *Deinonychus* and the smaller *Stenonychosaurus*. The human-sized *Velociraptor* was even capable of working as a team to bring down a much bigger dinosaur. These crafty carnivores were likely to have been some of the most intelligent dinosaurs around.

Brachiosaurus *had a very long tail and a long neck, which it probably used to reach treetop foliage to feed on. This dinosaur giant could grow up to 25 m long.*

What were the biggest land animals of all time?

Prehistoric reptilian sauropods, such as *Seismosaurus* and *Brachiosaurus*. These 50-tonne reptiles were as big as houses. They lived in herds, ate plants and had very long necks to reach up to nibble on treetops. Evidence from fossil footprints also suggests that they were able to run quite fast. *Mamenchisaurus*, a herbivore (plant-eater) whose bones have been found in China, had a neck 15 m long. Some of these giants had tails even longer than their necks. The biggest land mammal was *Baluchitherium*, a kind of mega-rhinoceros weighing 30 tonnes. The largest land animal of today, the modern African elephant, weighs only 7 tonnes!

Tyrannosaurus *preyed on weaker dinosaurs, and also ate carrion (dead animals).*

Mammals are not the biggest group of animals. But they are amazingly adaptable, and live in a wide range of habitats – on land, in the ocean and in the air – and in all sorts of climates. They have bigger brains (in relation to their body size) than other animals. The biggest sea and land animals are mammals – whales in the ocean and elephants on dry land.

The platypus lives in rivers in western Australia. It has webbed feet and a paddle-tail for swimming.

Which mammals lay eggs?

The only egg-laying mammals are the duckbilled platypus and the five species of spiny anteaters, or echidnas. These curious animals live only in Australia. The female platypus lays two eggs in a burrow, and suckles the young when they hatch. The female echidna lays one egg into a pouch on her body and the baby grows inside, sucking milk from her fur.

Do pouched animals live only in Australia?

No, some live in New Guinea and the Solomon Islands of the Pacific Ocean, and two kinds (opossums and rat opossums) live in the Americas. Mammals with pouches for rearing their young are called marsupials. Australia has the largest variety of marsupial animals, which includes kangaroos, koalas, wallabies, possums, wombats and bandicoots.

A baby kangaroo (a joey) grows inside its mother's pouch. It climbs back inside for safety, until it grows too big for the pouch.

What are carnivores?

Carnivores are flesh-eating hunting animals. Some of the best known hunters are the big cats – lions, tigers, leopards, jaguars, cheetahs – and many smaller cats. Most cats hunt alone, using stealth. Other families of carnivores include the dogs (wolves, jackals and foxes) and the weasels (otters, badgers, mink). Many marine animals such as sharks and dolphins are carnivores, hunting and feeding on fish and other living things in the water.

A leopard usually hunts at night, and after a kill drags its meal into a tree out of reach of scavengers such as hyenas.

Which mammals live in the sea?

Seals, dolphins and whales are sea mammals, whose ancestors lived on land millions of years ago.
Their front legs have become flippers or paddles for swimming, and instead of back legs whales have horizontal tail fins, or flukes. Seals and sea lions can still move on land, but whales and dolphins are now entirely water animals.

⬇ Like dolphins and other whales, killer whales are intelligent animals.

How do mammals give birth?

The placental mammals (the biggest mammal group) give birth to live young. Inside the female's body the developing young are nourished by an organ called the placenta. Most mammal babies are fairly well developed when born, though they still need parental care to begin with.

⬆ This baby rhino is a miniature replica of its massive mother, but will need her protection during the early months of its life.

Which is the biggest group of mammals?

Surprisingly, bats. There are 960 species of bats – the only mammals that truly fly. The largest bats are the fruit bats and flying foxes, which can have wings almost 2 m across, but most bats are small, about the size of a mouse. Many bats are nocturnal insect-eaters, but some also prey on small rodents, frogs and fish. Night-flying bats use echolocation to find their way in the dark and to locate prey. They send out high-pitched squeaks that are reflected as echoes from nearby objects.

⬇ Many bats have extra-large ears to pick up echoes as 'sonic images'. The bat homes in on its target, such as a moth. Many bats roost together in colonies, sleeping upside-down, dangling from their foot claws.

Birds are warm-blooded vertebrates (animals with backbones). Their feathers keep them warm and help them to fly. They walk on two back legs, while their front limbs have become wings. All birds lay eggs. And all birds' bodies are strong but light, ideal for flying – though not all birds fly.

Are all birds able to fly?

No, some birds have wings that are useless for flying. Some run or creep about, whilst others have wings adapted for swimming. Flightless land birds live in Africa (ostrich), South America (rhea) and Australia and New Guinea (emu and cassowary). The small, flightless kiwi lives in the forests of New Zealand, which was once home to a much bigger, flightless bird, the giant moa.

⊕ *The ostrich relies on fast running to escape enemies, but it can also give a vicious kick.*

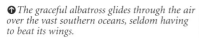

⊕ *The graceful albatross glides through the air over the vast southern oceans, seldom having to beat its wings.*

Which bird has the longest wingspan?

The wandering albatross of the southern oceans has the longest wingspan with long, thin wings that can measure more than 3 m from wingtip to wingtip. Its wings enable it to glide for enormous distances with little muscular effort. These majestic birds cannot take off very easily, so they launch themselves into 'upcurrents' of air from their clifftop nests. The marabou stork comes a close second with a wingspan of almost 3 m.

🔺 *A chinstrap penguin chases fish, using its wings like oars to 'row' through the water.*

🔻 *Storks, such as this yellow-billed stork, use their long beaks to probe for food in shallow waters and marshes.*

Do polar bears like to eat penguins?

They never get the chance. Polar bears are the top land predator of the northern hemisphere polar lands (the Arctic), while penguins live in the southern seas, as far south as Antarctica. Penguins cannot fly but their wings have evolved into flippers for swimming. A penguin is streamlined to dart after fish – and escape hungry leopard seals and killer whales.

Why do birds have beaks?

The bird jaw has become a beak, which has adapted to catch and eat all kinds of food. Reptiles and mammals have teeth, but birds do not. Birds of prey have hooked beaks, for tearing flesh. Fish-eaters such as herons have long spear beaks. There are specialized beaks designed for seed-eaters, nut-crackers, fruit-pickers and insect-snappers. Some birds also use their beaks as tools, to make nests or to bore holes.

➲ *The song thrush has one of the most melodious songs of all European birds.*

Why do songbirds sing?

Birds sing to tell other birds where they are, or to defend their territory – where it nests and finds food. Singing is the bird's way of telling other birds to 'keep out'. Singing also helps male birds to attract females during the breeding season. Early morning in spring is a good time to hear birdsong, but some birds sing at dusk, too.

Reptiles and amphibians are cold-blooded animals, which means they need sunshine to warm their bodies, and so are not found in really cold climates. In cool climates, these animals often hibernate during the winter. Many amphibians are water creatures, but reptiles are found in dry deserts, rainforests, swamps and even in saltwater oceans.

↟Crocodiles, such as this Indian gharial, hunt in the water, grabbing land animals and also preying on fish and water creatures.

How many reptiles are there?

More than 6,500 species. There are more lizards than any other reptiles – about 3,700 species. Next come the snakes (2,800). The biggest living reptile belongs to one of the smaller reptile families – the crocodiles – with only 25 species. There are about 3,000 species of amphibians, most of them frogs and toads. In general, amphibians are smaller than reptiles.

↡This picture shows some reptiles and amphibians. The poison arrow frog is small but deadly. The Komodo dragon (the biggest lizard) and Nile crocodile are giants by comparison and highly dangerous carnivores.

Eastern green mamba snake

Komodo dragon

Jackson's chameleon

Nile crocodile

Indian cobra

Desert tortoise

Golden arrow poison frog

Common frog

Spotted salamander

Frilled lizard

Shingleback lizard

How big can reptiles grow?

A large crocodile can weigh as much as 450 kg and live more than 100 years. As a reptile heavyweight, only a leatherback turtle outweighs a crocodile. The biggest lizard is the Komodo dragon, up to 3 m long. The longest reptiles are snakes. In 1912 a dead python was measured at 10 m long. The heaviest snake is the anaconda, at 200 kg.

➊ *Snakes, such as this pit viper, have heat-sensing pits in its head, to track prey in the dark or underground.*

What are amphibians?

Amphibians include frogs, toads, newts and salamanders. They can live on land or in water, and most return to water to lay their eggs, even if they spend most of their life on dry land. The eggs hatch into tadpoles, which grow legs and become adult animals, able to live on land or water. Amphibians were the first animals to move onto dry land in prehistoric times.

➲ *Frogs mate in the water and lay clusters of eggs in a jellylike mass of spawn.*

How do snakes hunt?

Snakes have poor eyesight and hunt mainly by using smell, sounds and special heat-detecting organs on their heads. Some snakes, like grass snakes, simply grab prey with their sharp teeth. Others, such as boas and pythons, kill by constriction (crushing the prey until it cannot breathe). Many snakes kill by biting with curved fangs, which inject deadly poison. All snakes swallow their food whole.

How long do tortoises live?

As long as a hundred years. A tortoise given to the ruler of Tonga by Captain Cook some time before 1777 lived until 1965, so it was at least 188 years old. Tortoises move slowly – they have no need to dash around because they carry protective shells with them. This slow lifestyle means tortoises use only a small amount of energy, and so can live on very poor vegetation.

Which lizards can change colour?

Chameleons are tree lizards and can change colour (camouflage) to match their surroundings for protection. They also change colour when alarmed or angry. Chameleons catch insects by uncoiling very long, sticky tongues at high speed. They also have eyes that swivel independently to give them the best all-round vision of any reptile.

➲ *Chameleons move slowly, clinging onto branches with their claws.*

Fish are the animals most perfectly adapted to living in water. They swim better than any other animal, and they can breathe by means of gills, rather than lungs. Fish can live in salty water (the ocean) or fresh water (rivers, lakes and pools). Some fish, such as eels and salmon, live in both. Sea fish tend to grow bigger than river and lake fish.

How many fish species are there?

Fish are the most numerous vertebrate animals (animals with backbones) and there are thought to be over 22,000 species. About a third of these species live in fresh water. There are three main groups of fish: jawless fish (such as hagfish); cartilaginous fish (sharks and rays); and bony fish – the biggest group.

A shoal of yellow snapper. Swimming in shoals means a small fish stands a better chance of avoiding becoming a predator's next meal.

The dogfish is a small relative of the great white shark.

Why does a dogfish have no bones?

A dogfish is a small shark and all sharks have a skeleton made of gristly material called cartilage. It is similar to bone, but more bendy and not so hard. Sharks have very rough skins, too, like sandpaper to the touch and, unlike bony fishes, they have no swimbladder to enable them to float without swimming.

Which river fish can strip meat from bones in minutes?

Many stories (mostly untrue) are told of fierce sharks, but the small piranha has razor-sharp teeth for chopping out flesh in chunks. This small fish lives in the rivers of South America. Unlike most predatory fish, piranhas hunt in shoals (groups). A shoal of piranhas can strip the flesh off a pig in less than a minute, leaving just the carcass.

The piranha is small, but ferocious when hungry.

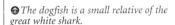

The coelacanth has been around since the time of the dinosaurs.

What is a coelacanth?

The coelacanth is a marine 'living fossil'. Scientists thought this primitive-looking fish died out 70 million years ago – until in 1938 a coelacanth was caught off East Africa. Since then, coelacanths have also been found living on the eastern side of the Indian Ocean, off the islands of Indonesia.

What do deep-sea fish look like?

Some look very strange. Their world is black and cold – no sunlight filters down below around 750 m. Food is scarce, so many deep-sea fish have wide gaping mouths, to make sure of catching whatever prey comes near. Some use 'fishing rods' to attract prey. Many deep-sea fish have special organs to make their own 'bio-light', to help identify one another in the darkness.

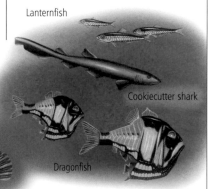

⊙ *Many deep-sea fish glow to confuse predators.*

Lanternfish

Cookiecutter shark

Dragonfish

⊙ *Anglerfish are dark-coloured for camouflage, but a glowing tip extends from its dorsal fin to attract prey.*

⊙ *The viperfish has a lure and huge jaws to grab the next meal, while lanternfish make their own light.*

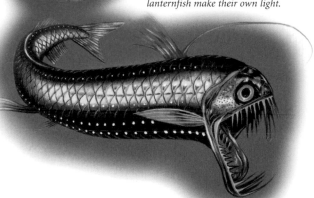

What is a devil fish?

This is another name for the giant manta ray. The manta ray looks fearsome, with a 'wing' span of up to 7 m across. Sailors in the past told stories of mantas rising up out of the ocean to shroud a ship in their wings and drag it underwater. In fact, the manta is a harmless giant that will even allow divers to hitch a lift clinging on to its body. The manta has broad fins for swimming effortlessly through the water, using its 'horns' to guide plankton into its gaping mouth.

⊙ *The manta is the largest of the rays. Rays and skates are fish with flattened bodies, and are related to sharks.*

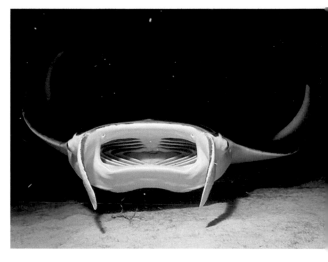

There are two main groups of animals – animals with backbones (vertebrates) and animals without backbones (invertebrates). About 96 per cent of all animals are invertebrates – they include insects, spiders, crustaceans, molluscs, worms, starfish and corals. Insects can live almost anywhere and eat almost anything. It is just as well that their body design limits their size, so that giant insects exist only in horror films.

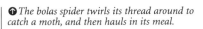

● The bolas spider twirls its thread around to catch a moth, and then hauls in its meal.

What makes an insect an insect?

Every insect has three pairs of legs and a body that is divided into three parts: head, thorax (middle) and abdomen. All insects have certain features in common. On the head are eyes, mouthparts and a pair of antennae or feelers. Most, though not all, insects have wings.

● A bombardier beetle, like all insects, has six legs. This beetle has an unusual defensive weapon – it sprays a jet of hot gas at an enemy.

Which animals have the biggest shells?

Giant clams of warm oceans have the biggest shells – over 1 m across. Insects have hard bodies, but many molluscs, such as snails and cone shells have elaborate, decorative shells. Crustaceans (crabs, lobsters and shrimps) also have shells. Like insects, crustaceans are arthropods (animals with jointed legs), and most of them live in the sea.

● The hermit crab has a soft body, and so makes its home inside the empty shell of a mollusc.

What do spiders eat?

All spiders are carnivores, and most feed on insects and other small creatures. Spiders catch their food in a variety of ways; some just chase their prey, but many spiders make silk web-traps to snare their victims. The bolas spider dangles a sticky ball from a silk thread. The sticky ball gives off a chemical smell similar to a female moth to attract male moths flying nearby. When the moth flies in, it gets stuck to the ball.

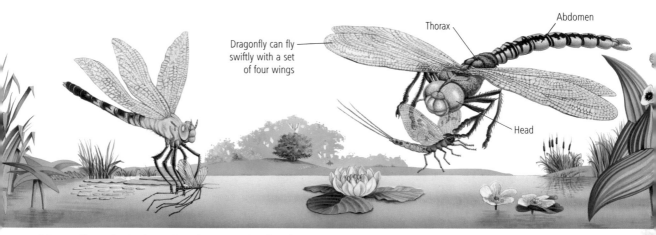

Dragonfly can fly swiftly with a set of four wings

Thorax

Abdomen

Head

⊕ *Dragonflies catch other insects in mid-air, using their front legs as a 'net'. They have eyes larger than any other insect to be able to spot prey.*

Which insects fly fastest?

The fastest fliers in the insect world are dragonflies, which can speed along at up to 90 km/h when in pursuit of their next meal. Second fastest are the bot flies, flying at around 50 km/h. The bumblebee flies at speeds of about 18 km/h.

⊕ *It takes 21 days for a bee to develop from an egg to an adult.*

What are social insects?

A few species of insects live in groups, or colonies, making them social insects. These insects include honeybees, some wasps, and all ants and termites. All the members work for the good of the colony, helping to build a nest and care for the young. Ants work together with the use of chemical pheromones, which send signals among the group. One beehive in summer will contain one queen, up to 60,000 worker bees, and a few hundred fertile males. Only one individual female, the queen, lays eggs.

⊕ *Honey bees build nests of wax sheets, called combs. Brood cells in the comb contain grubs that hatch from the eggs laid by the queen.*

Thousands of animals have died out naturally in the course of evolution. Several mass extinctions happened in prehistoric times – the biggest was 240 million years ago, when perhaps 96 per cent of living things vanished. Another, 65 million years ago, saw the disappearance of the dinosaurs. The rate of extinction has accelerated in the last 200 years and today over 5,000 species are endangered.

Why is the koala at risk?

Because it is a specialized feeder. This Australian marsupial eats only eucalyptus tree leaves. Being dependent on one food source is dangerous, because if the forests are cut down, the koalas cannot find anywhere else to live, or anything else to eat. A similar threat faces the Chinese giant panda, whose diet is mainly bamboo shoots. A shortage of bamboo means starvation for pandas.

What is the greatest threat to wildlife?

Habitat loss is the most serious threat to endangered animals and plants. For example, when tropical rainforests are felled for timber or agriculture, most of the wildlife dependent on the rainforest cannot survive anywhere else. They cannot find food or breed, and so their numbers start to decline. Many lost species are insects and other

⬆*A snow leopard needs a large hunting territory. Human interference, hunting for the fur trade and loss of its natural prey make survival difficult for big predators.*

invertebrates never studied by scientists. Changes to farm methods, housebuilding, hotel developments along the beaches, and over-hunting all threaten wild species.

➡*Koalas survived hunting in the early 20th century and are now a protected species.*

Which pigeons went missing for ever?

A flightless pigeon called the dodo lived undisturbed on the island of Mauritius in the Indian Ocean until European sailors arrived in the 1500s. Sailors killed the birds for food, rats and cats ate the eggs, and by 1680 the dodo was extinct. The most unexpected extinction was that of the passenger pigeon. Billions of these birds lived in North America until hunters began killing pigeons for food. Between 1850 and 1880 the vast flocks vanished and the last passenger pigeon died in a zoo in 1914.

The dodo was flightless and had no defence against humans or introduced predators.

Rhino horn is wrongly believed by some to possess magical properties, so the horns are used in medicine and in making weapons.

Why is oil in the water a killer to seabirds?

Seabirds that come into contact with the greasy surface of oily water cannot fly because their feathers become clogged with oil. This means that the birds cannot hunt to feed and soon die. Some birds are rescued by conservationists and cleaned up in order to be able to fly again, and eventually returned to the wild.

How can cutting off horns save some animals?

Removing the horns from rhinos living in game reserves does not hurt the animals, nor affect their lives seriously, but it makes them less of a target for poachers. Poachers in Africa kill rhinos for their horns, which are actually made of hair. The horns are used in traditional medicines in some countries, and in the making of ornamental weapons, such as knives. Poaching for rhino horn, elephant tusks and even elephants' feet is a serious problem in parts of Africa. By removing a rhino's horn, poachers have no need to hunt and kill them.

This seabird died as a result of having wings clogged with oil, which made it unable to fly and hunt for food.

There are about 375,000 kinds of plants. The biggest plant family is the flowering plants, or angiosperms, with over 250,000 species. Plants make their own food, using sunlight (photosynthesis). Fungi used to be classed as plants, but as they cannot make their own food, they are now put in a class of their own, which includes about 100,000 species.

🔻 *Tropical cycads are primitive cone-bearing plants that look rather like palm trees.*

What are the most abundant plants?

The flowering plants – grasses, cacti, trees, peas and beans, vines, potatoes and many wild and garden flowers. Flowers help plants to reproduce. The flower produces male and female cells (pollen and egg cells), and it also makes sure that seeds are spread – by attracting animals such as bees. The biggest groups of flowering plants are orchids,17,000 species; legumes (peas and beans) 16,000 species; and compositae (daisy-like flowers) 14,000 species.

Which plants have no flowers?

Mosses and ferns have no flowers. Instead of seeds, they produce spores, which fall to the ground and develop into a structure called a prothallus – it is this structure that produces male and female cells to make a new plant. Conifers have no flowers either. They are 'gymnosperms', and have cones containing pollen and seeds. Male and female cones may be on the same plant, as in most conifers, or on separate plants, as in cycads.

🔻 *Flowering plants, non-flowering plants and fungi grow together in woodlands.*

Bracket fungus

Birch sapling

Fern

Mushroom

Fly agaric

Bluebell

Cuckoo-pint

Foxglove

Acorn

How do fungi grow?

Fungi take food from other plants or feed as scavengers from dead, decaying matter, such as a fallen tree. Fungi contain no chlorophyll so they cannot make their own food, like green plants. Instead, they can grow on anything made of cellulose – such as food, clothes, wooden furniture, even old books – especially in damp places.

🔱 *Fungi, such as this cat-tail fungus, produce chemicals that feed on cellulose – the material of which green plant cells are made.*

🔼 *All we see of the water lily is its flower on the surface of the water, but underneath the surface, long stalks connect it to the roots on the river bed, like an anchor.*

How can plants live in water?

Over 90 per cent of a plant is water, so it is not surprising that plants manage to live in water perfectly well, so long as they can obtain sunlight. Some plants float on the surface, others root in the bottom of ponds or streams. Seaweeds growing in the oceans are very tough, to survive being pounded by waves or being dried and then soaked again as the tides come in and go out on the seashore.

➡ *Instead of a root, a seaweed has a 'holdfast' foot which sticks to a rock, to keep the plant in one place.*

🔽 *It is hard to imagine a lawn of bamboo, but lawn grass and bamboo are related plants.*

What is the tallest grass?

Bamboo looks like a tree but is actually a giant grass. It is the tallest grass (growing up to 25 m) and the fastest-growing plant, shooting up almost 1 m a day. Grasses have very small flowers, with no petals, and form the largest group of wind-pollinated plants. There are about 10,000 species.

Flowering plants are successful because they are good at spreading their seeds and are very adaptable.

Flowering plants live in most of the Earth's environments, including hot deserts and high mountains. There are more than 250,000 species of flowering plants, including flowers, vegetables, grasses, trees and herbs, which are all divided into two main groups: monocotyledons, such as grasses and bulb-plants, and the bigger group – dicotyledons.

↑ The huge flower of the rafflesia, which is also called the stinking corpse flower because of its pungent smell used to attract insects.

Which are the biggest flowering plants?

The biggest flower belongs to the smelly rafflesia of Southeast Asia. Its metre-wide flower smells like rotting meat, to attract insects. Some flowering plants are enormous – a Chinese wisteria in California has branches 150 m long and produces 1.5 million flowers every year.

How do plants live in dry deserts?

Some desert plants have long roots to reach deep underground where the water supply can be found. Others store water in their thick stems and fleshy leaves. Desert plants may look dead until the rain comes when they burst into life, grow and flower – and the desert briefly blooms.

↓ Cactus plants can grow in deserts, providing it rains occasionally.

Why does a sprouting plant grow upwards?

Because its leaves must reach the sunlight. A plant starts life as a a bulb or seed in the soil. Even if planted upside down, the roots will start to push downwards, under the influence of gravity. The shoot, bearing the leaves, pushes upwards towards the sunlight, to start making food for the growing plant.

➲ *A tulip starts life as a bulb, which sends out roots and a shoot. The leaves emerge into the sunlight and then, finally, the flower.*

Why do flowers have bright colours?

To attract animals, which transfer pollen from one plant to another. This is called cross-pollination. The chief pollinators are insects, which are attracted to flowers by their colours and scents. Insects do not see the same colours as us. To a bee a red flower looks grey, while a white flower probably looks blue. Birds, bats, rodents and even marsupials pollinate flowers in some parts of the world.

➲ *The dandelion produces the familiar fluffy seed-head. Blow it to 'tell the time', and you are helping the plant spread its seeds.*

Why do some plants have wings and parachutes?

To ensure the wind can carry a plant's seeds as far from the parent tree as possible. Dandelion seeds are so light that they blow about easily. The fruits of some other plants, such as maple trees, have winged seeds, which spin as they fall from the tree like the rotor blades of a helicopter.

➲ *When bees and other insects feed on flowers, pollen sticks to them, which they carry to other flowers of the same species.*

How do plants survive on windy mountains?

Plants such as mosses, shrubs and some flowers can survive the high winds and winter cold of mountains by staying small – they cling close to the ground. They have long roots to hold tight to the soil and to reach down to find as much moisture and food as possible. The trees best suited to alpine heights are conifers.

➲ *An alpine meadow in spring, with many flowers in bloom.*

There are two main groups of trees. Conifers, or cone-bearing trees, are known as softwoods and keep their leaves throughout the year. Broad-leaved trees are hardwoods, and those growing in cool climates lose their leaves in autumn. Trees play a vital role in maintaining life on Earth, because their leaves give off oxygen as part of the tree's food-making process.

How can you tell a bush from a shrub?

Shrubs are small, tree-like plants while bushes have more branches than shrubs, and are usually smaller. Shrubs have woody stems and several branches, spreading out near to the ground. Gardeners often grow bush roses, fruit bushes such as gooseberries, and ornamental shrubs such as fuchsias, azaleas and rhododendrons. Shrubs provide useful cover for wildlife, especially birds and small mammals.

Woodland with a mixture of trees and shrubs is a good habitat for animals.

Autumn leaves provide a brilliant colour show as the trees prepare for winter.

Why do some trees lose their leaves?

Losing their leaves in autumn helps trees save water as they 'shut down' their food-gathering system in winter. Food pipes inside the tree branches are sealed. Enough food has been stored within the tree to make buds grow in the spring. The leaf is cut off from its food supply and dies. The chlorophyll that keeps it green breaks down, and the leaves turn red, yellow and brown, before they fall to the ground.

Why do trees have bark?

Bark protects the living wood inside the tree. It keeps moisture in, so the tree does not dry out. It protects the tree from insects and parasites, and shields against extreme weather. The outer layer of bark is a tough, dead shell. The inner layer is soft and alive, and carries food through tiny tubes.

Where are the biggest forests?

The biggest forests are the tropical rainforest of Brazil and the cold boreal forest of Siberia. Many trees growing together make a forest. Once 60 per cent of the Earth was forested, but humans have cleared much of the ancient forest to build on. Forests are home to many plants and animals.

Forest life exists in layers from the floor through the shrub and understorey to the canopy (the tallest trees).

Why do conifer trees bear cones?

Male cones produce pollen, female cones produce eggs, which are sticky and attract the pollen. All conifer trees have cones. Seeds are made in the scales of the female cone, and spread by the wind. Most conifers are evergreen and grow best in cool climates. Typical conifers include spruce, pine and firs.

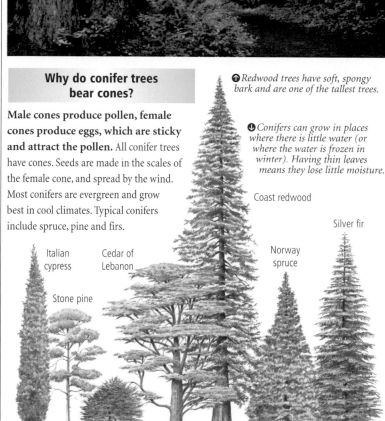

Redwood trees have soft, spongy bark and are one of the tallest trees.

Conifers can grow in places where there is little water (or where the water is frozen in winter). Having thin leaves means they lose little moisture.

Coast redwood

Silver fir

Italian cypress

Cedar of Lebanon

Norway spruce

Stone pine

Phoenician juniper

People need plants, as sources of food, for raw materials, for fuel, and to maintain the natural balance of the planet. Many plants have been altered by people through selective breeding. This process began when people first became farmers, about 10,000 years ago. Today's farm crops look very different from their wild ancestors.

⬆ *The sunflower turns its head throughout the day, following the Sun's path across the sky.*

Why are sunflowers useful as well as pretty?

Sunflowers produce useful foodstuffs, such as sunflower oil and sunflower seeds. Sunflowers have inspired artists, and children like to grow them to see how tall they become. A field full of sunflowers makes a brilliant sight, a mass of yellow blooms. So sunflowers are both a useful crop and a popular flower to grow.

What are tubers?

Tubers are food-stores, and probably the best-known tuberous plant is the potato. The tuber is the thick, swollen part of the stem, which grows underground. Potatoes were unknown in Europe until the first explorers brought them back from America in the 1500s. The eyes of a potato are tiny buds, which will sprout and grow into new plants if put into the soil.

➡ *Gardeners 'earth up' the plants to make sure the tubers are covered by soil in plants such as this potato plant.*

⬆ *Vast areas of what was once prairie in North America is now planted with wheat, one of the most important world crops.*

Which plants are staple foods?

Staple foods make up the largest part of a person's diet and include potatoes, wheat (made into bread and pasta) and rice. Potatoes and wheat are popular in western countries, while people in poorer parts of Africa and Asia rely almost entirely on plants such as rice, cassava and yams.

➲ *Terraced ricefields are a common sight in many parts of Asia.*

Which parts of plants can we eat?

The roots, bulbs, flowering heads and leaves of some plants are edible. Cauliflower and broccoli are the flowering heads of plants belonging to the cabbage family. Onions are bulbs. Carrots and parsnips are roots. We eat the leaves of lettuces, and the fruits of many plants, such as apples. Some plants are dangerous to eat – rhubarb leaves, for example, are poisonous, though the stems can be eaten. Mistletoe berries are poisonous, and so are yew and laburnum seeds.

⬇ *Pineapples are grown in Central America, Asia, Australia and Africa. The bit we eat is the fruit, which is normally seedless.*

⬇ *Rice is a cereal, like wheat, which needs warm, wet conditions in which to grow.*

How is rice cultivated?

Young rice plants are grown in flooded 'paddy' fields and the water is drained off before the rice is harvested. More than half the world's population eat rice as their main food. Once harvested, the rice grains are boiled and eaten, rather than ground into flour (like wheat grains).

Can we eat seaweed?

Seaweed is rich in vitamins and minerals, and many kinds are good to eat. In Wales, a red seaweed known as laver is boiled up into a jellylike mass, fried and eaten as 'laver bread'. The Japanese pioneered seaweed farming. Seaweed farmers drive rows of stakes into the shallow seabed to provide the plant with something to cling to. When the seaweed is harvested, it is used as an ingredient in various foods. If you see the names agar, algin or carrageenin on food packets, you will know those products contain seaweed.

➲ *A farmer harvesting seaweed, which is used in many food and cosmetic products. Ice cream is one of many foods that may contain seaweed.*

In order to find food, escape danger and to reproduce successfully, animals use a variety of natural strategies. For example, camouflage and protective colouration enable some animals to escape being seen or to appear so visibly that a predator is startled or scared away. The range of animal defences is amazing, from armadillo armour, porcupine's quills, mimicry and camouflage to lobster claws and the skunk's foul-smelling spray.

Why do some animals hibernate?

Hibernation is a strategy for surviving winter, when food is scarce. Bears fatten themselves up in autumn, then sleep in a cosy den. Badgers stay in their underground sets. Some animals, such as dormice, shut down their bodies so much that they appear to be dead. Hiberating animals live off the reserves of fat stored in their bodies until spring returns and warmer weather awakens them.

⬆ *Baby loggerhead turtles head for deep water. Many turtles are killed by waiting predators.*

Where do marine turtles lay their eggs?

Marine turtles lay their eggs on sandy beaches. The females dig a shallow hole, lay the eggs, cover them with sand, then crawl back to the water. When the babies hatch, they have to dig their way up to the light and air. They head straight for the water because waiting on the shore are a host of predators, such as seabirds, that seem to know just when the hatchlings will emerge.

⬇ *Woodland animals hibernate during the winter months, only emerging when the weather warms up.*

Why do some mammals live in groups?

Living together in a group is a good defensive strategy. An antelope has a better chance of escaping a lion if it stays in a herd – lots of eyes keeping watch are better than just one pair. Elephants have no real enemies (except some humans), but female elephants stay together to share the task of bringing up the young. Lions, unlike most cats, co-operate when hunting. So do wolves, wild dogs and hyenas who hunt in 'packs'.

❷A herd of elephants is usually led by an old female – the matriarch cow. The herd will look after an injured member and protect the young from predators such as lions.

Why do animals build homes?

Many animals have territories, but homes are usually only for rearing young. Females prepare a den or a nest for their young. Birds make the most ingenious homes, mostly in treetops or bushes. Fish, such as the male stickleback, guard their young fiercely. One of the most remarkable mammal homes is the beaver's underwater lodge. Built from mud and sticks, the lodge provides a dry, weatherproof home safe from land-predators.

❸North American beavers dam streams by cutting down small trees to make a pond. In the pond, they make their lodge with an underwater entrance.

What is migration?

Animals such as whales, fish, lobsters, caribou and butterflies all migrate – make seasonal journeys – to find reliable food supplies and the best breeding places.

The most remarkable migrants are birds, and many species migrate as the seasons change. Songbirds, seabirds, waterfowl and waders all migrate.

❸ The Arctic tern is the most-travelled bird. It breeds in the Arctic during the northern summer, then flies south for summer in the Antarctic. The round trip covers more than 25,000 km.

The record-breakers in the natural world come in all shapes and sizes. Many animals are unbelievably strong. Some insects and mammals have incredible appetites. The fastest animals can easily outrun a human sprinter. And no creature in the history of the Earth has been bigger than the majestic blue whale.

⬆ *The peregrine falcon reaches maximum speed in a dive to catch prey.*

What is the world's fastest animal?

The peregrine falcon, which in a dive or 'stoop' on its prey can reach a speed of more than 200 km/h. Ducks are probably the fastest fliers in level flight, reaching up to 100 km/h. The cheetah is the fastest land animal and the sailfish is the fastest fish, both clocking in at approximately 100 to 110 km/h. The cheetah cannot keep up its sprint for long, whereas the pronghorn antelope can sustain a speed of over 70 km/h for longer. In comparison, a top Olympic sprinter can reach about 43 km/h.

What is the world's biggest big cat?

The Siberian tiger is the biggest of the big cats. It is the most northern species of tiger, at home in the snow. It can measure 3.2 m from nose to tail and weigh up to 300 kg. Carnivores (meat eaters) include some of the most powerful predators in the animal world. The biggest land carnivores are bears and big cats.

What is the largest cactus?

Most cacti are fairly small, but the saguaro is an exception at a height of 18 m. It grows in the deserts of Arizona, California and Mexico. The saguaro has a column-like trunk from which sprout upturned branches. A big one can weigh up to 9 tonnes.

➡ *The Saguaro cactus is as tall as a tree.*

➡ *The Siberian tiger is a magnificent animal. It is an endangered species (at risk of extinction) and needs protection from hunters.*

Which are the most deadly sea animals?

Perhaps the most deadly sea creature to humans is the sea wasp jellyfish with a sting that can kill a person in less than 3 minutes. The most feared hunters of the ocean are great white sharks and killer whales, which eat seals and sea lions, and will even attack larger whales. Sharks lurk off seal beaches during the breeding season, while killer whales pursue fleeing seals into shallow surf and grab them off the beach itself. However, more people are killed every year by jellyfish than either of these larger animals.

◗ *The sea wasp jellyfish.*

What are the smallest animals?

◗ *Killer whales grab seals from shallow water and from along the shore's edge.*

The smallest bird is the 5 cm-long bee hummingbird, the smallest reptile is the dwarf gecko at half that size, and the smallest amphibian, the short-headed frog is just 1 cm long. The smallest horse, the Falabella, is only the size of a dog. Small means safe sometimes, for a small animal can hide where no large predator can follow. However, there are weasels small enough to pursue mice down their holes. There are tiny flies that lay their eggs on the bodies of larger flies. There are a whole host of mini-beasts, some of which can be seen only under a microscope.

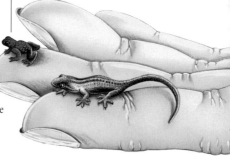

◗ *The world's smallest gecko at 2.5 cm, and the world's smallest frog at just 1 cm, shown to scale on a human hand.*

1 Is an animal that eats meat called a herbivore, a carnivore or an omnivore?

2 Do reptiles create their own body heat, or do they absorb it from the Sun and surroundings?

3 Which gas, essential to animal life, is produced by green plants: hydrogen, oxygen or carbon dioxide?

4 Did *Tyrannosaurus rex* sometimes walk on four legs?

5 Which came first: dinosaurs or birds?

6 Are green snakes poisonous?

FACTFILE

Smallest to **biggest**

There are about 4,500 mammal species, ranging in size from tiny shrews to whales. Biggest of all is the blue whale, which can grow to 33.5 m long.

Biggest **hoofed animals**

Name	Height	Weight
White rhinoceros	1.8 m	3,000 kg
Hippopotamus	1.5 m	1,400 kg
Giraffe	5.5 m	1,200 kg

Mammal **champions**

Record	Held by
Biggest rodent	Capybara
Longest hair	Yak
Largest bear	Polar bear
Smelliest mammal	Skunk
Sleepiest mammal	Dormouse
Slowest-moving mammal	Sloth
Heaviest tree-dwelling mammal	Orang-utan
Mammal most at home in mountains	Pika
Most armoured mammal	Armadillos and pangolins

NATURAL WORLD

Answers on page 157

153

7 Which animal were prehistoric woolly mammoths similar to: rhinos, elephants or sheep?

8 Which is larger, the African or the Asian elephant?

9 Do seals give birth at sea or on land?

10 Which furry animal flies on wings of skin?

11 Which is larger: a duck or a goose?

12 Can seagulls swim under water?

13 A giant tortoise, which can grow up to 1.2 m long, comes from which group of islands in the Pacific Ocean?

14 What does a cygnet grow into?

15 What baby reptile squeaks inside its egg: a lizard, crocodile or snake?

16 Do frogs hunt mainly by smell, hearing or sight?

17 Which turtles regularly return to the same spot to lay their eggs?

18 Are swordfish river or sea fish?

19 Does the parrotfish talk, or have beak-like teeth?

20 What is a tarantula?

Longest **gestation**

It takes a long time for a mammal baby to develop – nine months for a human, but longer for some other mammals.

Elephant	660 days
Whale	500 days
Rhinoceros	450 days
Walrus	480 days
Giraffe	430 days

➲ *Scientists assess a dolphin's reaction to various sights, sounds and situations in order to gauge their intelligence.*

Intelligent **mammals**

The most intelligent animals (not including humans):

1 Chimpanzee
2 Gorilla
3 Orang-utan
4 Baboon
5 Dolphin

21 Do most fungi like to grow in bright, dry areas, or in dark, damp areas?

FACTFILE

Feathered **friends**

Feathers are made of a horn-like protein called keratin, the same stuff your hair and nails are made of, but feathers are very light and very strong. A swan has about 25,000 feathers. Hummingbirds, which look as if they have scales not feathers, have the fewest of any bird – less than 1,000.

⬆A bird's skeleton is very light to help it glide through the air easily.

Design **secrets**

Bird bones are hollow but reinforced with cross struts. Birds have very efficient lungs and their digestive system works very fast because flying takes a lot of energy.

⬇A bird's wings make circular movements – the wing tips pushing forward on the upstroke.

22 Do pike swim in shoals?

23 Do earthworms eat insects or dead plant material?

24 Which sea creature usually has five limbs?

25 Was the dodo a type of bird or deer?

26 A pitcher plant catches and eats insects: true or false?

27 Which of the big cats has seen its numbers drop from 50,000 in the early 1900s to fewer than 6,000 left today?

28 Which bear has been reduced in number because of deforestation?

29 The sundew plant catches prey on its sticky tentacles: true or false?

30 Which of these is a type of plant: sponge, coral or kelp?

31 Do bluebells grow on beaches or in woods?

32 Which are taller, foxgloves or bluebells?

33 What is the world's largest bird?

34 Which large yellow flower is used in the making of cooking oil: marigold, sunflower or daffodil?

35 Are acorns the seeds of the oak or the holly?

36 Which member of the grass family provides Asia's main food crop: wheat, rye or rice?

37 Do willow trees like damp or dry conditions?

38 Which vegetable does not grow underground: carrot, pea or potato?

Oldest **birds**

In the wild, small birds have many predators. Many are killed in their first year. Bigger birds tend to live longer. Birds kept in captivity and wild birds ringed by scientists are studied to discover how long they can live. A Siberian white crane, a sulphur-crested cockatoo and a goose have been recorded to reach 80 years old.

Take **off**

Taking off for most birds involves flapping the wings to produce thrust and lift. Broad, rounded wings give the best lift and acceleration – useful for escaping a predator. Big birds, such as geese, run into the wind to generate enough lift to take off. Birds with long, narrow wings, such as swallows, can only take off from a high point – falling into the air and letting the air carry them.

Bird **brains**

Ravens and pigeons can work out simple counting sums. Parrots, budgerigars and mynahs can mimic human speech (though that is not the same as talking), and some parrots can name and count objects. The Galapagos woodpecker finch uses a twig as a tool to winkle out grubs from tree bark.

Record **eggs**

The ostrich lays the biggest egg. An ostrich egg is 20 cm long. The smallest bird egg, at 1 cm long, is laid by the hummingbird.

39 Which vegetable is made into a Hallowe'en lantern?

40 Do coconuts grow on plants or on trees?

41 How do poison-dart frogs warn off enemies: with bright colours, by hissing or by swelling up?

42 How do penguins recognize their young: by their appearance, their voice or their smell?

43 When do rattlesnakes rattle: when they are tired, to threaten enemies or when they are ready to breed?

44 What makes the walrus different from other pinnipeds?

45 Which is the world's largest frog: the African bullfrog, the Goliath frog or the giant tree frog?

46 What is the world's biggest eagle: the golden eagle, the harpy eagle or the bald eagle?

FACTFILE

⬆ *The ocean sunfish is the heaviest bony fish. It lays an astonishing number of eggs – about 300 million, most of which get eaten by other fish and sea animals.*

Giants of the **sea**

The biggest fish is the whale shark. It can grow up to 18 m in length. But this 15-tonne monster is a gentle giant and eats only tiny plankton. Some of its relatives are among the most powerful predators in the natural world. They include the mako shark, which grows up to 3.5 m in length, and the white shark and hammerhead shark, both of which grow up to 5 m in length.

➡ *The whale shark swims with its mouth wide open to filter krill from the water.*

Answers

1 Carnivore
2 They absorb heat
3 Carbon dioxide
4 No, its front legs were too tiny
5 Dinosaurs
6 No
7 Elephants
8 African elephant
9 On land
10 Bat
11 Goose
12 No
13 The Galapagos Islands
14 Swan

15 Crocodile
16 Sight
17 Sea turtles
18 Sea fish
19 Beak-like teeth
20 Spider (or arachnid)
21 Dark, damp areas
22 No, they live alone
23 Dead plant material
24 Starfish
25 Bird
26 True
27 Tiger
28 Giant panda
29 True

30 Kelp, which is a kind of seaweed
31 In woods
32 Foxgloves
33 Ostrich
34 Sunflower
35 Oak
36 Rice
37 Damp conditions
38 Pea
39 Pumpkin
40 On trees
41 With bright colours
42 Their voice
43 To threaten enemies

44 It has tusks
45 Goliath frog – up to 40 cm in length
46 Harpy eagle

Tails and **scales**

Fish swim using a side-to-side movement of their bodies. Muscles make up approximately 70 per cent of a fish's weight. A fish uses its fins for steering – the tail fin, for example, acts as a rudder. Like all animals, fish need oxygen – but they take in oxygen, which is dissolved in water, through their gills. The older a fish is, the bigger its scales – as the fish gets bigger, its scales get bigger, too.

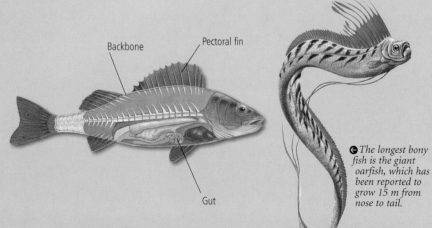

Backbone

Pectoral fin

Gut

⬅ *The longest bony fish is the giant oarfish, which has been reported to grow 15 m from nose to tail.*

SCIENCE & TECHNOLOGY

Science is a vital part of modern life. Almost everything we touch is the result of a special scientific invention. Without science, developments in communications, transport, energy, construction and countless other areas would not occur. Some aspects of science, such as mathematics and astrology, are ancient while others, such as computer science, are new and constantly changing.

Are atoms the smallest pieces of matter?

Could time stand still?

Why are there different colours of light?

Matter is anything and everything in the Universe. It includes all substances, items and objects, whether solid, liquid or gas – and not only here on Earth, but deep into space, to the Sun and beyond, in fact, all through the entire Universe. So there is plenty of matter! Studying what it is made of is one of the great quests of modern science.

- Neutrons
- Protons
- Electrons

Nucleus

Electrons move in areas called 'shells'

⬆ *Uranium is a very hard, heavy metal. Its atoms, such as this one above, are among the largest of all atoms, with 92 protons and about 146 neutrons in the nucleus, and 92 electrons to balance the protons.*

What are substances made of?

All substances consist of atoms. If you could chop up any substance smaller and smaller, the pieces would become too small to see. But if you could keep chopping, under the most powerful microscope, eventually you would reach the tiniest pieces or atoms of the substance. All matter is made of atoms.

Are atoms the smallest pieces of matter?

No, each atom is made up of even smaller parts, known as subatomic particles. There are three kinds of subatomic particles– protons, neutrons and electrons. Protons and neutrons clump together at the centre of the atom, called the nucleus. Electrons whizz round and round the nucleus. If an atom is split, it no longer has the features of the original substance.

➡ *The simplest and lightest atom of all is hydrogen. It has just one proton as the nucleus and one electron going around it. Helium is next, with a nucleus of two protons and two neutrons, and two orbiting electrons. Oxygen is more complex, with eight of each particle – protons, neutrons and electrons.*

What are quarks?

Some scientists believe that subatomic particles are made of even tinier pieces of matter known as quarks. For example, a proton is composed of three quarks. Other scientists believe that atoms, quarks and all other matter are made of far smaller vibrating lengths of energy called 'strings'. If an atom was the size of planet Earth, a 'string' would be the size of a shoelace. These 'strings' may join into 'superstrings' that could even stretch past lots of atoms. Scientists are beginning to investigate whether 'strings' really exist.

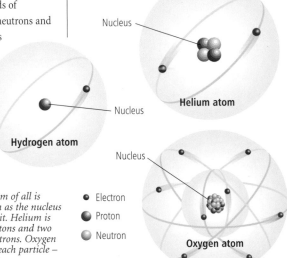

Nucleus

Helium atom

Nucleus

Hydrogen atom

Nucleus

- Electron
- Proton
- Neutron

Oxygen atom

H Hydrogen 1																		He Helium 2
Li Lithium 3	Be Beryllium 4											B Boron 5	C Carbon 6	N Nitrogen 7	O Oxygen 8	F Flourine 9	Ne Neon 10
Na Sodium 11	Mg Magnesium 12											Al Aluminium 13	Si Silicon 14	P Phosphorus 15	S Sulphur 16	Cl Chlorine 17	Ar Argon 18
K Potassium 19	Ca Calcium 20	Sc Scandium 21	Ti Titanium 22	V Vanadium 23	Cr Chromium 24	Mn Manganese 25	Fe Iron 26	Co Cobalt 27	Ni Nickel 28	Cu Copper 29	Zn Zinc 30	Ga Gallium 31	Ge Germanium 32	As Arsenic 33	Se Selenium 34	Br Bromine 35	Kr Krypton 36
Rb Rubidium 37	Sr Strontium 38	Y Yttrium 39	Zr Zirconium 40	Nb Niobium 41	Mo Molybdenum 42	Tc Technetium 43	Ru Ruthenium 44	Rh Rhodium 45	Pd Palladium 46	Ag Silver 47	Cd Cadmium 48	In Indium 49	Sn Tin 50	Sb Antimony 51	Te Tellurium 52	I Iodine 53	Xe Xenon 54
Cs Caesium 55	Ba Barium 56		Hf Hafnium 72	Ta Tantalum 73	W Tungsten 74	Re Rhenium 75	Os Osmium 76	Ir Iridium 77	Pt Platanium 78	Au Gold 79	Hg Mercury 80	Tl Thalium 81	Pb Lead 82	Bi Bismuth 83	Po Polonium 84	At Astatine 85	Rn Radon 86
Fr Frankium 87	Ra Radium 88		Rf Rutherfordium 104	Db Dubnium 105	Sg Seaborgium 106	Bh Bohrium 107	Hs Hassium 108	Mt Meitnerium 109	Ds Darmstadtium 110	Uuu Ununumium 111	Uub Ununbium 112						

Each left-to-right row is a period of elements with similar weights

La Lanthanium 57	Ce Cerium 58	Pr Praseodymium 59	Nd Neodymium 60	Pm Promethium 61	Sm Samarium 62	Eu Europium 63	Gd Gadolinium 64	Tb Terbium 65	Dy Dysprosium 66	Ho Holmium 67	Er Erbium 68	Tm Thulium 69	Yb Ytterbium 70	Lu Lutetium 71
Ac Actinium 89	Th Thorium 90	Pa Protactinium 91	U Uranium 92	Np Neptunium 93	Pu Plutonium 94	Am Americium 95	Cm Curium 96	Bk Berkelium 97	Cf Californium 98	Es Einsteinium 99	Fm Fermium 100	Md Mendelevium 101	No Nobelium 102	Lr Lawrencium 103

○ *All the known pure substances are arranged in a chart called the Periodic Table of chemical elements. They are arranged by their properties and weights. The lightest elements are upper left, the heaviest ones are lower right. The different colours represent the different type of element. For example, all the elements known as noble gases are shown in turquoise (first column on right). Each of the elements in this column are extremely stable, which means that they do not react dangerously with other elements.*

Each top-to bottom column groups elements with similar properties

What holds the parts of an atom together?

Protons and neutrons are held together in the nucleus by a basic attraction called the strong nuclear force. Protons have a type of electrical force called electric charge, which is positive. Electrons have a negative charge and neutrons have no charge. The positive protons attract the negative electrons and hold them near the nucleus. Most atoms have the same number of protons and electrons, so their charges balance each other. The atom has no charge – it is neutral.

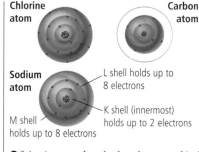

Chlorine atom

Carbon atom

Sodium atom

L shell holds up to 8 electrons

K shell (innermost) holds up to 2 electrons

M shell holds up to 8 electrons

○ *Scientists once thought that electrons orbited the nucleus at a different distance, like planets orbiting the Sun. Then the idea of 'shells' arose, where groups of electrons stay at a set distance from the nucleus. The modern view is that electrons move from one shell to another.*

Are all atoms the same?

Each kind of pure substance, known as a chemical element, has its own kind of atoms, which differ from the atoms of all other elements. So in an element, such as carbon, all the atoms are the same, with the same number of subatomic particles. Oxygen atoms are also all the same, but they differ from carbon atoms, with a different number of subatomic particles. There are more than 100 chemical elements, as shown in the table above. About 30 of these are manufactured.

A ll matter in the Universe is made of the atoms of pure substances, called chemical elements. These atoms join together or can be linked in countless ways to form the common objects and materials that we see and use every day – metals, wood, plastic, glass, water, rocks, soil and even the air around us.

❶ *Molecules of sodium chloride form crystals of salt, such as table salt, sea salt or rock salt.*

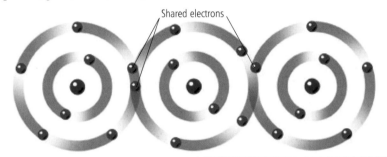

Shared electrons

❶ *When atoms join by covalent bonds, electrons orbit in one atom for part of the time, and the other for the rest of the time. The three atoms of a water molecule, two hydrogen and one oxygen, H_2O, have covalent bonds, as shown above.*

Do atoms join together?

Atoms usually join or bond with other atoms to form groups called molecules. In some cases the atoms come very close together and 'share' electrons, so that the electron sometimes goes around one nucleus and sometimes around the other. This is a covalent bond. Oxygen atoms floating in the air are joined in pairs by covalent bonds to form oxygen molecules O_2.

Are atoms ever alone?

On Earth, atoms are rarely found alone. Among the few examples are the 'inert gases' – helium, neon, argon, krypton and xenon. 'Inert' means 'inactive'. These gases form a tiny proportion of the air. Their atoms have all the electrons they need, with no need to share or swap. So they hardly ever join or bond, even with each other.

Sodium atom

❶ *In an ionic bond, one or more electrons pass from one atom to another. Molecules of common salt, sodium chloride, form in this way.*

How else do atoms join?

One or more electrons may 'jump' from one atom to a nearby one. This is known as an ionic bond. Atoms of the elements sodium and chlorine are linked by ionic bonds to form molecules of sodium chloride, NaCl, which we know as salt (table or cooking salt). Electrons are negative, so the sodium atom that loses its electron becomes a positive ion. The chlorine atom which receives an electron becomes a negative ion. Positive and negative attract and the sodium and chlorine stay close together.

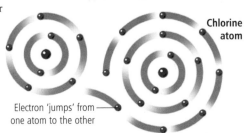

Chlorine atom

Electron 'jumps' from one atom to the other

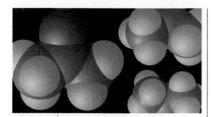

⊙ *The substance called acetone, also known as propanone, is commonly used in nail varnish remover. Each molecule of acetone has three carbon atoms (orange), one oxygen (pink) and six hydrogen (light green). It is written as the formula CH_3COCH_3.*

What is a compound?

A compound is a molecule with atoms from different chemical elements, rather than from the same chemical element. For example, an oxygen molecule, O_2, is not a compound. However, a salt molecule, NaCl, is a compound, because it consists of two or more different chemical elements. Most everyday substances are made from compounds.

⊙ *The tall towers at an oil refinery split crude oil into all its 'fractions'.*

How many atoms are in a compound?

The number varies from a few, to millions. Some substances, such as salt, have molecules with just two atoms each. If each sodium chloride molecule in a tiny grain of salt was increased to the size of the dot on this 'i', then the salt grain would be more than 2 km high. Other substances, such as plastic and wood, have giant molecules consisting of millions of atoms. Many of these are based on the element carbon. Carbon can join with up to four other atoms, so that it forms thousands of different compounds. Especially common are combinations of carbon and hydrogen, called hydrocarbons (CHs), and those of carbon, hydrogen and oxygen known as carbohydrates (CHOs).

➲ *Crude oil or petroleum, straight from the ground, is a mixture of hundreds of compounds. In an oil refinery it is heated so that it splits up into the gases of these compounds. These gases are turned back into liquids at various temperatures, at different levels in a tall tower called a fractionation column.*

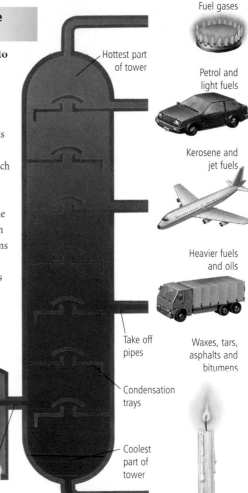

Fuel gases

Petrol and light fuels

Kerosene and jet fuels

Heavier fuels and oils

Waxes, tars, asphalts and bitumens

Hottest part of tower

Take off pipes

Condensation trays

Coolest part of tower

Crude oil turned into gases inside boiler

Science plays a huge part in the items we use every day – cars, televisions, tools, appliances, buildings, even furniture and clothing. They are all made from specially chosen materials, ranging from natural wood or stone to high-tech composites. Materials scientists specialize in putting together atoms, molecules and substances to create the right material for each job.

Copper is especially efficient at carrying or conducting electricity, it is second only to silver. It is braided so that it can be bent many times without cracking.

What are natural materials?

Natural materials are found around us, as part of nature, rather than being artificial or manufactured. Wood is a natural material and is important in making furniture, utensils and structures such as houses and bridges. Various kinds of rock and stone are also widely used, especially in the construction of larger buildings. Natural fibres, such as cotton, are woven into fabrics for clothes, curtains and other items.

Wood is often used in the construction of houses or boats, because it is a strong and durable material that can last against elements, such as strong winds and rain.

How is a material's strength measured?

It depends, because there are different kinds of 'strength'. Tensile strength resists pulling or stretching, compression strength resists pressing or squeezing, and torsional strength resists twisting. These different kinds of strength are measured by putting pieces of a material into a very powerful machine, a hydraulic test rig, which pulls, squashes or turns them until they crack and break. Every substance or material has a different combination of these strengths, suitable for different purposes.

What are other features of materials?

Another feature is flexibility or bendiness, which is the opposite of stiffness or rigidity. This is linked to elasticity – whether a material springs back to its original shape after being bent. Weight is another feature, especially density, which is the amount of weight in a certain volume. Durability is how long a material can last. A material is also categorized by its ability to conduct electricity.

Materials that carry heat or electricity, such as a metal spoon in a cup of hot liquid, are thermal or electrical conductors. Those that do not are insulators, such as a ceramic mug.

What material is most commonly used?

One commonly-used material is steel, an alloy (combination) of various substances based on the metal, iron.
Pure metals are also widely used, such as very light aluminium, for items ranging from aircraft to drink cans. Copper is used as a conductor of electricity in wires. Most materials in modern products are made by various industrial processes rather than being obtained from nature.

Iron ore, coke and limestone

❶Iron is obtained by heating iron ore in a blast furnace, and pouring off the wastes or slag. Pure iron is often combined with carbon and other substances to make steel.

Super-heated iron ore and limestone (the coke burns to create the heat)

Super-heated air blows into furnace

Hot gases to super-heater

Slag

Molten iron ore

❶Specialist metals are heated in furnaces and carefully hand-poured into moulds, where they cool and solidify into the required shape. Brass is an alloy (mixture) of copper and zinc.

Is a tin can really made of tin?

Only the outer coating is made of tin.
A 'tin' can is mainly steel, but steel can rust. So the steel can is coated with a thin layer of the metal, tin, which does not rust and so protects the steel beneath it.

❷Many metals and minerals form crystals as they cool from liquid to solid. The cooling process must be carefully controlled so the crystals lock together well for strength. Random-sized crystals would cause weakness in the material. Most crystals are tiny, only visible under a magnifying glass or microscope.

Our world is driven by energy. Without energy the world would be dark, cold, still and silent. We use it in many forms, including movement, sound, chemical bonds, electricity, heat, light, waves and rays. Energy is needed for anything to happen and it can be converted from its current form to various other forms to be used.

Where is energy?

Energy is everywhere and exists in everything. It has many forms. Chemical energy is released during chemical reactions. Food is a store of chemical energy, and when eaten can be used to power the movements of the human body. Potential energy is stored energy, ready to be used and converted into kinetic (movement) energy. Electrical energy is when a form of energy is converted into electricity. Solar energy comes from the Sun. There are many forms of energy.

⬆ *A typical power station changes chemical energy in the fuel into heat, then movement and then electricity. But some of the fuel energy is converted into excess heat, which is spread into the air by huge cooling towers.*

➡ *Wind turbines convert the kinetic energy of moving air into electricity. The wind obtained its energy in the form of heat from the Sun. In fact, nearly all the energy we use on Earth, in one form or another, comes from the Sun. Wind turbines generate their energy in a sustainable way, without using up valuable fuel resources.*

Can energy be made or destroyed?

A basic law of science says that energy cannot be created from nothing and equally cannot disappear. This applies throughout the Universe. However, energy can be changed from one form to another. For example, when a rocket takes off, the chemical energy in its fuel is changed into other forms of energy, such as heat, light, sound and movement energy. Energy can also be spread out so that it becomes weaker. When we say we 'use' energy, we mean that we convert some of it into the type we need. This generally converts the rest into a less useful type of energy that we cannot use. However, scientists say that energy is 'conserved' because the total amount of energy is always the same.

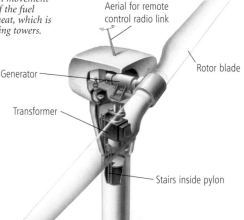

Aerial for remote control radio link

Rotor blade

Generator

Transformer

Stairs inside pylon

What happens in an energy chain?

An energy chain is the conversion of different forms of energy into a form that can be used. For example, coal, which is found deep underground, has a store of chemical energy. When burnt, this chemical energy becomes heat energy, which is used to make steam by heating water. The steam turns turbines to produce kinetic energy. This kinetic energy is converted in a machine called a generator in the power station to become electrical energy. Electrical energy is sent to homes and offices where it is used for light, and to power applicances, such as televisions and computers.

⊕Common fuels we burn for energy include oil, coal and gas. These were formed by the fossilization of decayed plants and other life-forms long ago. Their energy came as light from the Sun. Oil and coal are extracted from deep in the ground, formed beneath rock layers.

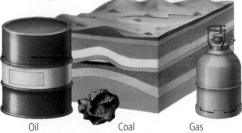

Oil   Coal   Gas

⊕A waterwheel changes the kinetic energy of running water into useful mechanical energy, to drive machines such as millstones, which grind grain into flour.

Can energy be created from atoms?

Energy can be made in one way – from matter or mass. Atoms, or usually parts of atoms, can be changed into energy. The different parts of atoms, such as neutrons, cease to exist in their current form and instead there is a large amount of energy in their place. The scientific law regarding the conservation of mass and energy states that any process or event has the same amount of mass and energy at the end as there was at the beginning of the process.

What is nuclear energy?

Nuclear energy is created in reactors inside nuclear power stations, nuclear-powered submarines, some spacecraft, and also in nuclear explosions. Nuclear fuel, such as uranium, generates enormous amounts of heat energy from the 'destruction' of the parts of its atoms. The energy produced is called nuclear energy because it comes from splitting the nucleus of an atom.

⊕Nuclear energy comes from the splitting or fission of the nuclei (centres) of atoms in nuclear fuel, such as uranium or plutonium. A fast-moving neutron smashes apart the nucleus, releasing heat, other forms of energy, and also more neutrons, which enable the fission process to continue.

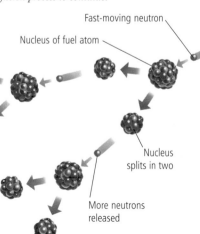

Fast-moving neutron

Nucleus of fuel atom

Nucleus splits in two

More neutrons released

When we switch on a light, turn on the computer, listen to the radio or watch television, we rely on our most convenient form of energy – electricity. It is convenient because it can be sent easily along wires and cables. Also it is readily changed into many other forms of energy, including light, heat, sound and movement.

Electrical energy or charge does not always flow. It can build up on the surface of an insulator, for example, after rubbing a plastic comb. This charge is called 'static electricity' and it attracts very light items, such as bits of tissue paper.

What is electricity?

Electricity is the movement or flow of the tiny parts of atoms called electrons, which have an electric charge. Electrons move around the central nucleus of an atom. But if an electron receives enough energy it can break away from its atom and 'hop' to the next one, where an electron has also broken away and jumped to the next atom, and so on. These moving electrons represent energy. As billions of them hop in the same direction from atom to atom, they cause a flow of electric current.

Electric current only flows if it has a pathway or circuit of conductors from its source and back again. Here, the circuit includes two wires and a bulb. The wires move the current to the bulb and back again.

Electricity flows along a wire as electrodynamic charge. If it has nowhere to flow, it collects on the surface of an object as electrostatic charge (known as static electricity). Van de Graaff generators (such as the one shown here) build up charges of millions of volts, which finally leap away as giant sparks.

Do all substances carry electricity?

No, only certain substances carry electricity. These substances are called conductors. Most metals, especially silver and gold, carry electricity well. Many other substances do not carry electricity. Instead, they have a high resistance to its flow and are known as insulators. They include wood, glass, plastic, paper, card and ceramics, such as pottery. Electrical wires usually have a conducting core of metal strands surrounded by a plastic sheath for insulation, which prevents the electricity from leaking.

How do batteries work?

Batteries change chemical energy into electrical energy. The links or bonds between atoms in chemical substances contain energy. As these break down in a chemical reaction, their energy passes to the electrons in the atoms and makes them move. This happens in a battery, but only when the electrons have somewhere to go, such as along a pathway or circuit of wires and components.

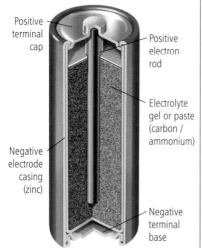

Positive terminal cap

Positive electron rod

Electrolyte gel or paste (carbon / ammonium)

Negative electrode casing (zinc)

Negative terminal base

↑ *A typical torch battery consists of two contacts or electrodes: the positive anode and negative cathode, with chemicals between them called the electrolyte. Chemical reactions between the electrodes and electrolyte cause the current to flow.*

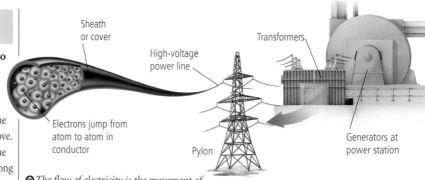

Sheath or cover

High-voltage power line

Transformers

Electrons jump from atom to atom in conductor

Pylon

Generators at power station

↑ *The flow of electricity is the movement of millions of electrons, which jump between atoms in the conductor – usually copper wire.*

What happens inside a power station?

In some power stations fuels such as coal, oil or gas are burned to make heat. This boils water into steam, which blasts past the fan-shaped blades or rotors of a turbine and makes them spin. The turbine is linked to a generator, inside which is a magnetic field, which rotates near a coil of wire, and this makes electricity in the wire. In hydro-electric power stations, running water spins the turbine blades. In wind turbines the propeller-like blades are whirled around by the wind to generate electricity.

What are DC and AC?

DC is direct current electricity and AC is alternating current electricity. Direct current electricity flows steadily in the same direction while alternating current electricity rapidly changes direction and flows one way then the other, 50 or 60 times each second. Batteries make DC. The mains electricity from wall sockets and light fittings is AC.

Transformers

← *Electricity from power stations is sent along huge cables, high above the ground, or buried below the surface. Its voltage is reduced by transformers, from hundreds of thousands of volts to only a few thousand for large factories, and just hundreds for homes, offices and schools.*

Magnets have no effect on many substances, such as wood, paper, plastic and even some metals, such as the aluminium used in drink cans. Yet when they are near an iron-based object, they pull it towards them with an invisible force. And when two magnets are near each other, they may attract (pull each other together) or repel (push each other apart).

North Pole

South Pole

Lines of magnetic force

Magnetism at its strongest at the pole

◯ A typical bar magnet is made of steel. Its lines of magnetic force curve from one pole to the other at each end. But a magnet can be any shape, including a u-like horseshoe, a disc with a pole on each side, or a ring with one pole on the outer rim and one on the inner.

What is a magnet?

A magnet is an object that produces a force called magnetism. The area where the force is felt is called the magnetic field. The force is strongest at two places in the magnet, called poles. The two poles are not the same, in fact they are opposites. One is called north or + and the other is called south or –. When two magnets come near, the north pole of one pushes or repels the north pole of the other, but pulls or attracts the south pole. The basic law of magnetism is that like poles repel, unlike poles attract.

How is magnetism made?

It is due to the movements of the same particles that cause electricity – the electrons of atoms. Electrons orbit their atom's nucleus, and spin around while the nucleus spins, too. Normally electrons spin in random ways, at different angles. But in a magnet it is believed that the electron spins are lined up, so their tiny forces combine to create the force of magnetism.

Which substances are magnetic?

A magnetic substance is one that is attracted by a magnet. The most common magnetic substance is iron. Steel contains mainly iron, so steel is magnetic too. A few less common metals are slightly magnetic, such as nickel and cobalt, and the much rarer metals, such as neodymium, gadolinium and dysprosium.

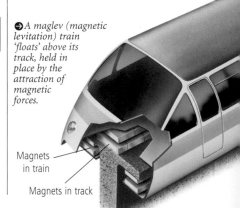

◯ The type of iron-rich rock called magnetite or lodestone has natural magnetism. Long, slim pieces of it were used for the first direction-finding magnetic compasses.

◯ A maglev (magnetic levitation) train 'floats' above its track, held in place by the attraction of magnetic forces.

Magnets in train

Magnets in track

⊕ *Big electromagnets can lift up heavy loads, such as car engines. They are also used at scrapyards for sorting iron-based or ferrous metals from other metals when recycling.*

Can magnets be switched on and off?

They can if they are electromagnets. Electricity and magnetism are two parts of the same basic or fundamental force, known as electromagnetism. Whenever an electric current flows in a wire, it creates a magnetic field around itself. If a wire is wound into a coil, with a piece of iron in the middle, this makes the magnetic field stronger and is known as an electromagnet. The magnetic field is present when the electricity flows, but when it is switched off, the magnetism disappears in an instant.

Are magnets common?

Very common. They are used in a simple way for holding paper onto appliances such as fridges, as knife-holders, for gathering and holding pins and nails, and as magnetic catches for doors. Large magnets are found in loudspeakers. Electromagnetism is used in many devices, such as remote-control cars, locks, electric generators and motors, videotapes, television sets, computers and their magnetic disc drives. Magnets are used in hundreds of different devices.

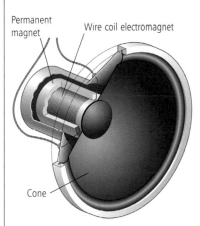

⊕ *A loudspeaker is a device that changes an electric current into sound. Electrical signals flow through a wire coil and turn it into an electromagnet, which pushes and pulls against a permanent magnet to produce sound.*

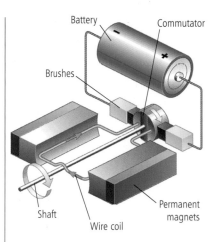

⊕ *A simple DC motor consists of a wire coil on a shaft between two magnetic poles. As it turns, the electric current flowing through the spinning wire coil is reversed by a barrel-shaped commutator switch.*

How does an electric motor work?

Using the push and pull of magnetism. A coil of wire inside an electric motor is positioned near two magnets. As the current flows, the wire becomes an electromagnet and its field interacts with the magnetic field of the surrounding magnets. The pushing and pulling forces produced by the magnets move the wire and so the motor spins. A rotating switch, the commutator, makes the flow of current through the coil change each turn to keep the motor spinning.

Electronic gadgets are all around us, from televisions, computers and mobile phones to washing machines and cars. Electronics is one of the fastest-growing areas of science, as the electronic chip becomes smaller and smaller, yet faster and more powerful.

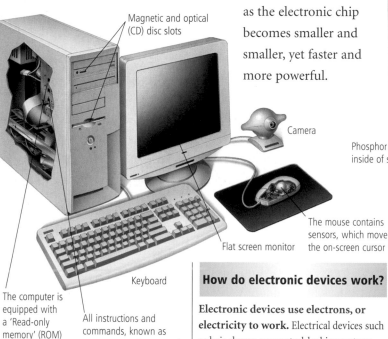

Magnetic and optical (CD) disc slots

Camera

The computer is equipped with a 'Read-only memory' (ROM)

All instructions and commands, known as programs, are interpreted and carried out in the CPU

Keyboard

Flat screen monitor

The mouse contains sensors, which move the on-screen cursor

Electron guns

Aerial

Phosphor dots on inside of screen

Focusing and scanning coils

Glass vacuum tube

➊ In a standard TV set, 'guns' fire streams of electrons at the inside of the screen. The electrons hit tiny dots of phosphor chemicals whose glow can be seen from the other side of the screen as the image. There is one electron gun for each set of coloured dots – red, green and blue. The beams pass electromagnetic coils or plates, which make the beams bend or deflect to scan the screen line by line.

➊ One of the smallest components in a typical personal computer is the central processing unit (CPU), where microprocessors interpret commands. The items connected by wires, called peripherals, include the keyboard, mouse, screen (monitor) and additional devices, such as scanners or cameras.

How do electronic devices work?

Electronic devices use electrons, or electricity to work. Electrical devices such as hair-dryers, car central-locking systems, food processors and microwave ovens often have moving parts, such as motors, electromagnets and gears, that we can usually see. They are electromechanical and so are powered by electricity. Electronic devices, such as transistors, have no moving parts except electrons, which are too small to see.

Do electronic devices use much electricity?

The electrons in an electronic device flow as an electric current, which is usually tiny. They measure from a few volts in strength down to only thousandths of a volt, and only fractions of an amp (measure of electrical amount). The electrons are mainly controlled by other electrons, as tiny electrical pulses or by magnetic effects.

What are ICs?

An IC – integrated circuit – is a circuit board where all the components and connections are made at the same time, fully joined together or integrated. Microscopic in size, the circuit can be made up of thousands of individual components. The components, such as switches, resistors, capacitors and transistors, are connected by wires or metal strips on the circuit board.

⊕ A PCB, printed circuit board, is made with all the metal connectors in position or 'printed' onto the insulator board. Microchips and other components are connected by inserting their metal 'legs' into sockets.

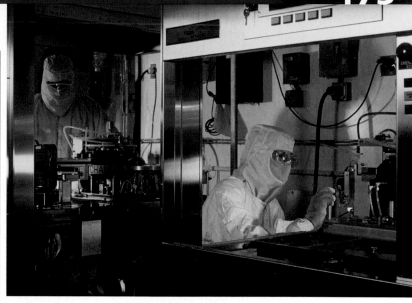

What is a microchip?

The 'chip' is a slice of a semiconductor material such as silicon and 'micro' means that all the components and connections of the integrated circuit on the chip are microscopic in size. Tiny parts of this material either carry electricity or not, depending on conditions such as changing temperature, or the presence or absence of electricity or magnetism nearby.

Integrated circuit

Plastic casing for insulation

'Leg' connecting pins

⊕ Electronic components must be made in extremely clean conditions. A few specks of dust could get inside the components and ruin the manufacture of microchips and electrical circuit boards.

What are CPUs?

Central processing unit microchips are the 'brains' of electronic devices, such as computers. Information is fed into the CPU as patterns of millions of tiny electrical signals per second. The microcircuits in the CPU analyze or process the signals and 'decide' what to do according to a set of rules built into the circuit design. The results are fed out as more electrical signals to various other parts of the equipment.

The air around us is full of rays and waves. We can only see one kind of them – light. The others include radio waves, microwaves, heat rays and even tiny amounts of X-rays. These are invisible, yet they are very similar to light rays in every feature, except for the length of each actual wave.

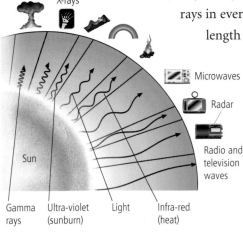

X-rays

Microwaves

Radar

Radio and television waves

Sun

Gamma rays

Ultra-violet (sunburn)

Light

Infra-red (heat)

◀ *Nearly all forms of electromagnetic radiation are given off by the Sun. As the wavelengths become smaller, from radio to gamma rays, the frequency – the number of waves per second – becomes larger. We also use many of these waves in various kinds of equipment, such as radio transmitters and microwave ovens.*

What is radiation?

Radiation is energy that is given out, or radiated, from a source. One type of radiation is a combination of electricity and magnetism, as electromagnetic waves. These are like up-and-down waves of energy. The different lengths of waves have different names, but they are all the same form of energy. We use them in hundreds of different ways, in communications, medicine, industry and scientific research.

Can radiation be emitted as particles, not waves?

Some types of radiation are emitted as particles. One type is known as alpha radiation, which is a stream of particles from inside atoms. Each alpha particle consists of two protons and two neutrons (similar to the nucleus of an atom of the very light gas, helium, which also contains two protons and two neutrons). Another type is beta particles, where each particle is an electron (or its 'opposite', a positron).

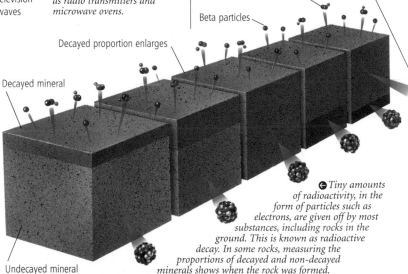

Nuclei of atoms become lighter

Alpha particles

Beta particles

Decayed proportion enlarges

Decayed mineral

◀ *Tiny amounts of radioactivity, in the form of particles such as electrons, are given off by most substances, including rocks in the ground. This is known as radioactive decay. In some rocks, measuring the proportions of decayed and non-decayed minerals shows when the rock was formed.*

Undecayed mineral

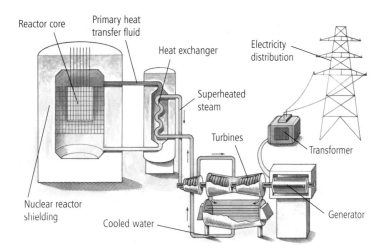

Reactor core

Primary heat
transfer fluid

Heat exchanger

Electricity
distribution

Superheated
steam

Turbines

Transformer

Nuclear reactor
shielding

Cooled water

Generator

Is 'radioactivity' radiation?

Yes, radioactivity is energy given off by atoms that are not stable or 'settled', because their subatomic particles are out of balance. Substances that naturally have a proportion of unstable atoms include radium, uranium and plutonium. These substances give off alpha and beta particles and gamma rays, which are extremely short electromagnetic waves.

🔵 *In a nuclear power station, the radiation given out by the splitting of fuel atoms includes vast amounts of heat. This boils water into high-pressure steam that spins turbine blades linked to the generator.*

How fast does radiation travel?

Radiation travels faster than anything else in the Universe. Its electromagnetic waves include light, and nothing can exceed the speed of light in a vacuum (such as the nothingness of space) – which travels about 300,000 km/sec. Many electromagnetic waves travel this fast – equivalent to seven times around the world in less than one second.

🔵 *If an electron beam is fired at certain metal objects, the beam gives off X-rays, which can penetrate solid objects, such as a hand, and cast an image of the interior, such as the bones inside a finger.*

Is radiation harmful?

Generally, no, but some types can be in certain amounts. Ultra-violet rays from the Sun can cause sunburn and skin cancers. Too many X-rays can damage the microscopic cells of living things and lead to illness, tumours and cancers. However, used very carefully, X-rays can also destroy growths and cancers: this is known as radiotherapy. Radioactivity may cause burns, sickness and many other ill effects. Too much of any radiation can be damaging. But in daily life, most forms of radiation are controlled in their amounts and strengths so as not to cause harm to living things.

🔵 *The magnetron in a microwave oven produces the type of radiation known as microwaves. The waves are up to 20 cm in length. They bounce or reflect off the paddles of the stirrer to spread evenly inside the oven.*

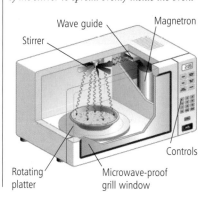

Wave guide

Magnetron

Stirrer

Controls

Rotating
platter

Microwave-proof
grill window

A simple description of light is that it is something we see with our eyes! Light is actually a form of energy, which is made up of electromagnetic waves. It is essential to our lives, so that we can look around to move about, eat, drink, learn and stay safe. We cannot survive in darkness, nor can most animals and plants.

What is light?

Light is a type of energy. We can imagine it as up-and-down waves of the form of energy known as electromagnetism. This is a combination of electricity and magnetism. So light waves are very similar in form to radio waves, microwaves, infra-red, ultra-violet and X-rays. Light waves are so short that about 2,000 of them would stretch just 1 mm.

◑ Light bounces or reflects off very smooth surfaces, in the same pattern and at the same angle as the rays hit the surface. This produces what we call a mirror-image. In this image, left and right are reversed. So in a mirror, we do not see our faces as other people see them.

Is light always in the form of waves?

Not always. Light energy also seems to be in the form of tiny 'packets', which are pieces of light energy known as photons, like the stream of bullets from a machine-gun. For some purposes scientists view light as a continuous form of energy, that moves in up-and-down waves. For other purposes, they view it as units of energy called photons. This is known in science as the 'wave-particle duality' of light.

◑ Different wavelengths or colours of light are bent or refracted by slightly different amounts as they pass at an angle into a glass prism. The waves spread out and reveal that ordinary 'white' light is really a mixture of all colours, known as the visible light spectrum.

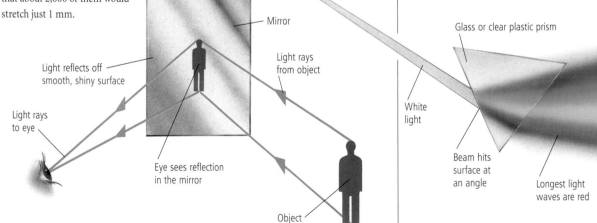

Mirror

Light reflects off smooth, shiny surface

Light rays from object

Light rays to eye

Eye sees reflection in the mirror

Object

Glass or clear plastic prism

White light

Beam hits surface at an angle

Longest light waves are red

Why are there different colours of light?

The colour of light depends on the length of its waves. The longest ones are each about 770 nanometres (0.00077 mm) in length. Our eyes detect these as red. The shortest light waves are 400 nanometres (0.0004 mm) and our eyes see these as violet. The wavelengths in between form all the other colours, from orange and yellow to green, blue and indigo. This range of colours is known as the light spectrum.

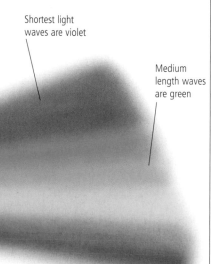

Shortest light waves are violet

Medium length waves are green

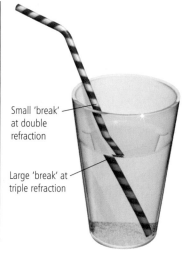

Small 'break' at double refraction

Large 'break' at triple refraction

🔾 *Light rays from the lower straw (beneath the surface of the water) are refracted as they pass through water, glass and air. From the upper straw they pass through only air and glass, so the path of light is different and makes the straw appear broken.*

Does light always travel in straight lines?

If nothing gets in its way, yes. But if light hits any objects or substances, various things can happen. If the object is see-through or transparent, such as a glass window or water, then the light carries on. It may bend where it goes from one transparent substance to another, known as refraction. If an object is opaque (not clear), such as a wooden door, then the light bounces or reflects off it.

How fast is light?

Light has the fastest known speed in the Universe – almost 300,000 km/sec. All electromagnetic waves go at this speed. But this is their speed in a completely empty space or vacuum. The speed of light is affected as it travels through different materials or substances. It travels slower through transparent substances, such as water and glass.

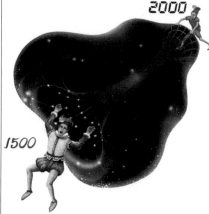

2000

1500

🔾 *One theory about space and time says that as an object moves faster and approaches the speed of light, then the passage of time for that object slows down. At light speed, time stops. Perhaps if the object went faster than light, time would go backwards. 'Short-cuts' in space called wormholes might make faster-than-light speed possible. So travelling through a wormhole could take you back in time, maybe 500 years or more!*

Loud shouts, soft whispers, repetitive noise, beautiful music, warning sirens, different voices, the crash of thunder – sounds are a huge part of our daily lives. The science of sound is known as acoustics, and it affects the design of modern buildings, as well as a vast variety of products, from televisions and water plumbing to cars, trains and planes.

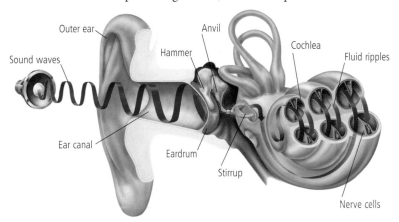

Outer ear

Anvil

Hammer

Cochlea

Sound waves

Fluid ripples

Ear canal

Eardrum

Stirrup

Nerve cells

What is sound?

Sound is energy in the form of movements of a substance or object. The to-and-fro movements many times each second are known as vibrations. Vibrating objects such as a loudspeaker make ripples of waves of high and low air pressure, which travel through the air to our ears. Since sound involves motion, it is a type of kinetic energy.

⬆ Invisible sound waves travel through the air and vibrate the eardrum, which passes the vibrations along the tiny ear bones into the cochlea. The vibrations cause ripples in the fluid within the cochlea, which make nerve signals that are sent to the brain to be processed.

Returning echo

Outgoing pulse

Can we see sounds?

We cannot see sound waves in the air, but we can see big vibrations in solid objects that produce sounds, such as loudspeakers or engines. We can also see the ripples on a liquid such as water, through which sound passes. However, the sounds we hear come from vibrations at the rate of more than 20 per second, known as 20 Hz. Our eyes cannot follow such fast movements so we see just a blur. A butterfly's wingflaps, at 10 Hz (ten per second), are too slow to produce sound for us to hear. A hummingbird's wingbeats at 100 Hz are fast enough to make a buzzing hum, but can only be seen as a blur.

⬇ A bat's squeaks and clicks are mostly ultrasonic – too high for our ears to detect. The sounds reflect from objects around and the bat works out whether the echoes indicate leaves and twigs to be avoided when flying or prey to be caught. This system is called echolocation and allows the bat to fly and feed – even in total darkness.

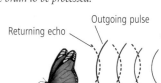

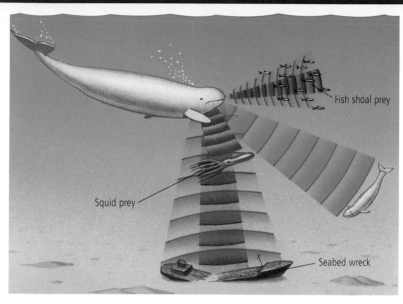

Squid prey

Fish shoal prey

Seabed wreck

⊕ *Hunting whales such as the beluga send out sonic clicks. These pulses bounce back as echoes to give the whale information about any objects that might be nearby.*

Can we hear all sounds?

No, our ears only respond to sounds with vibration speeds between about 20 and 20,000 Hz. The vibration speed or frequency, in Hz, affects the pitch of a sound. Low frequency sounds, such as the roar of a truck or rocket, are very deep and booming. High frequency ones, such as birds singing, are shrill. Sounds lower than about 20 Hz or higher than 20,000 Hz may be all around us, but we cannot hear them.

➔ *Some birdsong can exceed 100,000 Hz.*

How fast does sound travel?

The speed of sound depends on what it has to travel through. Its speed in the air varies with air temperature, pressure and humidity (moisture content), travelling an average of 344 m/sec. Sounds move at about 1,500 m/sec through liquids, such as water. It travels even faster through solid objects: 2,500 m/sec through hard plastic, 5,000 m/sec through steel, and about 6,000 m/sec through some types of glass.

Can sound reflect, like light?

Yes, sound waves reflect or bounce off hard, smooth, flat surfaces, such as walls and doors, just as light waves bounce off a mirror. If the returning sound or reflection is more than about one-tenth of a second after the original sound, we hear it separately and call it an echo. If the time gap for the reflection is less, it mixes with the original sound and makes it seem longer, which is known as reverberation.

⊕ *It is possible to hear more than one echo from a single sound. This usually occurs in caves, valleys or canyons where there are many different surfaces that can reflect sound. The sound waves bounce from wall to wall and enable us to hear several echoes.*

Machines are all around us, and are often used in everyday life. Jet planes roar overhead, cars whizz past on the road, cranes lift loads, gears are changed on cycles, vacuum cleaners suck and swings and seesaws are used in playgrounds. Machines work because forces make movements.

1 Kinetic energy is passed from the foot to the ball, applying a force to make the ball move

2 The momentum of the ball is affected by air resistance

3 The ball is pulled back down by gravity

➊ *The tendency of a moving object to carry on moving in a straight line is counteracted by other forces. For example, air resistance and gravity may act upon a moving object to break its momentum.*

What is a force?

It is a push, pull or other action that makes an object move, or tries to make it move. If you kick a ball, the force from your foot makes the ball move. The kinetic (movement) energy of your foot is passed, or transferred, to the ball. If you kick a wall, the kinetic energy of your foot does not make the wall move, but it is changed into energy that squashes against your foot.

➊ *The basic forms of matter (solid, liquid, gas and plasma) depend on the motion of atoms. Most pure substances can change their form as their temperature changes. For example, water (liquid) becomes ice (solid) when cooled enough, or steam (gas) when heated enough.*

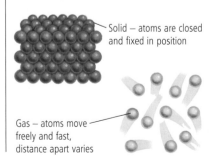

Solid – atoms are closed and fixed in position

Gas – atoms move freely and fast, distance apart varies

Do atoms move?

It depends on the substance or object they are in. If it is a solid, such as iron, or wood, the atoms are almost still and just move or vibrate slightly around a central point. In a liquid, such as water or oil, the atoms can move about, but they stay the same distance from each other, so the liquid keeps the same volume. In a gas, like the air around us, atoms can move even faster and also change their distances, so the volume of the gas can increase or decrease.

➜ *There is movement even at the subatomic scale. Electrons spin and whirl around the nucleus of an atom. The proton and neutron particles in the nucleus vibrate or oscillate (move from side-to-side) slightly.*

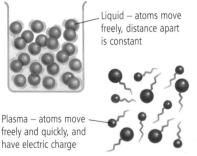

Liquid – atoms move freely, distance apart is constant

Plasma – atoms move freely and quickly, and have electric charge

Are there different kinds of motion?

Yes, depending on the direction or path of the moving object. The simplest kind of motion is movement in a straight line, known as linear motion. Angular motion is in a bend or curve, such as a car going around a corner. A special case of this is circular motion, where the object stays the same distance from a central point, like a wheel on an axle.

Reciprocating motion is a to-and-fro movement from a middle point, such as pistons in an engine or the vibrations in a loudspeaker.

A nutcracker is a form of lever that provides the effort (squeezing force) to break the load (nut)

An axe is a form of wedge

A screw is a turning type of wedge

A wheelbarrow enables heavy loads to be lifted using a wheel and axle, which reduce friction to make the task easier

⊕ *As a motorcycle travels in a curved pathway, the rider must lean into the corner. This counteracts the natural tendency of a moving object to keep going in a straight line. Otherwise the motorcycle would topple outwards, away from the corner.*

What is a machine?

In basic science, a machine is a device that allows a small force, known as the effort, to move a large object, the load. There are six types of simple machine – the ramp (a slope or an inclined plane), lever, wedge, pulley, screw, and the wheel and axle. Examples of four of these are shown to the left. Of the remaining two machines, the ramp eases the movement of heavy objects over a distance. Pulleys move loads by changing the direction and distance of the force, to be pulled down, rather than lifted up. All other machines work by using various stages that are a combination of these simple machines.

Do machines give us extra energy?

No, it is not possible for machines to create energy or motion from nothing. As you pull out a nail with a crowbar, your hands move a long way without much force, while the other end of the lever moves a little way with a much greater force. This is known as mechanical advantage. It breaks a task down into smaller, easier stages so it becomes much more manageable. Many machines have motors or engines, which provide the force, rather than our own muscles, so the task becomes even easier.

Many people wear wristwatches, and there are clocks in most rooms, which are there to tell us the time. We need to know the date and time so that we can arrive at school or work promptly, meet friends on agreed dates and at certain times, and in order to catch a bus, train or plane. However in science, there is much more to time than the tick of a clock.

⬆ *The ancient Egyptians made sundials more than 3,000 years ago. The marks showed hours. The length of the hours varied with the seasons, but people were used to such an idea and called them 'temporary hours'.*

When did people start measuring time?

At least 10,000 years ago, and probably well before that. Ancient peoples recorded sunrise and sunset each day, the changing phases of the moon each month, and the seasons of the year. They used these natural occurrences to devise calendars and predict important events, such as when a river might flood or the time to worship a certain god.

When were clocks first developed?

Ticking clocks similar to today's were devised in the 1300s. For centuries before, people had relied on simpler methods of timekeeping, such as hourglasses, or sundials. From the 1400s, however, explorers sailed on great voyages to find new lands. In order to track their positions, they needed to measure time precisely. In the 1700s, engineer John Harrison developed a series of very accurate clocks called chronometers (special clocks for use at sea to measure longitude). Accurate to less than 30 seconds in a year, even on a swaying ship, these began a new era of precise timekeeping.

Could time stand still?

Modern science predicts that yes, it might. We are used to time passing regularly, with every minute the same length, day after day, year after year. But Albert Einstein's theories said that time could change speed. The faster an object moves, the slower time passes. However, the speeds involved are enormous. If an object could move at the speed of light, then time might actually stop.

⬆ *John Harrison's 1759 version of the chronometer won a £10,000 prize. The prize had been devised by the British government in 1714 to promote research into the development of accurate timekeeping devices.*

⬅ *Simple timekeepers, such as hourglasses of trickling sand remained common until the 1300s when mechanical clocks were developed.*

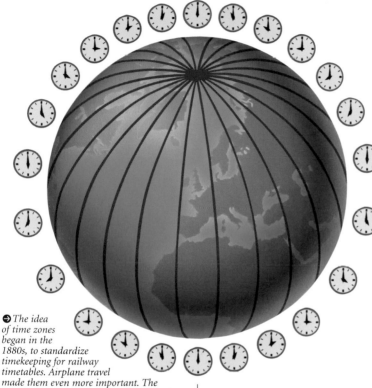

→ The idea
of time zones
began in the
1880s, to standardize
timekeeping for railway
timetables. Airplane travel
made them even more important. The
time is the same everywhere within one time
zone, but different to all the other time zones.

Is it the same time everywhere in the world?

No, because of the way the Earth spins around once every 24 hours. Otherwise at 8 a.m., the Sun might have risen in the UK, yet be setting in Australia, while the USA is completely dark. The world is divided into vertical strips called time zones. Some countries are within one time zone while others encompass several. Travellers need to adjust their watches or clocks as they move between zones to know the 'local' time. Some time zones 'bend' around islands or national borders.

Are time and space linked?

Yes, in modern science they are four parts or dimensions of the same whole. Three of these dimensions are in physical space – length, width and height. The fourth dimension is time. For example, to describe dangerous rocky rapids in a river, the length and width of the rapids, and the height that the water falls need to be measured. But the time of the measurement should also be recorded. Otherwise someone might arrive to see them in the dry season when the river and rapids have gone, and so the other measurements become irrelevant.

↓ Atomic clocks use the movement of atoms from substances such as caesium, which vibrate more than nine billion times each second, and are accurate to less than one second in a million years.

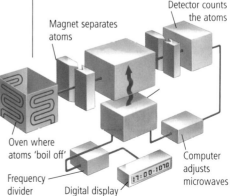

Detector counts
the atoms

Magnet separates
atoms

Oven where
atoms 'boil off'

Frequency
divider

Digital display

17:00.1070

Computer
adjusts
microwaves

Long ago, people travelled by foot and communicated face to face. It may have taken days to transport heavy goods just a few kilometres. Advances in transport and communication technology mean that we can now converse with a person on the other side of the world, using a videophone, or travel to be with that person within a day.

Communications satellite

Broadcast radio signals

➲ *Broadcast communications satellites send radio signals direct to many receivers over a wide area, for radio programmes and television channels.*

Uplink dish

Radio receiver

What is a comsat?

A communications satellite is designed to receive information such as radio programmes, telephone calls and television channels, usually sent to it in the form of 'uplink' radio waves. The satellite then strengthens or amplifies the signals and beams them back down again as radio waves. These satellites can be used as repeaters or relays to pass on information over great distances, or to broadcast to many receivers over a huge area. Most satellites are in geosynchronous orbits.

◐ *The world is encircled by communications satellites and criss-crossed by telecom wires, fibre-optic cables, and radio and microwave links. The telecom network links telephone calls, radio, television and computer data.*

Is the world really 'shrinking'?

Planet Earth itself is not getting smaller. But a 'shrinking world' means we can travel and communicate much faster than previously. In the late 1700s, a journey halfway round the world by sailing ship might have taken three months. In the late 1800s, a similar journey by steamship took six weeks. In the 1920s, pioneering aeroplane flights over the same distance took just two weeks. Today the journey time halfway round the world has 'shrunk' to less than 24 hours.

Will travel times continue to shorten?

In the near future, probably not. There are various plans for 'space-planes' that could travel around the world in just a few hours. However, the costs of developing such a massive project are phenomenal. In the 1960s, many people thought that supersonic (faster-than-sound) aircraft travel would become widely-used. But the only supersonic passenger plane was Concorde, which first flew in the same year as the subsonic Boeing 747 'Jumbo'. Concorde could fly from Paris to Washington in a record time of 3 hrs 32 mins.

➡ *Present-day cruise ships are massive, and are organized much like floating hotels.*

What are the fastest forms of transport?

Rockets and spacecraft are the fastest, with the space shuttle travelling at more than 24,000 km/h. The fastest jet warplanes travel at more than 3,000 km/h, but a passenger jet plane moves at about 900 km/h. On land, electric-powered 'bullet trains' exceed 300 km/h. Passenger hovercraft on the sea reach 70–80 km/h and fast passenger ships around 40–50 km/h. Most cars reach up to 150 km/h but speed restrictions and crowded roads mean that journeys are often much slower and safer.

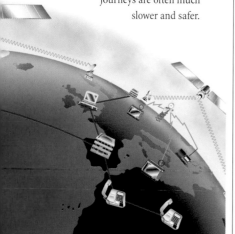

Will we have personal jump-jets or helicopters?

In the near future, probably not. There is only one working type of 'jump-jet' – the British Harrier multirole strike fighter. A newer US / British design, the JSF or Joint Strike Fighter, is taking years and costing billions to develop. Many important or wealthy people have personal helicopters. But the skills needed to fly a helicopter, and the strict limits on engineering, maintenance and safety mean that they are unlikely to become as common as cars in the near future.

Which form of travel is most luxurious?

Cruise liners offer amazing comfort and luxury, as 'floating hotels'. One of the biggest cruise liners is the *Queen Mary II*, which went into service in January 2004. It can carry 2,700 passengers at a top speed of 30 knots (equivalent to 55 km/h). The on-board facilities available to the passengers include 14 bars and clubs, six restaurants, a casino, theatre, swimming pools and even a planetarium.

⬇ *'Jump-jets' such as the Harrier and JSF are VTOL – vertical take-off and landing aircraft. The jet blasts come out of tilting nozzles, which can point down for take-off and landing, or to the rear for forward flight.*

Science and technology have filled our lives with machines, devices and gadgets. It seems incredible that just a few decades ago there were no CD players, satellite television or games consoles. Technical advances are moving at a tremendous rate with better and more efficient machines being constantly developed.

How do CDs and DVDs store information?

CDs (compact discs) and DVDs (digital versatile discs) hold information in the form of tiny bowl-like pits in the shiny underside surface. In a CD there are over 3,000 million pits in a spiral path or track about 5 km long. They can store about 70 minutes of high-quality music, over 700 megabytes of computer data or similar amounts of information. A DVD has more, smaller pits in different vertical layers and stores 4.7 gigabytes (4,700 megabytes) – enough for a full-length movie and its soundtrack. These pits are 'read' by a laser beam.

◑ Personal music players can store sounds on tape, compact disc (like this version), minidisc (similar to CD but smaller) or electronic microchip.

◓ A powerful microscope reveals the bowl-like pits and flat areas between them, in the surface of a CD (compact disc).

Detergent and additive trays

Controls

Drive belt

Motor

Hydraulic suspension

Door

Drum

Pump

Filter

◓ In western countries, such as the UK, about one household in two has a washing machine. About one in three households has a dishwasher.

Which labour-saving devices are most popular?

One of the most popular machines in daily life is the washing machine. In most developed countries, many households have one. Some people use industrial versions in launderettes. The machine washes clothes inside a revolving drum with hot water and soap, which are then rinsed away with clean water. A fast spin gets rid of excess water, so that the clothes can be hung to dry.

Can mobile phones get much smaller?

The main limits on mobile phone size are the rechargeable battery bulk and the size of the buttons so they are easy for our fingers to press. Also, screens for photos and videos cannot be too small. In the future mobile phones may become voice-operated so that they do not need buttons. For security it will only respond to the unique voice of its owner.

◉ Mobile phones have shrunk amazingly in the past 10 years, from the size of a housebrick to almost as small as a thumb.

Does medicine benefit from technology?

Yes, technology is very important in many aspects of modern medicine. For example, an endoscope is a flexible tube that can be inserted into the body to view its insides to achieve a more detailed and accurate diagnosis. Light to illuminate the interior is carried to the tip along optical fibres, which are bundled, flexible rods of transparent glass or plastic, thinner than human hairs. The image is carried from the tip to the eyepiece and screen by another set of optical fibres. There are also many kinds of scanners that can see inside the body.

◉ Doctors can see inside the body using various kinds of scanners, or directly by looking through an endoscope. The endoscope can also carry out treatments, such as sealing a cut using a laser beam.

Main unit feeds images to monitor or television

Hand console with controls

◉ Games consoles become more realistic every year, with faster action and better graphics, as well as more imaginative challenges. Some games can be played 'live' over the Internet with people anywhere in the world.

How fast does technology become out-of-date?

Technology is frequently updated, making existing versions out-of-date. For example, vinyl discs were used to play back recorded sound for more than 50 years. Cassette tapes also became popular for about 30 years. About 20 years later, CDs took over. Some 10 years after that, MP3-players arrived, storing sounds in electronic microchips. The world of technology continues to produce faster and more efficient machines.

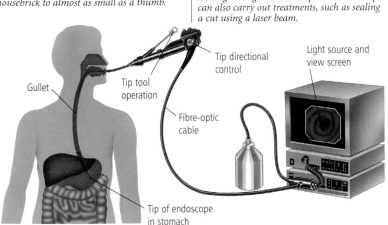

Gullet

Tip tool operation

Tip directional control

Fibre-optic cable

Light source and view screen

Tip of endoscope in stomach

1 What does water become when it boils?

2 Iron, steel and copper are examples of what?

3 What happens to water at 0°C?

4 What happens to butter when it is heated?

5 What is solid water called?

6 Which natural liquid is used to make nylon?

7 Which tool is used to push in and pull out nails?

8 Pierre and Marie Curie, who worked together to investigate radioactivity, shared which prize in 1903 with Henri Becquerel, who discovered radioactivity?

Atom **facts**

- A typical atom is about 0.2 nanometres (one billionth of a metre) across. So 10 million atoms in a row would stretch just 2 mm.

- The nucleus at the centre of an atom is tiny compared to the size of the whole atom.

- If the whole atom was a massive sports stadium, with the outermost electrons whizzing around the farthest seats, the nucleus would be the size of a human thumb in the middle.

- In a solid substance, the atoms are about 0.3 nanometres apart, so their outermost electrons almost touch.

Key **dates**

2500 BC Empedocles from ancient Greece suggested that all matter was made of mixtures of four elements – earth, air, fire and water.

2400 BC Greek philosopher, Democritus, developed the idea that it was possible to cut matter so small that it could not be cut any more. He named these pieces of matter 'atoms', meaning 'uncuttable'.

340 BC Greek thinker and scientist Aristotle added ether to the elements

1661 English scientist Robert Boyle described elements as "simple or perfectly unmingled bodies".

9 What supports a building?

10 Which will feel hotter after stirring a hot drink: a plastic or metal spoon?

11 What is used to attach a door to its frame but lets it open and close?

12 What gives your body energy?

13 What is the name for a machine made of ropes and wheels used to lift heavy loads?

14 What is an example of natural electricity?

15 What does 'AC' stand for in electrical matters?

16 Does a conductor let energy flow, or stop it flowing?

17 A magnet has an east and west pole: true or false?

18 What is special about a compass needle?

19 What navigational device uses a magnet suspended or floating in liquid?

20 In what kind of station is electricity made?

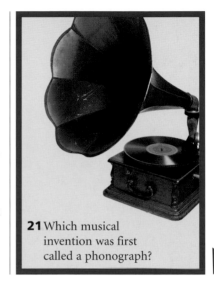

21 Which musical invention was first called a phonograph?

◆ *Dalton studied gases as well as chemistry, and from the age of 15, he kept daily records of the weather.*

1787 French chemist Antoine Lavoisier defined a chemical element as "the last point which analysis can reach". He listed all the known elements and introduced chemical symbols.

1808 English physicist John Dalton suggested that each pure chemical element had its own kind of atom.

1868–69 Russian scientist Dmitri Mendeleév listed all the known elements, and devised a chart, the Periodic Table, to categorize them.

➔ *Lavoisier began the system of using symbols for chemicals in 1787.*

22 What is used to make electricity in a hydro-electric power station?

23 What did Thomas Edison invent to create light in 1879?

24 What are the straight lines that light travels in called?

25 What type of rays are used to take a photograph of your bones?

26 Which type of radiation can cause sunburn or skin cancer?

27 What is kinetic energy?

28 Who developed the first hot-air balloon, launched in 1783?

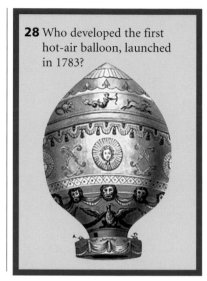

29 What is the curved glass in spectacles called?

30 The seven colours of the spectrum combine to make what colour light?

31 Light bends when it goes through water: true or false?

32 Which word describes how loud sound is?

33 How do you make a sound on a percussion instrument?

34 In what year was the aircraft invented?

FACTFILE

Changing **energy**

In science, energy is the ability or capacity to do work or to cause change. Work is usually described as the changing of energy from one form or system to another, often resulting in some type of movement. In everyday life we think of 'work' as something useful, with a purpose. But this is not so in science. For example, an apple hanging on a tree has the type of energy known as potential energy, because of its position high above the ground. If the apple falls, its potential energy is changed into the energy of movement, known as kinetic energy, and 'work' has been done in the process, as it fell from the tree. This work happens whether the apple falls to the ground, or if it hits something on its way down.

↑ *Potential energy is found in a bird as it sits on a perch before flying away. The potential energy becomes kinetic energy once the bird takes off into the air.*

35 What has sails that turn round in the wind to work machinery?

36 Which English scientist developed the first modern theory about how gravity works?

37 Could we live on any other planet apart from Earth?

38 How many hours are there in a day?

39 Length, breadth and width are three dimensions: what is the fourth?

40 What kind of boat floats on air?

41 Do the thick or thin strings on a guitar sound lowest?

Measuring **energy**

- The main unit for measuring both energy and work is the joule.

- The calorie was an older unit used especially to measure heat energy and the chemical energy contained in foods.

- One calorie equals 4.2 joules, and one kilocalorie or kcal equals 4,200 joules (4.2 kJ).

◔ *It takes a massive amount of energy to launch a spacecraft – approximately 100 billion joules.*

- A 100-watt light bulb requires one joule of electrical energy each second.

- A typical light bulb left on for 24 hours takes about 5 million joules.

- An average person needs about 5 to 10 million joules of energy each day from foods, to stay active and healthy.

- A split-second bolt of lightning releases 2,000 million joules.

42 What is the name for the strip where an aircraft lands?

43 What did Alexander Graham Bell invent in 1876?

44 What do radios and televisions have for picking up signals?

45 Does a computer programmer develop hardware or software?

46 How many joules are there in a bolt of lighning?

47 What is used to receive signals from a satellite?

Making laser **light**

'Laser' means 'light amplification by stimulated emission of radiation'. A laser beam is made by putting pulses of energy into a substance called the active medium. The input energy can be electricity, heat or even ordinary light. The atoms of the active medium gain more and more energy, which suddenly reaches a certain limit or threshold, and is given off as a burst of laser light.

🔊*In one type of laser, energy is put into the active medium of a ruby rod as flashes of ordinary light.*

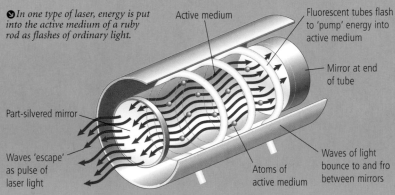

Active medium

Fluorescent tubes flash to 'pump' energy into active medium

Mirror at end of tube

Part-silvered mirror

Waves 'escape' as pulse of laser light

Atoms of active medium

Waves of light bounce to and fro between mirrors

Answers

1 Steam	16 It lets it flow	30 White light	45 Software
2 Metals	17 False – it has a North	31 True	46 2,000 million joules
3 It freezes	and a South pole	32 Volume	47 Satellite dish
4 It melts	18 It is a magnet	33 You bang or rattle it	
5 Ice	19 Magnetic compass	34 1903	
6 Oil	20 In a power station	35 A windmill or wind turbines	
7 Hammer	21 Gramophone	36 Sir Isaac Newton	
8 Nobel Prize for Physics	22 Water	37 No	
9 Foundations	23 The light bulb	38 24	
10 Metal spoon	24 Rays	39 Time	
11 Hinge	25 X-rays	40 Hovercraft	
12 Food	26 Ultra-violet rays	41 The thick strings	
13 Pulley	27 Movement energy	42 Runway	
14 Lightning	28 The Montgolfier brothers	43 The telephone	
15 Alternating current	29 A lens	44 Aerials	

Types of **light**

Laser light differs from ordinary light in a variety of ways:

In laser light all the light waves are the same length and the same colour. A laser gives out light of one pure colour only. All of the peaks and troughs of the waves of laser lights are level or aligned, and the waves are all parallel, which means they stay the same distance from each other, no matter how far they travel.

In ordinary light, even what seems to be a single colour of light has a mixture of wavelengths, and therefore a mixture of colours. The peaks and troughs are mixed up and not aligned, and the waves spread out or diverge so the whole beam gets wider.

Light **speed**

Light speed varies greatly with the substance or medium through which it passes.

Medium	Speed (km/sec)
Vacuum	299,792
Air	299,700
Water	225,000
Window glass	195,000
Decorative (lead crystal) glass	160,000
Diamond	125,000

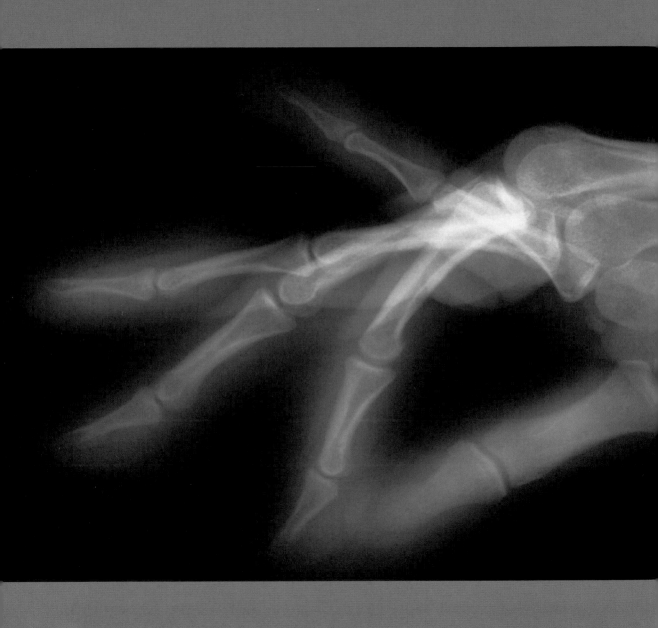

THE HUMAN BODY

There are more than six billion people in the world, and each person has unique characteristics. Inside, however, they are all made in the same way. Beginning life as a single cell, the human body grows and develops to become an incredible machine, more complex than any computer, with systems that are constantly active even when the body appears to be at rest.

What is skin made of?

How does the tongue taste different flavours?

How much blood is in the body?

What do we know more about than anything else in the world? You! Perhaps not you as an individual, but the way you live, eat, drink, think, feel happy and sad, daydream and sleep – the human body. There are more than six billion human bodies in the world, and each and every one of those has unique characteristics but, inside, they are all made and work in much the same way.

How can we learn about the body?

Modern medical science uses hundreds of complex machines and tests to find out more about the body every year. They include scanners, chemical tests, microscopes and electrical monitors. Scanners and X-ray machines see inside the body. Chemical tests on the blood and other parts show the substances they contain. Microscopes reveal the smallest cells and even genes. Electrical devices, such as heart (ECG) and brain (EEG) monitors, show readings as wavy lines on a paper sheet or screen for doctors to examine.

➲ *A typical body cell is far too small to see without a microscope. Yet it contains many even smaller parts, called organelles.*

What are organs?

Body organs include the heart, brain, stomach and kidneys and are the body's main parts or structures. The biggest organ within the body is the liver, while the largest organ of the whole body is the skin. Usually, several organs work together as a body system.

Cell membrane (outer covering)

Nucleus (control centre)

Internal membranes (make cell products)

Mitochondria (energy centre)

➲ *Inside the arm are many organs and tissues, including bones, blood vessels and nerves. Muscles and connective tissues link all these parts together.*

What are body systems?

A body system is a group of parts that work together to carry out one job or particular task to help keep the body alive and working well. For example, the heart, blood vessels (tubes) and blood make up the circulatory system. This pumps or circulates blood all around the body, to supply every tiny part with essential substances such as oxygen and nutrients, and to collect wastes for removal.

Humerus (upper arm bone)

Radial artery and vein

Radius (forearm bone)

Carpals (wrist bone)

➲ *Some body parts, such as bones and joints, can be replaced by artificial versions made of tough plastics, stainless steel and titanium. Artificial or prosthetic joints are shown here coloured in white.*

Can body parts be replaced?

Some body parts can be successfully replaced to enable the person to move about easily again. For example, people who have trouble with one or both of their hips, knees, shoulders, elbows or any of their fingers can be given metal or plastic artificial joints in place of the damaged body parts. Broken bones can be held together with plates, strips and screws. Some blood vessels can be replaced by manufactured plastic tubes. Internal organs, such as the heart, lungs, liver or kidneys, can be replaced. The new organs often come from deceased people who donated them before their death.

What are tissues?

Tissues are groups or collections of microscopic cells that are all the same type and do the same job. Examples include muscle tissue, which can shorten or contract to cause movement, nerve tissue, which carries nerve signals, and connective tissue, which fills the gaps between other tissues. Most organs are made of several kinds of tissue.

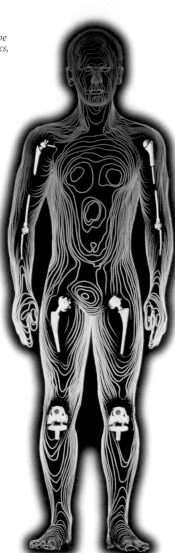

What are cells?

Cells are the smallest living parts of the body. They are like microscopic 'building blocks' in many shapes and sizes, which carry out different jobs. There are some 200 different kinds such as nerve cells, muscle cells and blood cells. On average, about 100 cells in a row would stretch across this 'o'. The whole body contains more than 50 billion billion cells.

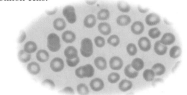

➊ *Under a light microscope, magnified about 1,500 times, red blood cells appear as blobs with pale centres. This is due to their dished shape, rather like a doughnut.*

➊ *Physiologists study how the body uses energy during strenuous activity such as swimming, when the heart beats faster, the lungs breathe more quickly and the muscles work harder.*

When you look at a human body, most of what you see is dead. The surface layer of the skin, and the hair and nails, were once made of living cells. But these gradually die off and then get rubbed or worn away as we move about, change clothes or wash and rub dry with towels, as part of daily living. The only visible parts of the body that are truly alive are the eyes.

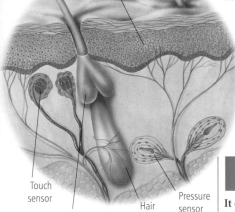

Hair shaft

Epidermis

Touch sensor

Sebum gland

Hair follicle

Pressure sensor

⊖ *The epidermis, the tough outer layer of skin, is mostly dead. The dermis below contains hair follicles, sweat glands, tiny blood vessels, and micro-fibres of elastin for flexibility, and collagen for toughness.*

⊕ *When undertaking hard physical work, the rubbing on the skin of the hands may be greater than normal. The epidermis (outer layer of skin) may develop calluses (rough patches of skin) against further damage.*

What is skin made of?

Like the rest of the body, skin is made of billions of microscopic cells. These cells form two layers, the epidermis on the outside and the dermis below it. The epidermis is tough and hard-wearing. The dermis is thicker and contains millions of microscopic sensors that detect different kinds of touch on the skin.

Why doesn't skin wear away?

It does – but it is always growing to replace the bits that wear away and are rubbed off. The tiny cells at the base of the epidermis continually multiply to make more cells. These gradually move upwards, filling with the tough substance keratin as they die, to form the hard-wearing surface. The whole skin surface is gradually worn away and replaced every four weeks.

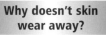

How thin is skin?

Skin can be between 0.5 and 5 mm thick. The thinnest skin is found on the eyelids and other delicate, sensitive parts of the body. The thickest skin is on the soles of the feet. This can be 5 mm or more, and grows even thicker in people who often walk and run in bare feet. It grows thicker to adapt and protect the soles of the feet from damage.

⊖*An enlarged view of the skin shows surface flakes that are about to be rubbed off.*

How quickly does hair grow?

In most people, if a single head hair was left uncut, it would grow about 1 m long, over four to five years. Then the hair naturally falls out of its follicle, which is the tiny pit in the dermis where it grows. However, this does not mean a bald head, since the follicle soon starts to grow a new hair. Follicles over the scalp do this at different times, so there are always plenty of hairs – in most people.

⬇️*A hair is alive and growing only at its root, down in the base of the follicle. The shaft that sticks out of the skin is dead, and is made of flattened cells stuck firmly together.*

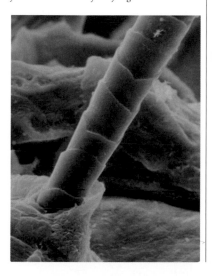

Why do we have fingernails?

To form a firm layer at the back of the fingertip. This stops the flexible fingertip from bending too much, so we can feel, press and pick up small items more easily and without damage. A nail grows at its root, which is under the skin at its base, and slides slowly along the finger.

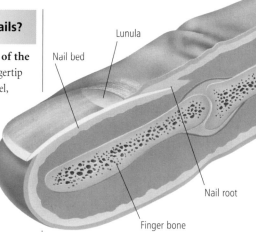

Lunula

Nail bed

Nail root

Finger bone

⬆️*A nail has its root under the skin and grows along the nail bed, which is the skin underneath it. The paler, crescent-like area is the lunula or 'little moon'.*

⬅️*Black hair is coloured by lots of melanin.*

⬅️*Reddish hair has carotenoid colouring substances.*

➡️*Light hair has less of the pigment melanin.*

Why do people have different coloured hair?

Hair colour depends on the genes inherited from parents. The colour of both hair and skin is due to natural pigments, mainly the very dark brown substance melanin, contained in cells known as melanocytes at the base of the epidermis. In some people the melanocytes are more active and make more melanin, and so the skin and usually the hair are darker.

Bones provide the strong framework that supports the whole body and holds its parts together. Without bones you would flop down on the floor like a jellyfish! All of the bones together are called the skeleton, and this gives protection as well as support.

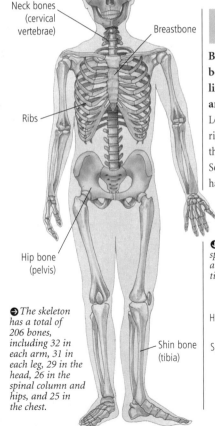

Neck bones (cervical vertebrae)

Breastbone

Ribs

Hip bone (pelvis)

Shin bone (tibia)

➲ *The skeleton has a total of 206 bones, including 32 in each arm, 31 in each leg, 29 in the head, 26 in the spinal column and hips, and 25 in the chest.*

What do bones do?

Bones form a framework inside the body, which holds it upright, makes limbs such as the arms and legs strong and protects many internal organs. Long bones in the arms and legs work as rigid levers, so when muscles pull on them, they can push, lift or make other movements. Some bones are protective. The skull forms a hard case around the delicate brain, and the backbone, ribs and breastbone make a strong cage around the heart and lungs.

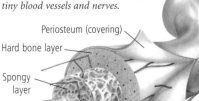

➲ *A typical bone has a hard outer layer, a spongy, honeycomb-like middle layer, and marrow at the centre, as well as tiny blood vessels and nerves.*

Periosteum (covering)

Hard bone layer

Spongy layer

Marrow

Orbit for the eye

Cranium

Zygoma (cheekbone)

Mandible (lower jaw)

➲ *The skull consists of 22 bones (including the lower jaw) linked by joints called sutures, which fix the bones firmly like glue. The sutures show up as faint wiggly lines.*

What is inside a bone?

A typical bone has three layers, which consist of collagen, minerals and bone marrow. On the outside is a 'shell' of compact or hard bone. This contains crystals of minerals such as calcium and phosphate for hardness, and fibres of collagen that allow the bone to bend slightly under stress. The middle layer is spongy or cancellous bone, with tiny spaces like a honeycomb. In the middle, the jelly-like bone marrow makes new cells for the blood.

What happens if a bone breaks?

It starts to mend itself straight away! Bones are made of living tissues, and once the parts of the bone are put back into their natural positions, usually by a doctor, microscopic cells called osteoblasts begin to make new bone that fills the break or gap. After a few months the gap is joined and the bone is repaired.

Are there different kinds of joints?

Yes, there are several different kinds, such as synovial joints, which allow movement, and suture joints, which do not. Synovial joints are found throughout the body, especially in the shoulder, elbow, hip and knee. These allow various kinds of movements, depending on their design. The elbow and knee are hinge joints, which allow only a to-and-fro movement. The shoulder and hip are ball-and-socket joints, which enable more flexibility such as twisting.

➔ *In the shoulder the ball-shaped end of the upper arm bone fits into a cup-like socket formed by the shoulder blade and collarbone.*

Collarbone

Upper arm bone

What is inside a synovial joint?

In a synovial joint the ends of the bones have a covering of shiny, slippery cartilage. The joint also contains oil-like synovial fluid, which is made by a bag-like covering around the joint, the synovial capsule. This fluid moistens the cartilage, making movements smooth, with hardly any rubbing and wear. The bones are prevented from moving too far or coming apart by strap-like ligaments, which are strips of strong tissue holding the bones and joints together.

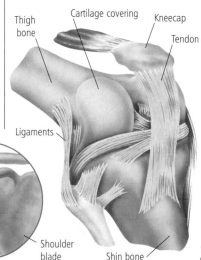

Thigh bone

Cartilage covering

Kneecap

Tendon

Ligaments

Shoulder blade

Shin bone

➔ *Regular exercise and movement help make joints flexible and supple to keep them healthy.*

Do bones change with age?

Yes, a baby's bones are softer and more flexible than an adult's. They tend to bend, rather than snap, under stress, which is helpful because young children tend to fall over or suffer bumps quite often. A baby's skeleton also contains more than 340 bones compared to 206 in the adult skeleton. This is because in early life some bones merge with others to form one bone. All bones are fully formed and at their strongest between about 20 and 45 years of age. In later life the bones become stiffer and more brittle, so they tend to crack rather than bend.

➔ *Strap-shaped ligaments criss-cross the outside of the knee joint to hold the bones in place.*

Every movement, every breath, every mouthful you chew – all of these actions and more are carried out by the body's muscles. A single muscle can do only one task, which is to get shorter to pull on body parts. But working together in very precise and co-ordinated ways, the body's hundreds of muscles carry out thousands of different activities every day.

Occipitalis

Deltoid

⊖ The muscles just under the skin are called the superficial layer. Beneath them are the intermediate or middle layer of muscles, and then the deep layer muscles, which are next to the bones.

Latissimus

Gluteus

Vastus

Gastrocnemius

How many muscles are there in the body?

There are about 640 muscles in the body. The biggest ones are in the torso, hips, shoulders and thighs. As you move you can see them bulging under the skin. But some muscles are much smaller. Each eyeball has six small ribbon-shaped muscles behind it, so it can swivel to look around.

⊕ Inside a muscle are bundles of myofibres, each about as thick as a human hair. Every myofibre is made of even thinner myofibrils, which contain numerous strands of the substances actin and myosin. These slide past each other to make the muscle contract.

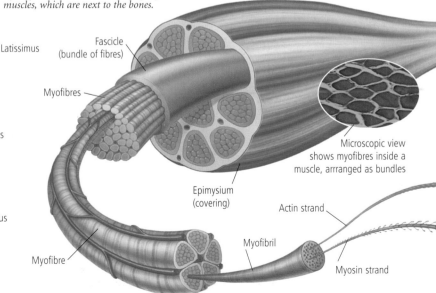

Fascicle (bundle of fibres)

Myofibres

Myofibre

Epimysium (covering)

Myofibril

Microscopic view shows myofibres inside a muscle, arrranged as bundles

Actin strand

Myosin strand

Can muscles push?

No, they can only pull, or contract. Most muscles are long and slim, and connected at each end to bones. As the muscle contracts it pulls on the bones and moves them, and so moves that body part. Then another muscle on the other side of the bone contracts, to pull it back again. Muscles work like this in pairs or teams to move body parts to-and-fro.

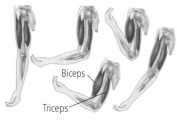

Biceps

Triceps

⊙ *Most muscles are arranged in opposing or antagonistic pairs to pull a bone one way and then the other, like the biceps and triceps in the upper arm.*

How fast can muscles work?

Very fast – as quick as the blink of an eye! But the speed depends on the type of muscle. 'Fast-twitch' muscles in the fingers, face and eyes can contract in less than one-twentieth of a second. They are speedy but soon tire. 'Slow-twitch' muscles, such as those in the back, take longer but can keep contracting for a greater period of time.

What controls muscles?

The brain controls muscles by sending nerve signals along nerves to the muscles, to tell them when to contract, by how much, and for how long. Luckily we learn many common movements such as walking, speaking and chewing early in life, so that we can do them almost without thinking. The brain is still in control, but it is the lower or 'automatic' part of the brain, which does not need our concentration or conscious awareness. Even standing requires muscle power, as the neck and back muscles tense to keep the body balanced and upright.

Why do muscles get tired?

Blood carries oxygen and energy to the muscles in order to keep them active, but the blood flow is sometimes too slow and so the muscles get tired. If the heart cannot pump blood fast enough to active muscles, the supplies run short and the muscles become tired or fatigued and can no longer work. Also, a busy muscle makes a waste product, lactic acid, which is taken away by blood. Again, if the blood supply is insufficient, lactic acid builds up in the muscle and may cause cramps.

Can the body make more muscles?

No, but the muscles it has can become larger, by undertaking exercise and activity. This helps the muscles stay healthier and the body become stronger, with added muscle power. Exercise also makes the heart pump faster and the lungs breathe harder, which has many benefits for the whole body. In fact the heart itself is mostly muscle, and the movements of breathing are muscle-powered, too. So any form of exercise helps to keep all muscles fit and healthy.

⊙ *As a tennis player serves, muscles are working not only in the arms, but in the neck, back and legs, to keep the body well-balanced and supple, in order to run forwards without causing injury.*

Yʏou might not think you are doing much at the moment – except reading, of course. But many parts of the body are busy. One of the vital processes that never stops is breathing, every few seconds during the day and all through the night, too. Along with the heartbeat, it is the body's most essential activity.

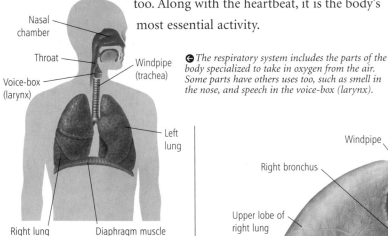

Nasal chamber

Throat

Voice-box (larynx)

Windpipe (trachea)

Left lung

Right lung   Diaphragm muscle

🔄 *The respiratory system includes the parts of the body specialized to take in oxygen from the air. Some parts have others uses too, such as smell in the nose, and speech in the voice-box (larynx).*

Why do we need to breathe?

To get oxygen into the body. Oxygen is a gas which forms one-fifth of air. The body needs it for an inner chemical process that happens in every microscopic cell. It breaks down the high-energy substance glucose to release its energy for powering life processes. Oxygen is required for glucose breakdown. Since the body cannot store oxygen, it must always obtain new supplies.

Where does breathed-in air go?

Through the nose and down the throat, into the windpipe (trachea) in the neck, and then along air tubes called bronchi into the two lungs in the chest. All of these parts form the body's respiratory system. Breathing is sometimes called respiration or bodily respiration.

🔽*Air flows to and from the lungs along the windpipe, which branches at its base into two bronchi, one to each lung. The heart fills the scoop-like space located between the lungs.*

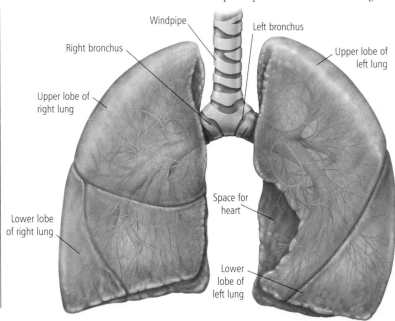

Windpipe

Left bronchus

Right bronchus

Upper lobe of left lung

Upper lobe of right lung

Space for heart

Lower lobe of right lung

Lower lobe of left lung

What are the lung's smallest parts?

Alveoli, which are shaped rather like miniature balloons. There are about 250 million alveoli in each lung! Each alveolus is wrapped in a network of even smaller blood vessels – capillaries. Oxygen from the air in the alveolus can seep easily into the blood in the capillaries, to be carried away around the body by the blood circulation.

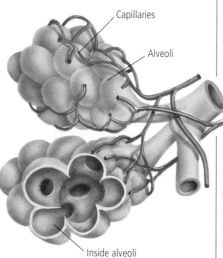

Capillaries

Alveoli

Inside alveoli

⊙ *The bubble-like alveoli are in groups or bunches at the ends of the narrowest air tubes, wrapped in blood capillaries. They make up about one-third of the total space taken up by the lungs.*

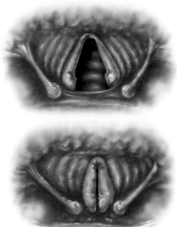

⊙ *The two vocal cords are in the voice-box in the neck. Each one sticks out from the side like a flexible flap. The cords have a triangular-shaped gap between them for normal breathing (top), and move almost together for speech (bottom).*

What is in breathed-out air?

Less oxygen but more carbon dioxide than is present in breathed-in air. There is about 16 per cent oxygen, compared to 21 per cent in breathed-in air. But there is much more carbon dioxide, more than 4 per cent compared to almost none in breathed-in air. Carbon dioxide is a waste product made by the breakdown of glucose for energy. If it builds up it will poison the body. So it is collected by the blood, passes into the air in the alveoli and is breathed out.

When is breathing out noisy?

When you talk, sing, hum, shout and scream. These sounds are made by the vocal cords inside the voice-box (larynx), at the top of the windpipe. As air passes up the windpipe, it blows through a narrow gap between the strip-like vocal cords and makes them vibrate to produce sounds. Breathing out harder makes the sounds louder, and stretching the cords longer makes the sounds higher-pitched.

⊙ *The basic sound of the voice comes from the vocal cords. But the shape and position of the air chambers in the throat, mouth, nose and sinuses (air-filled spaces in the skull bone) all affect the voice quality, so we all sound different.*

The body needs to breathe fresh air every few seconds to stay alive. But it cannot live on fresh air alone. Its other main needs are food and drink. The body needs food which contain many substances, used to help the body grow and repair itself, as well as provide the energy to move about. Drink is needed to continually replenish the supply of water in the bloodstream.

Why do we need to eat?

To provide energy for life processes, and to obtain many kinds of nutrients for bodily growth, maintenance and general health. Taking in food and breaking it into tiny pieces, small enough to absorb into the body, is known as digestion. Ten or so main parts, called the digestive system, work together to carry out this task. As swallowed food is moved through the digestive system, nutrients are absorbed into the bloodstream.

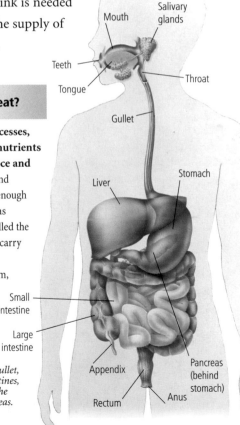

➎ *The digestive system includes the mouth, teeth, tongue, throat, gullet, stomach, the small and large intestines, which together form a long tube, the digestive tract, the liver and pancreas.*

Mouth
Salivary glands
Teeth
Throat
Tongue
Gullet
Liver
Stomach
Small intestine
Large intestine
Appendix
Pancreas (behind stomach)
Rectum
Anus

How many teeth do we have?

The human body has 52 teeth – but not all at once! The first set of 20 grow from around the time of birth to three or four years of age. They are called milk or deciduous teeth. From about six or seven years old, they fall out naturally as the second set of 32 teeth grow. These are larger and stronger, and are called the adult or permanent teeth.

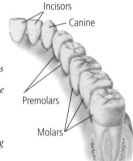

Incisors
Canine
Premolars
Molars

➎ *In each side of the jaw, the adult set of teeth includes two incisors at the front for biting, one taller canine for tearing, and two broad premolars, plus three wider molars for crushing and chewing.*

➎ *In the centre of a tooth is a soft pulp of blood vessels and nerves. Around this is tough dentine. On the outside of the top part, the crown, is even harder enamel. The roots fix the tooth into the jawbone.*

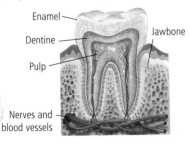

Enamel
Dentine
Pulp
Jawbone
Nerves and blood vessels

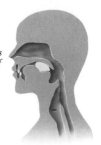

➲ *Swallowing involves a complicated series of muscle actions as the tongue pushes the lump of food (shown in yellow) into the throat, past the entrance to the windpipe and down the gullet.*

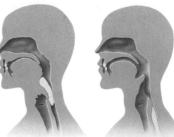

1 Tongue presses food to back of mouth

2 Food passes over the top of the windpipe

3 Food is pushed down the gullet

What happens before swallowing food?

The teeth bite off lumps of food, chew them and mix them with watery saliva (spit) to make the food soft and easy to swallow in small lumps. Food is swallowed into the gullet (oesophagus), a muscular tube that pushes it down through the neck into the stomach where it is churned around with gastric juices.

What does the stomach do?

The stomach breaks down food in two main ways. It is a muscular bag that can squeeze, mash and squash the food into a soft pulp. It also attacks the food by adding strong chemicals called acids and enzymes, which break down the food into a soup-like substance called chyme.

Which is the body's longest organ?

After the stomach, the semi-digested food flows into the body's longest part – the 6 m-long small intestine. This is coiled up in the middle of the lower body. It adds more enzymes and other chemicals to break the food into the smallest nutrients. These seep through the small intestine lining into the blood, and are carried away for use around the body.

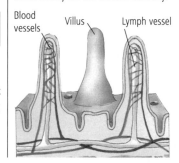

Blood vessels   Villus   Lymph vessel

➲ *The inner lining of the small intestine is covered with small, finger-like parts, villi, each about 1 mm long. These provide a huge surface area for absorbing nutrients into the blood.*

Which is the biggest internal organ?

The liver, which is to the right of the stomach. It receives blood that is rich in nutrients, and processes or alters these nutrients so they can be stored or used around the body. To the left of the liver, under the stomach, is the pancreas. It makes powerful digestive juices that flow into the small intestine. The pancreas produces about 1.5 l of digestive juices each day.

➲ *The liver is a large, wedge-shaped organ with a plentiful blood supply, carried by the portal vein, direct from the intestines. It makes a fluid, bile, which is stored in the gall bladder and then flows into the small intestine, where the bile helps to digest fatty foods.*

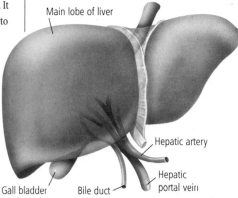

Main lobe of liver

Hepatic artery

Hepatic portal vein

Gall bladder   Bile duct

The body is a busy place. Every second there are thousands of chemical processes inside every tiny cell, which use energy, nutrients and other raw materials, and produce unwanted wastes. The circulatory system is a complex network of blood vessels, such as arteries, veins and capillaries, specialized to bring these raw materials to every part of the body and take away the wastes – and it never stops.

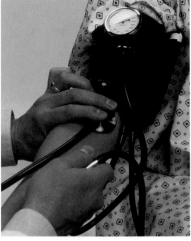

🟢 *Blood pressure can be measured by placing a cuff around the top of the arm and inflating it briefly. The reading then appears on a gauge that is connected to the cuff.*

Which part of the body never rests?

The heart does not stop beating throughout life. It is a muscular bag that pumps blood round and round the body. The heart is divided into two pumps, left and right. The right pump sends used or stale blood to the lungs to pick up oxygen. The blood comes back to the left side, is pumped all around the body to deliver the oxygen, and then returns to the right side to complete the circulation. It takes blood an average of one minute to complete the whole journey.

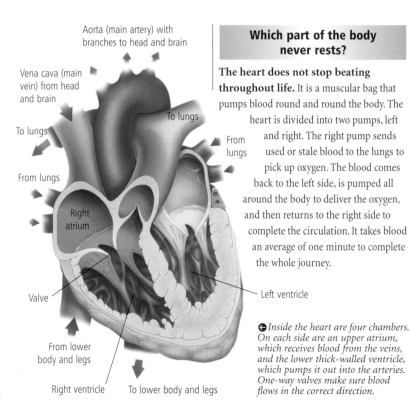

Aorta (main artery) with branches to head and brain

Vena cava (main vein) from head and brain

To lungs

To lungs

From lungs

From lungs

Right atrium

Valve

Left ventricle

From lower body and legs

Right ventricle

To lower body and legs

To lungs

From lungs

🟢 *Inside the heart are four chambers. On each side are an upper atrium, which receives blood from the veins, and the lower thick-walled ventricle, which pumps it out into the arteries. One-way valves make sure blood flows in the correct direction.*

How fast can the heart beat?

At rest the heart pumps about 60–75 times each minute, but after plenty of exercise this rises to 130 times or more, before returning to the resting rate. The speed of the heartbeat varies according to the body's needs. With each beat blood is pushed under pressure into the vessels and makes them bulge. This bulge can be felt in the wrist as the pulse. Doctors measure the pressure during and between heartbeats to tell how healthy the heart is.

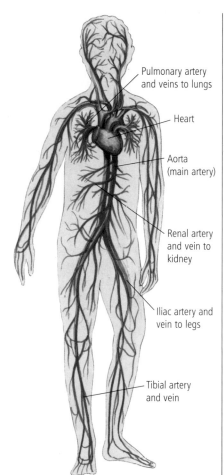

- Pulmonary artery and veins to lungs
- Heart
- Aorta (main artery)
- Renal artery and vein to kidney
- Iliac artery and vein to legs
- Tibial artery and vein

◑ *The circulatory or cardiovascular ('cardio' for heart, 'vascular' for blood vessels) system includes a network of blood vessels which transport blood to every part of the body.*

How much blood is in the body?

About one-twelfth of the body's weight is blood. For most adults this means from 4–6 l. About 55 per cent of blood is a pale liquid, plasma, containing dissolved oxygen, nutrients and hundreds of other substances. The remaining 45 per cent of blood comprises microscopic cells.

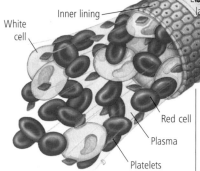

- White cell
- Inner lining
- Tough outer cover
- Muscle layer
- Elastic layer
- Red cell
- Plasma
- Platelets

◑ *Red cells are the most numerous blood cells and have a rounded, dished shape. White cells can change their shape as they surround and attack germs. Platelets are much smaller, resembling pieces of cells.*

How many jobs does blood have?

Blood has more than 100 jobs to do. One of the most important is to carry oxygen in its billions of red blood cells. Blood also distributes nutrients, carries dozens of natural substances called hormones that control body processes, spreads warmth around the body, carries white cells that fight disease, and collects carbon dioxide and other wastes.

What is a clot?

Blood clots or goes lumpy to seal a cut or wound. At the damage site, a substance in blood, called fibrin, forms a tangled web of micro-fibres. Blood cells, known as platelets, help to form the clot, which stops blood leaking away. The clot hardens into a scab, which protects the area as the damage heals over the next few days, then falls off.

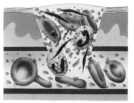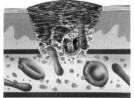

◑ *Where there is a wound, red and white cells tangle in fibres (left). The lump hardens to seal the gap (right).*

Wastes are produced by all living things, including the human body. Each day the body takes in 1–2 kg of foods, and 2–3 l of water. The unwanted parts and by-products from these 'inputs' must be removed daily, too. Otherwise after a year, the body would weigh more than one tonne and would be full of horrible, smelly wastes!

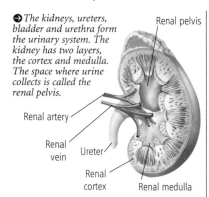

➔ *The kidneys, ureters, bladder and urethra form the urinary system. The kidney has two layers, the cortex and medulla. The space where urine collects is called the renal pelvis.*

Renal pelvis

Renal artery

Renal vein

Ureter

Renal cortex

Renal medulla

What do the kidneys do?

The two kidneys make the waste liquid, urine. Inside each kidney are one million microscopic filters called nephrons. Each has a tiny bunch of blood capillaries, which pass water and many substances into a long, looped tube. In the tube some of the water and substances are taken back into the body, leaving the unwanted water and wastes as urine. This flows from the kidney down a tube, the ureter, to the bladder.

How do wastes leave?

The body removes its wastes in three main ways – respiration, defecation and urination. Respiration (breathing), gets rid of carbon dioxide. Defecation, or bowel movements, removes the undigested and leftover parts of food and drink from the intestines. Urination gets rid of amounts of urine, a liquid containing urea and other unwanted substances filtered from the blood.

How much urine does the body make each day?

On average, the body makes about 1,500 ml of urine every 24 hours. The urine collects in the bladder until there is about 300 ml, when you feel the need to empty the bladder. This happens by urination along a tube to the outside, the urethra. However, the amount of urine varies hugely, depending on how much you drink, and if water is lost as sweat rather than as urine.

What do hormones do?

Hormones are natural body chemicals that control many internal processes and make sure the organs and systems work together. Hormones are made in parts called endocrine glands and travel around the whole body in the blood, but each hormone affects only certain parts, known as its target organs.

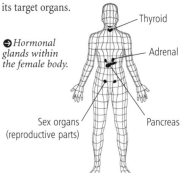

➔ *Hormonal glands within the female body.*

Thyroid

Adrenal

Pancreas

Sex organs (reproductive parts)

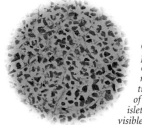

⬅ *In the pancreas, this collection of millions of tiny clumps of cells called islets, only visible under a microscope, make the hormone insulin, while the cells around them make digestive juices.*

⊙*Lymph nodes vary from less than 1 mm to about 20 mm across. They contain lymph fluid, which flows slowly around the body through lymph vessels. The nodes enlarge or swell greatly during illness as they fill with disease-fighting white cells.*

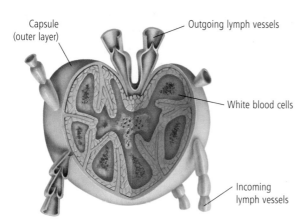

Capsule (outer layer)

Outgoing lymph vessels

White blood cells

Incoming lymph vessels

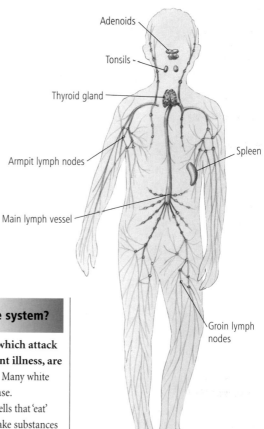

Adenoids

Tonsils

Thyroid gland

Armpit lymph nodes

Spleen

Main lymph vessel

Groin lymph nodes

⊙ *The immune system includes many lymph nodes, found particularly in the neck, chest, armpits, lower body and groin. There are also lymph tissues in the adenoids, tonsils and the spleen, which sits behind the stomach.*

Is blood the only liquid flowing around the body?

No, lymph fluid also flows through the body. Lymph fluid carries wastes of metabolism, and white blood cells, which destroy harmful substances such as germs. However, unlike blood, the fluid only moves one way. It begins as liquid around and between cells and tissues. It collects in small tubes called minor lymph vessels. These join to form major lymph vessels. The largest lymph vessels empty the lymph fluid into the main blood vessels near the heart. The body contains about 1–2 l of lymph fluid.

What is the immune system?

The body's self-defences, which attack invading germs and prevent illness, are called its immune system. Many white cells take part in fighting disease. Macrophages are large white cells that 'eat' germs whole. Lymphocytes make substances known as antibodies that stick to germs and disable them. Basophils are involved in allergic reactions and blood clotting. White cells are especially numerous in small areas called lymph nodes, which are sometimes called 'lymph glands'.

A re you a sensitive person? Of course – your body has senses! The five main ones are sight, hearing, smell, taste and touch. They provide information about what is happening around and on the body, and in the nose and mouth. There are also tiny sensors inside the body that give information about the positions of the muscles and joints.

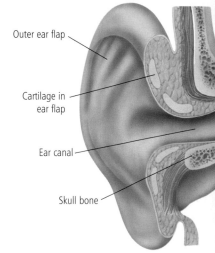

Outer ear flap

Cartilage in ear flap

Ear canal

Skull bone

Lachrymal tear gland

Retina

Lens

Sclera

Lachrymal duct

Pupil

Iris

🔵 *Tear fluid is made in the lachrymal glands and drains from the inner eyelids through the lachrymal ducts into the nose. Inside the eye is the light-sensitive lining, the retina.*

🔼 *The vibrations of sound waves pass along the ear canal to the eardrum, and along the tiny ear bones (ossicles) to the coiled cochlea, which converts them to nerve signals.*

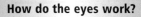
How do the eyes work?

The eye changes the brightness and colours of the light rays it sees, into a code of electrical nerve signals, which it sends to the brain. The light rays pass through the domed, clear front of the eye, the cornea, then through a hole, the pupil, in a ring of coloured muscle,

🔵 *The eye's own lens, just behind the dark hole or pupil, can become thicker or thinner to focus on near or far objects. When the lens is not working properly, some people need extra lenses, so spectacles or contact lenses help them see clearly.*

the iris. The iris makes the pupil smaller in bright conditions, preventing too much light from entering the eye and damaging the inside.

What numbers 125 million in the eye?

Microscopic light-detecting cells called rods and cones, which make nerve signals when light rays shine on them. The 120 million rods see well in dim light but not colours. Up to six million cones work only in brighter light, but see colours and fine details. All these cells are in a curved sheet, which is as big as your thumb-tip and thinner than this page, called the retina. The retina lines the inside of the eyeball.

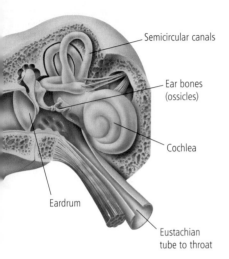

Semicircular canals

Ear bones
(ossicles)

Cochlea

Eardrum

Eustachian
tube to throat

Can we hear every sound?

No, some sounds are too high-pitched (ultrasonic) or too low (infrasonic) for our ears – but some animals such as dogs and horses can hear them. Sound waves in air travel along the tube-like ear canal and hit the eardrum, making it vibrate. The vibrations pass along three tiny bones, the ossicles, into the fluid inside the snail-shaped cochlea, deep in the ear. The vibrations shake micro-hairs sticking up from delicate hair cells in the cochlea, and these produce nerve signals, which are sent to the brain.

What is inside the nose?

An air space called the nasal chamber, as big as your two thumbs. In its roof are two patches, each about as large as a thumbnail, called olfactory epithelia. Each of these has more than 25 million microscopic olfactory receptor cells. Tiny smell-carrying particles called odorants float through on breathed-in air and land on the cells, causing them to send nerve signals to the brain. However, each of the millions of cells responds to only a few kinds of odorants.

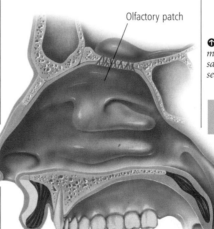

Olfactory patch

◑ *The hairy-looking patches called olfactory epithelia, which detect smells, are in the top of the air space known as the nasal chamber, inside the nose and above the mouth.*

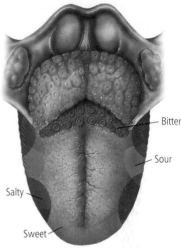

Bitter

Sour

Salty

Sweet

◑ *The taste buds at the tip of the tongue sense mainly sweet flavours. Those at the sides detect salty and, behind them, sour, with bitter tastes sensed mainly across the tongue's rear.*

How does the tongue taste different flavours?

As we eat, about 10,000 taste buds scattered around the tip, sides and rear of the tongue detect tiny particles in foods called flavourants. Each taste bud has around 25 gustatory receptor cells. If a suitable flavourant lands on a cell, it sends nerve messages to the brain. The tongue tastes flavours similarly to how the nose smells odours.

The body has its very own 'Internet'. This sends millions of signals along thousands of routeways called nerves, to-and-fro between its hundreds of parts, and to and from the one part which controls all the others – the brain. The brain is linked to the body by the main nerve, the spinal cord.

Which body parts could stretch halfway to the Moon?

The body's complicated network of branching nerves. If all the nerves could be joined together end to end, including the tiniest ones visible only under a microscope, they would stretch this far! Nerves are like shiny, pale cords. They are made of bundles of even thinner parts, nerve cells or neurons, which pass messages between each other. Each nerve has a tough covering to prevent squashing or kinking.

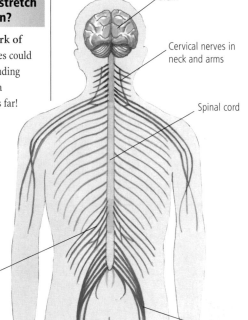

Brain

Cervical nerves in neck and arms

Spinal cord

Abdominal nerves

Sciatic nerve to leg

❯ *The nervous system controls and co-ordinates all body processes and activities. Its main parts are the brain and main nerve, the spinal cord, which together are called the central nervous system, and the hundreds of nerves that branch from them all through the body, the peripheral nervous system.*

What is a motor nerve?

A motor nerve carries nerve signals from the brain, out to the rest of the body. Nerve signals or impulses are tiny bursts of electricity that travel along nerves, carrying information. Most of these go to the muscles, telling them when to contract, by how much and for how long. Some motor signals go to glands, such as the sweat, salivary and tear glands, instructing them to release their contents. Sensory nerves carry signals the other way, from the eyes, ears and other sense organs, to the brain.

❯ *A single nerve cell or neuron has a wide part, the cell body, with branching parts known as dendrites, which receive signals from other nerve cells. One long fibre-like part, the axon, passes the signals to other nerve cells.*

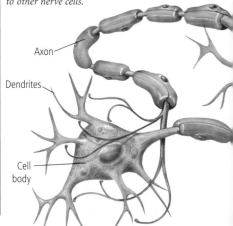

Axon

Dendrites

Cell body

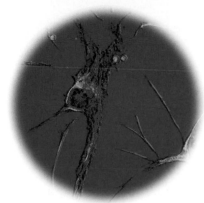

🔾 *Under the microscope, a nerve cell growing in a glass dish sends out tentacle-like dendrites to 'search' for other nerve cells.*

How many nerve cells are there?

Hundreds of billions, including about 100 billion in the brain itself. The optic nerve from each eye to the brain has more than one million nerve fibres, and other nerves also have huge numbers. Also some nerve cells pass messages to more than 10,000 others, at synapses. So the possible number of pathways for nerve signals around the body is too big to imagine – and the connections continuously change, too.

🔾 *As a person plays the guitar, the brain sends thousands of nerve signals every second along motor nerves to the muscles in the arms, hands and fingers, controlling movement with amazing speed and precision.*

How fast do nerves work?

The fastest signals, such as those from the skin, warning of damage and pain, go at more than 100 m/sec. This enables quick reflex action to protect the body from harm. However, the speed varies with the type of nerve it is and the information it carries. Other signals, such as those controlling how the stomach and guts work, can travel as slow as 1 m/sec.

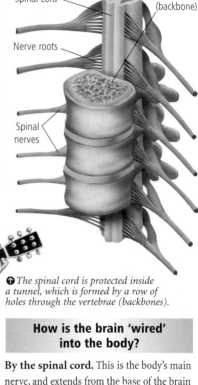

🔾 *The spinal cord is protected inside a tunnel, which is formed by a row of holes through the vertebrae (backbones).*

How is the brain 'wired' into the body?

By the spinal cord. This is the body's main nerve, and extends from the base of the brain down inside the backbone (spinal column). Thirty-one pairs of nerves branch from it, on each side, out into the body. There are also 12 pairs of nerves that branch from the brain itself, mainly to parts such as the eyes and ears. These are called cranial nerves and some extend down to the chest.

The brain never truly 'sleeps'. Even while most of the body is relaxed and still at night, the brain is busy. It controls the beating of the heart, the breathing lungs, body temperature, the digestive system and many other internal processes. The more we find out about the brain and its processes, the more complicated it seems.

How does thinking happen?

Thinking seems to happen as a result of nerve signals passing between many different parts of the brain. There is no single part in the brain where thoughts occur. Especially important is the cortex, which is the wrinkled grey outer layer of the large, bulging parts known as cerebral hemispheres. Under these are the lower parts of the brain, which are concerned less with consciousness or awareness, and more with 'automatic' processes such as controlling heartbeat and breathing. The smaller, lower, wrinkled part at the rear of the brain is the cerebellum. It organizes nerve signals sent to muscles, to ensure that all the body's movements are smooth and co-ordinated.

Where are memories stored?

As with thinking, there is no single 'memory centre' in the brain but many parts working together to store memories, as pathways for nerve signals through the incredible maze of nerve cells. However, a curved part called the hippocampus is important in changing short-term memories, such as a phone number we need for just a few seconds, into long-term memories that we can recall weeks or months later.

Cortex of cerebral hemisphere

Sulcus (groove)

Corpus callosum (links two hemispheres)

Thalamus

Hyphothalamus

Hippocampus

Pons

Cerebellum

Brain stem

↑ *About nine-tenths of the brain is the large dome of the two cerebral hemispheres. The outer cerebral cortex is where many conscious thoughts happen. Inside are blob-like parts called ganglia.*

Are bigger brains more intelligent?

No, there is no link between brain size and intelligence. It also depends what we mean by 'intelligence'. Some people are not especially successful at mathematics or science, but they may be brilliant at music or painting, or making money, or developing friendships. Every person has different abilities, talents and ways of behaving.

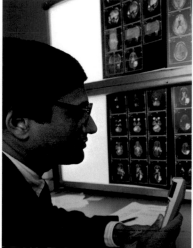

🡱 *Doctors examine brain scans to locate problems such as a stroke, when the blood supply to part of the brain fails and its nerve cells are damaged.*

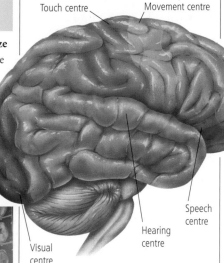

Touch centre   Movement centre

Speech centre

Hearing centre

Visual centre

🡱 *Different parts of the cortex deal with nerve signals that are either coming from the senses or being sent to muscles.*

What is the 'mind's eye'?

It is the place where we can imagine scenes and views that our eyes might see – even with our eyes closed. Different parts of the brain's cortex receive information from different senses. Information from the eyes goes to the lower rear of the cortex, called the visual centre, where the brain works out what is being seen. Other cortex centres are shown above. The movement centre is also called the motor cortex.

What happens during sleep?

EEG (electroencephalogram) recordings of the brain's nerve signals or 'brain-waves' suggest that, during sleep, the brain could be assessing recent events and memories, and deciding which ones are less important and can be forgotten. At certain times the body's muscles twitch and the eyes flick to-and-fro even though they are closed. This is called rapid eye movement or REM sleep and is when dreams occur.

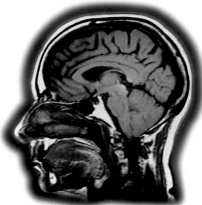

🡱 *This MR head scan shows how the wrinkled cerebral hemisphere dominates the brain. The lower rear of the brain tapers into the brain stem and then into the spinal cord in the neck.*

About four weeks after a new baby is born, we say it is 'one month old'. But really it has been ten months since its body began to form. After fertilization, the unborn baby spent nine months developing and growing inside its mother. People look carefully at babies to see who they resemble most, the mother or the father. This resemblance is due to the inheritance of genes.

How does the body begin?

In the beginning, every human body begins as a single cell. This is a tiny speck, smaller than the dot on this 'i', called the fertilized egg. It is made from the joining of two cells, the egg cell from the mother and the sperm cell from the father. As the human body develops over the following months and years, it is built up from billions and billions of microscopic cells, which are all formed by the splitting or division of other cells.

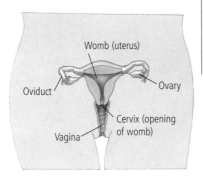

Where do eggs come from?

Egg cells are contained inside a woman's body in rounded parts called ovaries, one in either side of the lower abdomen. Each ovary contains many thousands of egg cells. Each month one of these eggs develops and becomes ripe or ready to be fertilized. The ripe egg is released into a tube, the oviduct (fallopian tube), and passes slowly towards the womb, in a process called ovulation. The lining of the womb is thick and rich with blood, ready to nourish the egg if it is fertilized by a sperm cell. If not, the egg and the womb lining are lost through the birth canal or vagina, as the monthly menstrual flow or period.

↻ *The parts of the body specialized to produce a baby are known as the reproductive organs. In the woman, egg cells are contained in the two ovaries. Each month the menstrual cycle causes one egg to ripen and pass along the oviduct into the womb, where a sperm cell may join with it.*

Where do sperm come from?

Sperm cells develop and are contained inside a man's body. They are made continually in rounded parts called testes, which hang below the lower abdomen inside a bag of skin called the scrotum. Millions of sperm cells are made each day. The sperm develop and are stored in a coiled tube called the epididymis. The sperm live for about one month. If they are not released from the body during sex, they gradually die and break apart as new ones are made.

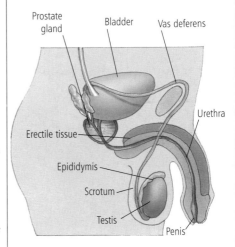

↑ *In a man's reproductive organs, sperm are made in the two testes. During sex they pass along the vas deferens tubes, which join and continue as the urethra, to the outside.*

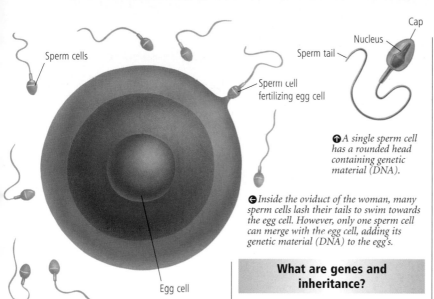

Sperm cells

Cap

Nucleus

Sperm tail

Sperm cell fertilizing egg cell

Egg cell

➊A single sperm cell has a rounded head containing genetic material (DNA).

➋Inside the oviduct of the woman, many sperm cells lash their tails to swim towards the egg cell. However, only one sperm cell can merge with the egg cell, adding its genetic material (DNA) to the egg's.

How do egg and sperm join?

During sex (sexual intercourse), sperm cells enter the woman's vagina, swim through the womb and into the two oviducts where a ripe egg may be present. The journey begins inside the man's body where millions of sperm cells pass from the testes and epididymis, along tubes known as the vas deferens, to another tube called the urethra, which is inside the penis. Fluid containing the sperm leaves the end of the penis, but only one sperm can join with the egg at fertilization to start the new baby.

What are genes and inheritance?

Genes instruct the human body how to develop and carry out its life processes, and inheritance is the passing of these genes from parents to offspring. Genes are in the form of a chemical substance called DNA (de-oxyribonucleic acid). The egg cell contains genes from the mother, and the sperm cell contains the father's genes. When egg and sperm join at the time of fertilization, the genes come together and the fertilized egg can begin to develop into a baby.

Which kind of features are inherited?

Some physical body features are inherited from parents, such as the colour of the eyes, skin and hair, the shapes of the nose and ears, and overall body height. But some of these features can be controlled by several genes. This means a child's hair colour or ear shape is not always the same as either of the parents – it may be more similar to one of the grandparents. Even identical twins, with the same genes, have slightly different features.

➌The full set of genes is contained in 23 pairs of chromosomes (below left). In reproduction the pairs split so that only 23 go into each egg or sperm (below centre). At fertilization, sets of 23 come together to form 46 (below right). The last pair of chromosomes determine the sex of the baby. The combination shown here is XY, with the large X and smaller x-like Y, and results in a boy. Two larger sex chromosomes, XX, would produce a girl.

Each human body starts as a tiny speck, the fertilized egg. Nine months later it is six billion times bigger – a newborn baby, which can cry loudly when it is very tired or hungry! The time of development in the mother's womb is known as pregnancy.

➲As the speck-like fertilized egg develops into a baby, most of the body parts form within the first two months. The mother's abdomen begins to bulge from about 16 weeks after fertilization. She can feel the baby moving from about 18 weeks, as it twitches its arms, kicks its legs and bends its neck and back.

Which body parts develop first?

An unborn baby develops 'head-first', starting with the brain and head, then the main body, then the arms and legs. Life begins when the fertilized egg divides into two cells, then four, eight, and so on. After a few days there are hundreds of cells, and after a few weeks, millions. These cells build up the various body parts.

When does the heart start to beat?

The unborn baby's heart begins to beat after only four weeks, although it has not yet taken on its full shape. From the time of fertilization to eight weeks later, the developing baby is known as an embryo. The lungs, intestines and other parts are also taking shape around this time. In fact, by eight weeks all the main parts have formed, even the fingers and toes – yet the tiny body is only the size of a grape.

Can an unborn baby hear?

From before halfway through pregnancy, the unborn baby may be startled and move suddenly by a loud noise, indicating that it can hear. From eight weeks after fertilization until birth, the unborn baby is known as a foetus. It spends most of this time growing in size and developing smaller body parts such as eyelids, fingernails and toenails. In the womb it is dark, with nothing to see, yet the eyes are working, too, even though the lids are closed.

How does the unborn baby breathe?

It does not – it is surrounded and protected by bag-like membranes and fluids. However, it still needs oxygen to survive. This comes from the mother. The baby's blood flows along the twisted, rope-like umbilical cord to a plate-shaped part, the placenta, in the lining of the womb. Here the baby's blood passes very close to the mother's blood and oxygen can easily seep or diffuse into the baby's blood, which then flows back along the umbilical cord to its body. The baby is fed by nutrients in the same way.

What happens at the start of birth?

As the time of birth approaches, powerful muscles in the wall of the womb begin to shorten or contract. This squeezes the baby through the opening or neck of the womb, called the cervix. The cervix was tightly closed during pregnancy but now widens, or dilates, to let the baby through. The contractions of the womb continue to push the baby along the birth canal, or vagina, until it emerges and is born.

⬆ *In order to keep fit whilst pregnant, and to prepare for birth, an expectant mother can undertake certain exercises and develop special breathing techniques.*

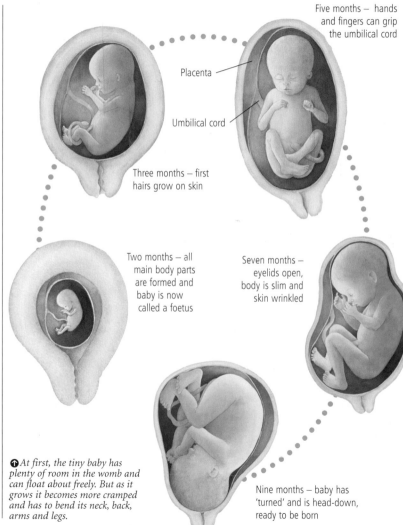

Five months — hands and fingers can grip the umbilical cord

Placenta

Umbilical cord

Three months — first hairs grow on skin

Two months — all main body parts are formed and baby is now called a foetus

Seven months — eyelids open, body is slim and skin wrinkled

⬆ *At first, the tiny baby has plenty of room in the womb and can float about freely. But as it grows it becomes more cramped and has to bend its neck, back, arms and legs.*

Nine months — baby has 'turned' and is head-down, ready to be born

A newborn baby is about one-twentieth of the size of a fully-grown adult. But growth is about far more than getting bigger. Body shape and proportions change, muscles become stronger and movements more skilled. From the moment of birth, the baby learns an incredible amount almost every day.

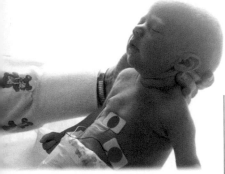

⬆ *A newborn baby is given an extensive medical check-up, in this case with sensor pads to monitor heartbeat rate. The baby's head is so large and heavy compared to its neck and body muscles, it needs to be carefully supported to prevent damage.*

What does a newborn baby do?

A new baby seems to do little except cry, feed on its mother's milk and sleep. At first it probably sleeps for about 20 hours in every 24. But the baby can carry out various automatic actions, or reflexes. It grips something that touches its hand and turns its head towards anything that touches its cheek. If startled by a loud noise, it throws out its arms and cries. And when its bladder and bowels are full, it empties them straight away!

When does walking start?

On average a baby can walk at around one year of age. Most babies learn to do more complicated actions, such as walking and talking, in the same order. But the times may differ widely, and being early to talk or late to walk is rarely a problem. Most babies can sit up by themselves at five to six months, stand whilst supported at seven to eight months, crawl at eight to nine months, and walk at about one year old. These movements are called motor skills.

⬆ *Babies can smile as young as a few weeks old, and can laugh within the first year. On average, babies start to talk from about ten months old.*

When does talking begin?

Like motor (movement) skills, the process of learning to talk happens at widely varying ages in different babies. Some can say several simple words like 'dada', 'mama' and 'cat' by the age of ten months, while others may not begin to form words until 13 to 14 months. Putting words together, like 'teddy bear' starts at about 14 to 15 months. By 18 months old the average toddler knows 20 or more words.

⬅ *Some babies crawl at six months – but some never do. They may use other methods such as rolling over or shuffling along on their bottoms to move about, before they begin to walk.*

When does the body grow fastest?

After birth, the fastest time of growth is during the first year, when body weight increases about three times. Then growth gradually slows until the age of about 9 to 12 years, when it speeds up again. This time of fast growth through the early teenage years is known as puberty. It includes rapid development of the reproductive or sexual parts, as these begin to work.

⬇ *Teenagers may interact with one another to develop social skills, which can become the basis for future relationships in life.*

⬆ *Young children often think little about risks and dangers, such as falling over during play – which could cause a serious injury and even life-long harm. Adults need to point out the hazards and the need for safety precautions such as protective clothing and equipment.*

When is the body fully-grown?

Most people reach their full height by about 20 years of age. The muscles reach their full development at about 25 years. However, some physical activities involve co-ordination, training, practise and mental preparation as well as simple muscle power. Some sports people do not reach their peak until 30-plus years of age. Body weight is more variable – certain people alter their body weight, up and down, throughout life.

⬇ *The body grows not only physically, but also mentally – in the mind. This involves social skills such as making friends, respecting the opinions of others, understanding right and wrong and working out risks.*

1 Is your body made up of 50 per cent water, 70 per cent water or 90 per cent water?

2 Where is your skin thickest?

3 The science of the body and its parts is called what?

4 Which two parts of your body do you brush every day?

5 What do you have five million of growing on your body?

6 You would find cuticles at the base of which parts of the body?

7 A tendon connects a muscle to what type of body part?

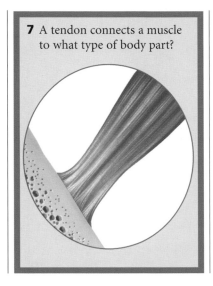

8 How many bones make up the skeleton?

9 How many pairs of ribs do you have?

10 Which is the longest bone in the body?

11 What pulls your bones and lets you move?

12 Where are your strongest muscles?

13 Which muscle is in the back of the leg, situated below the knee?

FACTFILE

Artificial **joints**

In some people, joints become stiff and painful due to disease, injury or stressful use over a long period of time. In many cases, these natural joints can be replaced with artificial ones – joint prostheses. These are usually made of supertough plastics and strong metals shaped like the original joint.

➲ *This artificial knee joint has two rounded plastic 'knuckles' at the base of the thigh bone, and a metal plate on top of the shin bone.*

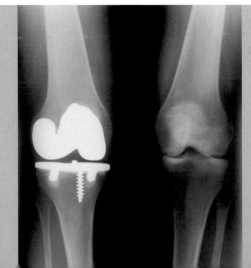

The **spine**

The spine (spinal column) is the body's central support. It is made of 26 block-like bones called vertebrae, one on top of the other, which hold up the skull and head while allowing the main body to flex and bend. The spinal column also protects the body's main nerve, the spinal cord, which links the brain to all body parts. The spinal cord is inside a tunnel formed by the gaps or holes within the vertebrae.

14 Which gas does your body take in when you breathe?

15 Does incoming air pass through the lungs or the windpipe first?

16 What does exhalation mean?

17 What is the name of the first part of the small intestine?

18 Is your stomach above or below your intestines?

19 Which is longer: your small or large intestine?

20 What are the five senses?

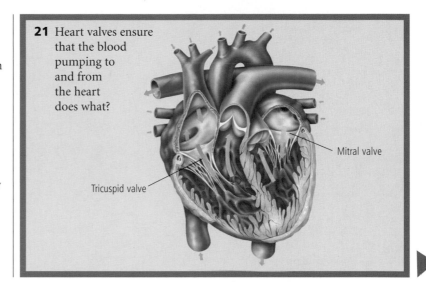

21 Heart valves ensure that the blood pumping to and from the heart does what?

Mitral valve

Tricuspid valve

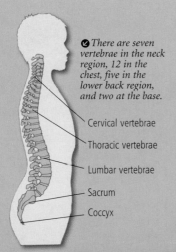

There are seven vertebrae in the neck region, 12 in the chest, five in the lower back region, and two at the base.

Cervical vertebrae

Thoracic vertebrae

Lumbar vertebrae

Sacrum

Coccyx

Amazing **bone facts**

• Most of the body parts are about two-thirds water, but bones are only one-fifth water.

• The skull has 22 bones, including 14 in the face and eight in the domed brain case or cranium.

• The smallest bones are the three tiny ossicles inside each ear.

• The longest bone is the thigh bone or femur, making up about one-quarter of the body's total height.

• The broadest bone is the hip bone or pelvis.

• Most people have 12 pairs of ribs, but about one person in 500 has 13 or 11 pairs.

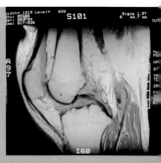

A scan through the knee joint shows the oval-shaped patella or knee cap on the left, the joint itself in the centre and the rear leg muscles to the right.

22 Which part of the throat tightens across the airway and vibrates in order to produce sound?

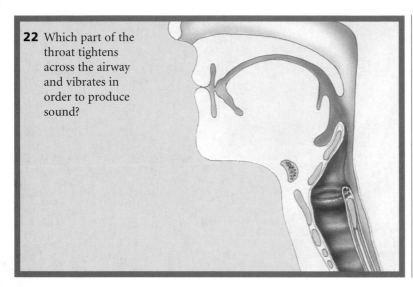

23 What causes a bruise to turn blue?

24 What carries blood away from the heart?

25 Which type of blood cells carry oxygen?

26 What forms over a cut when it is healing?

27 What should you do before you eat or drink?

28 What do we call an automatic response by a muscle, which does not involve thinking?

FACTFILE

Breathing **muscles**

Half a litre of air passes in and out of the lungs every time you breathe. Breathing uses the sheet-like diaphragm below the chest, and the strip-like intercostals between the ribs.

When breathing in, the diaphragm becomes flatter, pulling down the bases of the lungs. The intercostal muscles force the ribs up and out, pulling on the lungs. Both these actions stretch the lungs to suck in air. To breathe out, both muscle sets relax. The stretched lungs spring back to their smaller size, blowing out air.

➲ *The action of breathing in (near right) is powered by muscles and so uses energy. Breathing out (far right) is due to the stretched lungs becoming smaller, like an elastic band contracting, and so does not need muscle power.*

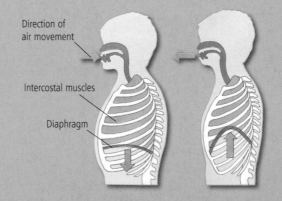

Direction of air movement

Intercostal muscles

Diaphragm

29 If you take medicine orally, how do you take it?

30 Which nerve connects your eye to your brain?

31 Why is blinking good for your eyes?

32 Do you get goose pimples when you are hot or cold?

33 Which part of your body helps you keep your balance?

34 What does the spine protect?

35 What is amnesia?

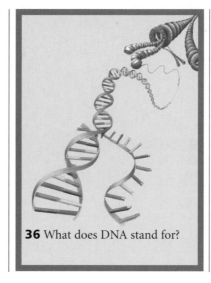

36 What does DNA stand for?

37 Where is the cerebellum?

38 What is the term for three babies born at the same time from the same mother?

39 A baby grows in which organ of the mother's body?

40 If a disease is hereditary, how does someone catch it?

41 What is the name of the tube that supplies nourishment to a baby before it is born?

42 How many months are there between conception and birth?

When we **yawn**

- Yawning occurs when the body is resting, and has not been breathing deeply for some time, so more oxygen is needed. The body takes an extra-deep breath – the yawn.

- Yawning moves the jaw and face muscles and makes more blood flow to the brain, for greater alertness.

- Some people open their mouths so wide when yawning that they can dislocate or 'detach' their jaws and cannot close the mouth again.

Amazing **facts**

- As you rest or sleep, you breathe once every three or four seconds.

- After much exercise, you may breathe as fast as once each second.

- Deeper breathing moves 2–3 l of air each time.

- Restful breathing moves less than 10 l of air in and out of the lungs each minute, compared to more than 150 l during strenuous breathing.

- No matter how much you breathe out, about 0.5 l of air stays in your lungs.

- After holding your breath for a time, it is the amount of carbon dioxide in the body, dissolved in the blood, which causes gasping for air – not the lack of oxygen.

43 What do we call a baby that is born before it is fully developed?

44 What is a newborn baby's main food?

45 Do you grow more when you are awake or when you are asleep?

46 What happens to a boy's voice when it breaks?

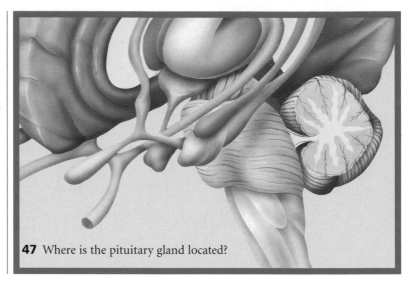

47 Where is the pituitary gland located?

FACTFILE

Blood **facts**

Red blood cells

Monocyte (white blood cell)

Lymphocyte (white blood cell)

Basophil (white blood cell)

⊗ *Red cells cannot change their shape, but the various white cells can, to enable them to attack germs invading the body.*

In a drop of blood as big as this 'o' there are:

• About 20 million red blood cells, also called erythrocytes. Each one contains the substance haemoglobin, which easily joins to and carries oxygen. A typical red blood cell lives for about three months.

• Around 20,000 white blood cells, known as leucocytes. There are many kinds of white blood cells and most fight germs and illness (see page 23). Some live a few days, others for many years.

• Between one and two million platelets, or thrombocytes, needed for blood clotting.

Answers

1 70 per cent
2 The soles of your feet
3 Anatomy
4 Your hair and teeth
5 Hairs
6 Fingernails and toenails
7 Bone
8 206
9 12
10 Thigh bone
11 Muscles
12 In your jaw
13 The calf muscle
14 Oxygen
15 Windpipe

16 Breathing out
17 Duodenum
18 Above
19 Small intestine
20 Sight, hearing, touch, smell and taste
21 Flows one way
22 Vocal cords
23 Blood from broken veins
24 Arteries
25 Red blood cells
26 A scab
27 Wash your hands
28 A reflex
29 By mouth

30 Optic nerve
31 It keeps them clean
32 Cold
33 Your ears
34 Spinal chord
35 Loss of memory
36 De-oxyribonucleic acid
37 The brain
38 Triplets
39 Womb (uterus)
40 It is inherited
41 Umbilical chord
42 Nine
43 Premature
44 Milk

45 Asleep
46 It sounds deeper
47 The brain

Types of **blood vessels**

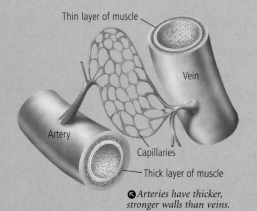

Thin layer of muscle

Vein

Artery

Capillaries

Thick layer of muscle

❷ *Arteries have thicker, stronger walls than veins.*

Arteries carry blood away from the heart. They have thick walls to withstand the surge of blood with each heartbeat. They carry blood to the major parts or organs. Arteries divide into **arterioles** – smaller versions of arteries. They are about the same thickness as human hairs. Arterioles divide into **capillaries** – less than 1 mm long and far too thin to see. Oxygen and nutrients seep from blood through their walls into surrounding tissues. Capillaries join to form **venules** – which carry the slower-moving blood, now under much less pressure. Venules join further to form **veins** – wide, thin-walled and floppy, which take blood back to the heart.

At any moment about 66 per cent of all the body's blood is in the veins, 29 per cent in the arteries and 5 per cent in the capillaries.

AROUND THE WORLD

Our world is a varied landscape with a multitude of countries and cultures. For over two million years humans have built towns and cities to live in, and worked the land. Some continents, such as Europe, are very crowded, while nobody lives permanently in frozen Antarctica. Fewer than one in ten people in the world live in North America, yet it has the biggest economy.

Where is the Forbidden City?

Which is the highest mountain in Africa?

Why do people visit Machu Picchu?

Our world is a varied landscape with diverse countries and cultures. Mountains, rivers, deserts, seas, oceans, rainforests, grassland and extreme weather are just some of the Earth's features. For more than two million years humans have populated the Earth, building towns and cities to live in, and working the land to produce food and materials to sustain life.

⊕ *Beaches in the Mediterranean are packed during the summer, when mostly European holidaymakers head for the sea.*

Where are Asia's high and low points?

Asia has the highest mountain on Earth, Mount Everest, and the lowest point, the Dead Sea. In fact, the ten highest peaks (all more than 8,000 m high) are in the Himalayas, the greatest mountain range in Asia. But not all Asia is mountainous. There are huge areas of flat grasslands and desert, and the lowest point on Earth is the shore of the Dead Sea (in Israel and Jordan) – 400 m below sea level.

Where is the world's largest desert?

The world's largest desert is the Sahara, in northwest Africa. The Sahara Desert covers an area of over 9 million sq km, stretching across the northern third of the African continent. It continues to grow as the areas surrounding it are overgrazed by animals and so turn to dust. Temperatures during the day can reach 50°C and yet drop to freezing during the night. Despite years without rain in the Sahara, certain animals and plants have adapted to be able to live in these conditions.

Which is the most densely populated continent?

More than 700 million people live in Europe, which is only slightly bigger than Australia, making Europe the most densely populated continent for its size. The most densely populated area stretches from southeast Britain, through northern France and into the Netherlands, where there are approximately 410 people per sq km. This figure is in vast contrast to a country such as the USA in North America, where there are about 27 people per sq km.

⊙ *The Himalayan mountain range has formed over 25 million years, and continues to grow at a rate of 5 cm every year.*

Where is the world's largest rainforest?

The Amazon rainforest of Brazil, Peru and Bolivia, in South America, covers more than 6 million sq km. It is home to more than 1,500 varieties of fish, more than 22,000 species of plants and a vast variety of insects, birds, reptiles and mammals. Local people and scientists use as many as 2,000 of the plant species found in the Amazon for use in medicine. Natural resources, such as gold, diamonds and rubber can also be found in the rainforest.

➍ *Spider monkeys are just one of the many mammal species that are found in the Amazon rainforest.*

Where is the world's coldest place?

In July 1983, a record –89°C was recorded near the Vostok Scientific Station in Antarctica. The average annual temperature on the continent is –57°C, and 98 per cent of the land is covered in ice, which accounts for 90 per cent of the world's ice.

Where is the world's longest coral reef?

Covering more than 350,000 sq km, the Great Barrier Reef is found off the northeast coast of Australia. More than 2,000 species of fish live among the many thousands of individual reefs, which are built from the remains of marine life. Some parts of the reef are up to 25 million years old.

➊ *Temperatures in Antarctica rarely reach above 0°C. Inland, Antarctica has one of the driest climates on Earth, receiving no rain and barely any new snow each year, which means that only a few small plants and insects can survive there.*

Which continent experiences extreme weather conditions?

North America has some of the worst hurricanes, deepest snowfall and is home to one of the hottest places on Earth. In 1998 Hurricane Mitch reached 290 km/h, killing 11,000 people and destroying more than 93,000 buildings. The greatest snowfall ever recorded was 11.5 m, measured in California in 1911. In contrast, Death Valley in California can reach a temperature of 57°C. Furthermore, an average of 800 tornadoes a year rage across U.S. states such as Kansas, Missouri, Iowa and Nebraska.

sia is the world's biggest continent, both in land area and in the number of people who live there. It fills about one-third of the planet's land area. About six in every ten people on Earth are Asian. Asia's terrain is vast and varied and includes the world's highest mountain range, the Himalayas, as well as desert, steppe grassland, tundra, boreal (northern) forest and jungle.

Which country is also a subcontinent?

India is a subcontinent and is home to about one-fifth of the world's population. The Indian subcontinent comprises India itself, which has more than one billion people, plus the countries of Pakistan, Bangladesh, Bhutan, Sri Lanka, Nepal and the Maldives. India also has 14 major languages and more than 400 other languages and regional dialects. Over the last 5,000 years the land has been invaded many times, and as migrating people have settled there a varied and diverse culture has emerged. India is now the world's largest democracy and has given rise to some of the world's most popular religions. The climate is hot and dry, but the monsoon season bring heavy rains and often flooding.

map key

1	Armenia	15	Myanmar (Burma)
2	Azerbaijan	16	Nepal
3	Bahrain	17	North Korea
4	Bangladesh	18	Oman
5	Bhutan	19	Qatar
6	Cambodia	20	Singapore
7	Cyprus	21	South Korea
8	Georgia	22	Syria
9	Israel	23	Tajikistan
10	Jordan	24	Thailand
11	Kuwait	25	Turkmenistan
12	Kyrgyzstan	26	UAE
13	Laos	27	Uzbekistan
14	Lebanon	28	Yemen

Hanoi in Vietnam is modernizing rapidly, and its trade is increasing with Europe and the US. Traditionally, sampans, boats are used to transport goods to market.

Where is Hanoi?

Hanoi is the capital of Vietnam, in Southeast Asia. It is in the north of this long, narrow country. Ho Chi Minh City is the major city in the south. It used to be called Saigon until in 1976 it was renamed after Ho Chi Minh, who led North Vietnam in a long and bitter civil war against South Vietnam and their American allies.

What is a zen garden?

A zen garden is a simple outdoor space containing natural materials, neutral colours and clean lines designed to promote peace and serenity. Zen is a form of Buddhism, which developed in China from about 500 AD. Zen Buddhism was introduced to Japan in about 1100 AD and became influential in Japanese culture and has since become very popular in western countries.

Zen gardens often contain one flower, such as a lotus, and small, pruned trees, such as bonsai.

Where do Sinhalese people live?

Sinhalese people live in Sri Lanka, the island at the southern tip of the Indian subcontinent. About 72 per cent of the population are Sinhalese, who are mainly Buddhist. The largest minority group in Sri Lanka are the Tamils who originated in southern India and are mostly Hindu. Sri Lanka was a British colony from 1802 until 1948 and was called Ceylon until 1972. Sinhalese and Tamil are the country's two official languages and tea is one of its most profitable exports.

Many Sri Lankan people are employed on plantations to pick tea leaves. Tea is one of Sri Lanka's main exports.

Asia was the home of great ancient civilizations, such as those of the Indus Valley and the Tigris-Euphrates region. The greatest imperial power in Asia was China, but by the 1800s much of Asia had come under European colonial rule. Japan was the first Asian country to 'westernize' its industries, and by the 1950s it had become one of the world's leading economic powers.

↑ The Forbidden City in Beijing was once the emperor's private world, kept a secret from the people and foreigners. Beijing has been China's capital since 1421 when the emperor Yung Le made the city his base.

Why does Asia have some of the world's richest countries?

Much of Asia's wealth comes from its manufacturing nations such as Japan, China, South Korea, Malaysia and India; and its oil-producers, such as Saudi Arabia, Brunei and Kuwait.
The manufacturing countries have large populations, many of whom work for low wages, so the average income per person is less than in Europe or North America. The oil-rich states have smaller populations, so average incomes are higher. The two richest rulers in the world are the King of Saudi Arabia and the Sultan of Brunei. The Middle East possesses more than 65 per cent of the world's oil reserves.

➔ The city of Tokyo is the business centre of Japan. Its many industries help to make Japan one of the world's richest nations.

Where is the Forbidden City?

The Forbidden City is the old imperial section of Beijing, in China. It forms a square that is surrounded by a moat and wall. Inside the boundaries are palaces that were once used by the Chinese emperors, but they are now open to the public as museums. Ordinary Chinese people and foreigners were once banned from entering the city. Only officials and nobles could gain entrance. One million workers took ten years to build the walled city, with its great halls, temples, pagodas and gardens.

❶ *Istanbul is the gateway between Europe and Asia. Because the continents are joined, it is a super-continent known as Eurasia.*

Why is Korea divided into North and South?

At the end of the Second World War (1945) Korea was occupied by Russia and America, who divided the country into communist North Korea and democratic South Korea. Korea is a peninsula, or strip of land, on the east coast of Asia, bordering China. Its old name was Joseon. The Korean War (1950–53) failed to settle disputes, and the two Koreas remain separated by a heavily guarded border control.

❶ *Seoul in South Korea is a busy, modern city. South Koreans enjoy a much higher standard of living than people across the closely guarded border, in the North.*

❶ *Singapore skyscrapers rise from a small island linked to the mainland by a causeway.*

Which is the only city situated on two continents?

Istanbul, in Turkey, lies in both Europe and Asia. It stands on both banks of the strait called the Bosporus, which separates the two continents. The Asian part of the city is one and a half times smaller than the European part. Istanbul had been called Byzantium and (from AD 330) Constantinople, and was the capital of the eastern half of the Roman Empire. It became Istanbul in 1453 when the Turks captured it.

Who founded Singapore?

Singapore was founded in 1819 by Sir Stamford Raffles. He built a British trading base on what had been a small fishing village, which then flourished as a small republic at the tip of the Malay peninsula. It became a major port, and is now a busy trade centre. The people are mostly Chinese and Malay.

Africa is a huge continent, covering about 20 per cent of the Earth's land surface. Only Asia is bigger. Africa comprises 53 different countries and more than 600 different tribal or ethnic groups. Africa's landscape is varied, with the world's largest desert, the Sahara, and the world's second longest river, the Nile. It has vast expanses of tropical grasslands or savanna, as well as rainforest.

map key

1	Benin	11	Liberia
2	Burkina Faso	12	Malawi
3	Burundi	13	Republic of Congo
4	Central African	14	Rwanda
	Republic	15	Senegal
5	Djibouti	16	Sierra Leone
6	Equatorial Guinea	17	Swaziland
7	Gambia	18	Togo
8	Ghana	19	Tunisia
9	Guinea-Bissau	20	Western Sahara
10	Lesotho		

Which is Africa's largest city?

Cairo, in Egypt, is Africa's largest city, with more than 15 million people living there. It outranks other big cities in the continent, such as Algiers (Algeria), Lagos (Nigeria) and Johannesburg (South Africa). Like other cities of northern Africa, Cairo has Islamic mosques, open-air markets (bazaars) and tall, modern buildings. All over Africa cities are growing rapidly, as people leave the countryside to look for work in towns.

Cairo has grown into a large, modern city, but old mosques (Muslim places of prayer) remain.

Which are Africa's most valuable minerals?

Gold, diamonds, coal, oil and gas are among the many valuable minerals that are mined in various parts of Africa. South Africa is mined for gold, diamonds, coal and cobalt. Algeria, Libya and Nigeria provide oil and gas. Diamonds are mined in Sierra Leone and copper is found in Zambia. Africa also produces iron ore, tin, bauxite (aluminium ore) and manganese.

Which is the highest mountain in Africa?

At 5,895 m high, Mount Kilimanjaro, a dormant volcano in Tanzania, is the highest mountain in Africa. It is so high that, even though it is very near the Equator, its peak is always snow-covered. Its name in Swahili is *Uhuru*, which means 'freedom'.

⊃ This section of the Victoria Falls is called the Devil's Cataract. The falls were named after Britain's Queen Victoria by 19th-century explorer David Livingstone, who travelled across much of Africa, and mapped out various parts of the continent.

How much of Africa is desert?

About 40 per cent of this hot continent is desert. The Equator crosses the middle of Africa and in most places it is hot all year round. There are great rivers and lakes in Africa but, in contrast, large areas of it are very dry and this has led to the spread of deserts. The Sahara is the biggest desert in the world, and stretches across north Africa. In the southwest of Africa are the smaller Namib and Kalahari deserts.

⊙ Mount Kilimanjaro rises above the savanna in northern Tanzania, close to the Kenyan border, its snow-capped peak clearly visible. It formed over one million years ago.

What is 'the smoke that thunders'?

Victoria Falls is Africa's most famous waterfall and its African name Mosi-oa-tunya, means 'smoke that thunders'. This refers to the cloud of spray that rises above the Victoria Falls as the Zambezi River tumbles over a sheer rock wall. The rumble of the falls can be heard far away and sounds like distant thunder. The falls are 108 m high and 1,500 m wide.

By 1900 Africa was almost completely colonized by European countries. The colonial boundaries became the boundaries of new independent African nations, as African peoples sought self-government from the 1950s. Libya was the first African country to win its independence in 1951. In South Africa, the white minority controlled the government until the 1990s, under a system known as apartheid.

⊙ *A Zulu from South Africa wears traditional warrior dress, comprising of a short spear, or assegai, and an ox-hide shield. A regiment of Zulu soldiers is known as an impi.*

Who are the Zulus?

The Zulus are a people who live in South Africa. In the early 1800s, they were a small tribe, mainly cattle-herders, but a chief named Shaka led a powerful army to fight against the Boers (Dutch settlers) who were taking their land. In 1879, the Zulus were defeated by the combined armies of the Boers and British in the Zulu War. Today the Zulus are citizens of the Republic of South Africa.

Where do the Masai people live?

The Masai are a tribal group of people in Kenya, East Africa. Traditionally, they lived as cattle-herders. Masai men were famous for their skill at hunting lions, armed only with spears. Many African countries have a mixture of tribal groups. There are about 50 ethnic groups in Kenya alone, including the Kikuyu, who are the biggest tribe.

What causes famine in some parts of Africa?

Famine can be caused by drought or civil war. The regions hit hardest by drought include Ethiopia, Chad and Mali, which may go for a year or more without rain. Farmers rely on the seasonal rains to make their crops grow and so the lack of rain means that the soil becomes dry and vegetation dies. This leaves the local population with very little to eat. Civil wars are also responsible for famine because they disrupt farming and trade, thus increasing the risk of famine in some areas.

⊙ *Masai women wear colourful headbands and beaded collars for tribal ceremonies. Many other traditional African costumes are now seldom seen except for tourist displays.*

Why are Africa's game parks so important?

Tourism is a major source of income for African countries, as tourists flock to the game parks to see the amazing variety of wildlife. Lions, giraffes, rhinos, elephants, hippos, antelope and many more animals are found in game reserves across Africa. The reserves protect the animals from poachers, who shoot elephants for their ivory tusks and rhinos for their horns. People used to go to Africa on safari to shoot 'big game', but now many of these animals have become endangered and so are protected inside game parks, such as the Kruger in South Africa and the Tsavo in Kenya.

◑ *Big cats, such as the cheetah, can be spotted by tourists travelling through game reserves in South Africa, Tanzania and Kenya.*

Which African leader fought for an end to apartheid?

Nelson Mandela was imprisoned for 26 years for campaigning for the end of apartheid. Apartheid was a social system in place in South Africa that separated black and white citizens. Mandela was jailed in 1964 for being a senior member of the ANC (African National Congress). In 1990, South African president, F. W. de Klerk, released Mandela.

● *Mandela became the first black president of South Africa in 1994. Under his leadership, apartheid gradually began to break down.*

Where is Timbuktu?

Timbuktu is an ancient trading city south of the Sahara Desert in the African country of Mali. The name means 'place of Buktu'. According to legend, a slave named Buktu was left there to guard her master's goods. Timbuktu was once rich and prosperous, a stopping place for camel travellers crossing the Sahara, carrying gold and salt. It later fell on hard times.

◐ *Many people in Timbuktu live in traditional mud-brick houses.*

Europe is the smallest continent, not counting Australia, and the most densely populated. It has the longest coastline of all the continents (more than 60,000 km), with mountains in the north and south enclosing a central plain. There are 42 independent countries in Europe, some are large (Russia, Ukraine, France and Spain) and others, such as Liechtenstein, are tiny.

Where does Europe end?

Europe has sea on three sides (north, west and south), but it merges with the Asian landmass on the eastern side. There are natural land barriers forming a boundary between Europe and Asia. These boundaries include the Ural Mountains and the Caspian Sea, in Russia. Europe is separated from the continent of Africa by the Strait of Gibraltar, which lies between Morocco in Africa, and Spain in Europe.

Where is Scandinavia?

Scandinavia is the region of northern Europe with a shared geography and history. The countries of Scandinavia are Norway, Sweden, Denmark, Finland and Iceland, which is an island in the Atlantic Ocean. The Scandinavian countries are famed for their landscapes of fjords (Norway), lakes (Sweden), forests (Finland), busy fishing ports (Denmark) and hot springs (Iceland).

map key

1	Albania	9	Lithuania
2	Andorra	10	Luxembourg
3	Belgium	11	Macedonia
4	Bosnia-Herzegovina	12	Moldova
5	Croatia	13	Netherlands
6	Estonia	14	Slovenia
7	Latvia	15	Switzerland
8	Liechtenstein	16	Yugoslavia

❶ *St Petersburg is Russia's second largest city, and boasts the world's biggest art gallery, the Hermitage Museum (shown above) and a famous opera and ballet theatre.*

Where do people walk on land that was once sea?

The Netherlands. The name Netherlands means Low Countries, and this region is very low-lying. Sea walls or dykes have been built to stop the sea flooding the land, and water has been pumped from flooded parts to turn salt marshland into fertile agricultural land. The reclaimed land is known as polders. About 40 per cent of the country has been reclaimed from the sea and 25 per cent of this is used for housing and roads. It takes about eight years after draining the land for it to be suitable for farming and building on.

❷ *Merchants built the network of over 100 canals that cross the Dutch city of Amsterdam.*

Which is the biggest country in Europe?

Russia is so big that it is shared between Europe and Asia, so strictly speaking only part of Russia is 'European'. Even so, at 4.7 million sq km, the European region of Russia is seven times bigger than the next biggest country in Europe, the Ukraine. Next come France, Spain and Sweden.

How many countries make up the British Isles?

The British Isles is made up of two independent countries: the United Kingdom and the Republic of Ireland. The United Kingdom consists of Great Britain (the island containing the nations of England, Scotland and Wales) and Northern Ireland (part of the island of Ireland).

❶ *The Tower of London is in the capital city of England. Building of the Tower was begun by William the Conqueror in 1078, when London was already 1,000 years old.*

Europe was the birthplace of ancient Greek and Roman culture, and later European ideas and technology were spread by explorers, traders and empire-builders to other continents. Europe was the first continent to undergo the Industrial Revolution, in the 1700s. It was also the cradle for two terrible world wars, 1914–18 and 1939–45. Since 1950, the European Union has become the dominant economic force in Europe.

⬆ *The Rock of Gibraltar is a 426-m high mass of limestone. Gibraltar was once an important naval base, but is now a favourite tourist location.*

In which city is the Kremlin?

The Kremlin is the medieval centre of Moscow, which is the capital of Russia, and used to be the home of the Russian tzar (**emperor**). The name kremlin means fortress, and the first wooden fortress was built on this spot more than 800 years ago. The walls now in place date from the 1400s. Cathedrals and palaces were built around the Kremlin fortress. In 1917, the Kremlin became the headquarters of the world's first communist government, which then collapsed in 1991.

⬅ *St Basil's Cathedral, with its cluster of domes, is one of Moscow's landmarks.*

Where is the Rock of Gibraltar?

Gibraltar is a rocky landmark at the southern tip of Spain, at the point where the Mediterranean Sea and Atlantic Ocean meet. About 30,000 people live there. The Rock (as Gibraltar is known) was held by the Arab and Berber Moors and the Spaniards until 1713, when it was ceded to Britain by treaty. Spain wants Gibraltar back, but local people voted to stay British.

➡ *The colony of Gibraltar is represented by this flag and covers an area of 6.5 sq km.*

⊙ *Some members of the European Union have discussed the creation of a European federal state, represented by the current European Union flag. However, most member states prefer their national independence and wish to keep their own flags and currencies.*

⊙ *The Colosseum in Rome is the biggest Roman amphitheatre (open-air arena): 49 m high and 157 m across. Inside there was room for 80,000 spectators.*

Which is Europe's smallest country?

Europe's, and the world's, smallest independent state is the Vatican City, official home of the Pope (the head of the Roman Catholic Church). Fewer than 1,000 people live in the Vatican City. It has its own police and the Pope's bodyguard force, the Swiss Guard, who wear traditional uniforms. It also has a national anthem, stamps, coins, flag and a radio station.

⊙ *The Vatican's main buildings are St Peter's (shown below), one of the world's largest churches, and the Vatican Palace.*

How did the European Union begin?

The European Union evolved from a series of economic agreements, such as the common market, set up by various European nations, from the 1950s. The founder members of the EU were France, Germany, Italy, Netherlands, Belgium and Luxembourg. More countries joined and by 2004 the EU had 25 member-states and its own parliament. A common currency (the euro) is shared by some member states.

Which European city was once the heart of the Roman Empire?

The city of Rome, in Italy, was once the heart of the Roman Empire. The Romans conquered most of Europe over 2,000 years ago, and imposed their laws and culture on the peoples who lived under their rule. This had an enormous effect on later European history. The remains of some buildings from ancient Rome, such as the Colosseum and the Pantheon, still stand today in Rome, the capital of Italy.

The third largest continent, North America extends from Greenland and Alaska in the Arctic north, through Canada and the United States, to Mexico in the south and the islands of the Caribbean Sea. The landscape of North America includes bleak polar regions, towering mountain ranges such as the Rockies, vast grassy plains or prairies (now ploughed for cereal crops), forests, mighty rivers and the Great Lakes.

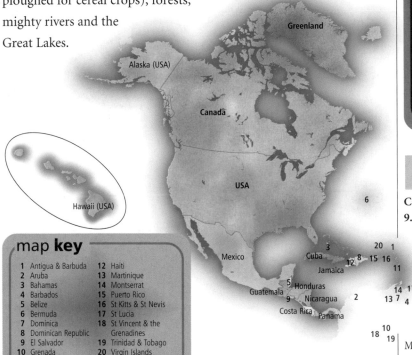

US states

Alabama	Louisiana	Ohio
Alaska	Maine	Oklahoma
Arizona	Maryland	Oregon
Arkansas	Massachusetts	Pennsylvania
California	Michigan	Rhode Island
Colorado	Minnesota	South Carolina
Connecticut	Mississippi	South Dakota
Delaware	Missouri	Tennessee
Florida	Montana	Texas
Georgia	Nebraska	Utah
Hawaii	Nevada	Vermont
Idaho	New Hampshire	Virginia
Illinois	New Jersey	Washington
Indiana	New Mexico	West Virginia
Iowa	New York	Wisconsin
Kansas	North Carolina	Wyoming
Kentucky	North Dakota	

map key

1	Antigua & Barbuda	12	Haiti
2	Aruba	13	Martinique
3	Bahamas	14	Montserrat
4	Barbados	15	Puerto Rico
5	Belize	16	St Kitts & St Nevis
6	Bermuda	17	St Lucia
7	Dominica	18	St Vincent & the
8	Dominican Republic		Grenadines
9	El Salvador	19	Trinidad & Tobago
10	Grenada	20	Virgin Islands
11	Guadaloupe		

Which is North America's largest country?

Canada, with an area of more than 9.97 million sq km, is North America's largest country. The United States is a little smaller, at 9.37 million sq km, but the population of Canada is only 11 per cent of that of the USA. Canada shares a 6,400 km long land border with its southern neighbour, the USA. The Rocky Mountains stretch almost 5,000 km southwards from Canada, south into the United States.

⬆ *Red rocks rise hundreds of metres out of the otherwise flat Monument Valley, which is situated in both Utah and Arizona.*

Why is the USA called the land of the skyscraper?

The USA is home to some of the world's greatest cities, and many of the world's tallest buildings. In many US cities, such tall buildings create dramatic skylines, particularly in Chicago, along the shore of Lake Michigan and in New York City, on Manhattan Island. Chicago once boasted America's tallest building, the Sears Tower, which has 110 floors and stands 1,707 m high with its topmost masts.

Where is Monument Valley?

Monument Valley is in the dry, western American state of Utah but also crosses into Arizona. In the valley can be found some of the most spectacular scenery in the United States. Over thousands of years, the huge crags of sandstone have been eroded by the wind and rain, making the valley an ideal location for shooting 'western' films.

Where are four presidents cut into stone?

In the Black Hills of South Dakota, in the midwest United States. A sculptor named Gutzon Borghum carved the heads of four US Presidents into the granite rock of Mount Rushmore. Each head is about 18 m high and can be seen from almost 100 km away. Work started on the monument in 1927 and lasted until the 1960s.

⬅ *The four presidents on the Mount Rushmore National Memorial are (left to right): George Washington, Thomas Jefferson, Theodore Roosevelt and Abraham Lincoln.*

⬆ *The Niagara River tumbles into a gorge. Spray and foaming water rise into the air, often forming rainbows.*

Where are the Niagara Falls?

There are two falls on the Niagara River: the Horseshoe Falls on the Canadian side and the American Falls on the US side. The Horseshoe Falls are 792 m wide and 51 m high. The American Falls are 305 m wide and about 54 m high. The most water (about 85 per cent) crashes over the Horseshoe Falls. Each year millions of tourists head for Niagara Falls, which have been an attraction ever since European explorers first saw them in the late 1600s.

North America includes countries with diverse cultures and traditions. Canada and the United States have historic ties with Britain, but Canada also has a large French-speaking minority. Both countries have populations of Native Americans, who retain many of their traditional cultures and languages, as well as people of African, Asian and European origin. In Mexico, people speak Spanish – this is also a legacy of the country's past.

Who were the Aztec and Maya?

The Aztecs were a native people living in what is now Mexico, around 1300 AD: the Maya were a native people living in Central America around the same time. The Aztecs built a city called Tenochtitlán,

⬆ *Chichén Itzá is an ancient sacred site of the Maya of Central America. The Maya people built stepped-pyramid temples in their cities.*

upon which Mexico City now stands. The Aztecs were conquered by the Spaniards in 1521, who destroyed their temples. Each of the Mayan Kingdoms had a capital city that was built entirely from stone.

Who were the first Americans?

The first people to live in North America were the Native Americans and Inuit, whose ancestors came from Asia, probably before the last ice age. When Europeans invaded in the 1500s, the natives fought a fierce battle to keep their land. However, today Native Americans form less than one per cent of the population of the USA. Most Americans today are those whose ancestors came from Africa, Asia and Europe.

⬇ *Today, about one-fifth of Native Americans live on land known as reservations, which has been given back to them by the government.*

🔼 *The Caribbean Sea is in the Atlantic Ocean. Caribbean islands have a tropical climate. Many of the islands are formed from volcanic rock and contain vast coral reefs.*

Where is the Panama Canal?

The Panama Canal opened in 1914, providing a shipping short cut between the Atlantic and Pacific oceans. The Panama Canal is 81 km long, and using it saves ships more than 12,000 km travelling around the tip of South America. The Canal was dug across the isthmus (narrow neck of land) of Panama. The area was so jungle-covered and hot that, after work started in 1881, it had to be halted after eight years because so many workers died of disease and exhaustion. The canal cuts through the continent at its narrowest part.

How did the Caribbean Sea get its name?

When Spanish explorers arrived in the New World from Europe in 1492 they called the sea in which they discovered the islands, 'Mar Caribe', after the Caribs who lived there. The Caribs were Native American people who had settled on the islands we now call the 'West Indies' and on the mainland of South America. Within a few years the Caribs were completely wiped out by wars, enforced slavery and diseases brought by the Europeans. Most Caribbeans today are the descendants of Africans and Europeans.

How did Greenland get its name?

When Viking sailors first saw the island, they were encouraged when they saw the green grass and so settled. Most of Greenland today looks white, not green, because the island is almost entirely covered by ice and snow. Only the coast has a small amount of vegetation in summer. The name Greenland also encouraged others to follow and start settlements. Greenland today actually belongs to the European country of Denmark.

🔼 *Inuit people of the Arctic traditionally make ice-houses as temporary hunting lodges. They hunt and fish in the sea for food.*

The fourth largest continent, South America, is almost twice as big as Canada. It has the world's largest tropical rainforest, the world's longest river, and the Andes Mountains, as well as areas of grasslands. It has a rugged, forested interior, and volcanic eruptions and earthquakes are frequent. Most South Americans are descendants of the ancient civilizations, such as Aztec and Maya, or of European, African or Asian descent. The main languages spoken on the continent are Spanish and Portuguese.

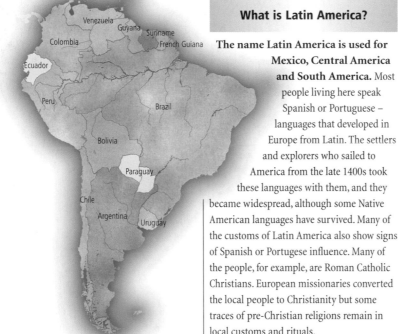

What is Latin America?

The name Latin America is used for Mexico, Central America and South America. Most people living here speak Spanish or Portuguese – languages that developed in Europe from Latin. The settlers and explorers who sailed to America from the late 1400s took these languages with them, and they became widespread, although some Native American languages have survived. Many of the customs of Latin America also show signs of Spanish or Portugese influence. Many of the people, for example, are Roman Catholic Christians. European missionaries converted the local people to Christianity but some traces of pre-Christian religions remain in local customs and rituals.

What is Argentina's biggest city?

Argentina's biggest city is its capital, Buenos Aires. The city has a population of more than ten million people and a very busy port. It was founded in 1536 as a port on the Rio de la Plata, and the name is spanish for 'fair winds'. Buenos Aires is famous for its broad streets and wide plazas, or squares, such as the Plaza de Mayo. Many people have moved from the countryside to live in towns or cities, such as Buenos Aires, where more employment and higher wages can be found.

⬆ *Residential districts are called barrios, and one called La Boca is noted for its colourful painted houses. Many of the city's poorest inhabitants live in shanty towns on the outskirts of the city.*

Why do people visit Machu Picchu?

One of the most amazing insights into South America's past is the lost city of Machu Picchu, built by the Incas in the 1400s. The terraced city high in the Andes Mountains was one of the last refuges for the Inca people after their empire was conquered by Spain in the 1500s. It had stone houses, a royal palace and army barracks, and around it were fields cut into the mountain slopes. The city was abandoned and forgotten, until it was rediscovered by an American archaeologist in 1911.

The ruins of Machu Picchu lie northwest of the city of Cuzco, Peru, in mountains more than 2,000 m high.

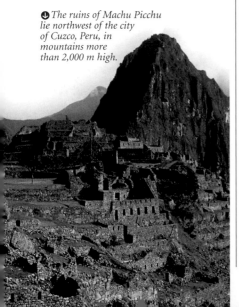

The huge statue of 'Christ The Reedemer' overlooks Rio de Janeiro from atop Corcovado mountain. Founded by the Portuguese in 1565, this Brazilian city is the second largest of Brazil, and has one of the main seaports of South America. Rio is famous for its music, beaches and vibrant carnivals.

Where do most South Americans live?

About 75 per cent of South Americans live in cities. Many of the cities are badly overcrowded like São Paulo in Brazil, which has some of the worst slums in the world. However, much of South America is thinly populated. Few people live in the high Andes Mountains or in the Amazon rainforest – though settlement there is being encouraged.

Where can you see Sugar Loaf Mountain?

Sugar Loaf is a curiously-shaped mountain overlooking Rio de Janeiro, the second biggest city in Brazil after São Paulo. Sugar used to be sold in solid blocks of this shape. On Corcovado Mountain, another peak across Guanabara Bay, stands a 30-m statue of 'Christ The Redeemer', which can be seen from most parts of the city.

Australia, New Zealand, Papua New Guinea and the Pacific island groups of Melanesia, Micronesia and Polynesia form Oceania. Australia is the world's sixth largest country and is populated by people of mostly aboriginal, European and Asian descent. It is the only country that is also a continent in its own right. To the south of Oceania lies the much bigger and uninhabitable landmass of Antarctica.

Papua New Guinea

Solomon Islands

Australia

Tasmania

New Zealand

Which country is the biggest wool producer?

Australia produces more wool than any other country in the world. More than one-quarter of the world's wool is shorn from sheep roaming the sheep stations (farms) of Australia. Australia has a vast and dry interior, but is also rich in pasture ideal for sheep-grazing. There are approximately 150 million sheep in Australia. Some sheep stations can reach up to 15,000 sq km in size. The sheep that produce most wool are Merino, a breed originally from Spain and able to thrive in an arid climate.

What is it like in Antarctica?

The ice-covered continent of Antarctica is bare and empty due to its harsh climate. It was first seen by Captain Cook in 1773, but it was not until the 20th century that Roald Amundsen (1911) and Robert Scott (1912) reached the South Pole. In the 1950s a land expedition crossed Antarctica and today there are scientific bases used by visiting scientists to study the climate, geology and wildlife. Antarctica is protected from exploitation by an international treaty, deeming it to be a 'continent for science' only.

Antarctica

Where is Polynesia?

Polynesia is a region in the Pacific Ocean. There are perhaps as many as 30,000 islands in the Pacific, the world's biggest ocean. The three main groups of islands are Melanesia in the west, Micronesia in the north, and Polynesia in the east. Polynesia covers the largest area – the easternmost island in Polynesia is Easter Island, which is more than 6,000 km from New Zealand.

Easter Island is famous for its 50-tonne stone heads made between AD 900 and 1600. Why they were made is a mystery.

What is Ayers Rock?

Ayers Rock is a reddish sandstone landmark in Australia's Northern Territory. It is about 2.4 km long, 1.6 km wide, and 8 km around the base. The rock rises 335 m from the sandy plain in which it stands. Aboriginal people thought the rock was sacred, and made wall paintings in caves there. Europeans first saw the rock in 1872.

Where do people called kiwis live?

The New Zealanders are nicknamed kiwis. The flightless bird of New Zealand called the kiwi has become one of New Zealand's national emblems, and a friendly nickname for its people. With about 60 million sheep and eight million cattle, New Zealand is one of the major exporters of wool, meat and many dairy products. as well as the main producer of the kiwi fruit.

The aboriginal people of Australia call Ayers Rock Uluru, which means 'great pebble'.

About 10 per cent of New Zealanders are Maoris, whose ancestors came from the eastern Pacific in about AD 850. The Maori culture is still very much alive in New Zealand, with their traditions and language being upheld.

Every society needs a structure to make laws, defend its citizens, fix taxes and spend money for the good of all. That is why governments exist. The first governments were headed by powerful rulers, such as a king. The ancient Greeks had the first democracy – or rule by the people – though neither women nor foreigners could vote. Democracy in various forms is practiced across the world, though ideas differ as to what 'democracy' really means.

The Capitol building in Washington is the seat of the United States Congress, the law-making body for the nation. The President's home is nearby, in the White House.

What is the difference between a republic and a monarchy?

In a republic, a parliament or assembly are elected by members of the public who vote; in a monarchy, even though the government can still be elected, the unelected king, queen, emperor or empress is the head of state. The crown (the symbol of monarchy) is hereditary, and passes through a royal family, from parent to child. Today, they are not usually elected. A president is either the head of the government (as in South Africa) or the head of state (as in France), or both. The President of the USA is head of both state and government and acts like chief executive.

What is a dictatorship?

A dictatorship is a type of government in which a person or group of people rules a country with absolute power. There are often no legal restrictions over a dictator's power and they govern by decree rather than by election. Dictatorships can be established through violence and maintained through physical force and a limitation of people's freedom of speech and behaviour. Dictators are often in control of the media, and will allow only their messages and information to be published or broadcast to the public.

Which is the world's biggest communist country?

China is the world's largest communist country, though in recent years it has embraced a capitalist economy. China has had a communist government since 1949. The communist leader Mao Zedong tried to destroy 'old China' with a cultural revolution in the 1960s, but today's Chinese leaders are less revolutionary and more interested in economic growth. Communism allows only one political party, the Communist Party, and tries to control most aspects of people's lives.

Why do people vote?

People vote to elect a head of state, government or local councillor (someone to represent their views at council level). In a democracy, people over a certain age are allowed to vote. Some non-democratic countries do not allow their citizens the right to vote: instead, these people are told who will govern them. People across the world have had to fight for their right to vote, in particular women. Known as suffragettes, women fought for equal voting rights with men and had to overcome fierce opposition in order to win. Even today many countries will not allow women to vote.

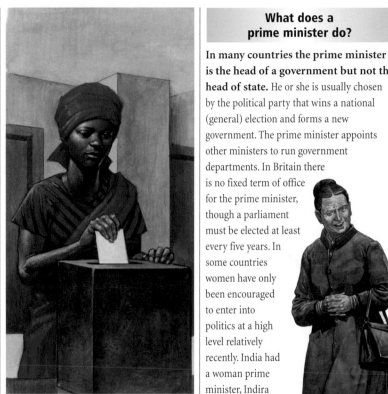

◔ *In a free election, such as those held in some African countries, voters mark a ballot paper, which is then put into a box. Electronic and postal voting is also sometimes allowed.*

➲ *The world's first woman prime minister was Sirimavo Bandaranaike of Sri Lanka. She first took office in 1960. Her husband had also been prime minister but was assassinated in 1959. When her daughter, Chandrika Bandaranaike, became president of Sri Lanka in 1994, she reinstated her mother as prime minister.*

What does a prime minister do?

In many countries the prime minister is the head of a government but not the head of state. He or she is usually chosen by the political party that wins a national (general) election and forms a new government. The prime minister appoints other ministers to run government departments. In Britain there is no fixed term of office for the prime minister, though a parliament must be elected at least every five years. In some countries women have only been encouraged to enter into politics at a high level relatively recently. India had a woman prime minister, Indira Ghandi, elected in 1966.

The world's many religions teach various beliefs about the creation of the world, the afterlife, why evil exists and good behaviour. The religions with the greatest number of followers are Christianity, Islam, Judaism, Buddhism, Confucianism, Hinduism, Shinto and Taoism. Other world religions include Sikhism, Jainism Baha'ism and Zoroastrianism.

⊙ The Wailing Wall in Jerusalem is the last remnant of the ancient Temple of Solomon, and is a special, holy place for Jews who come from across the world in order to pray there.

Where did Christianity begin?

Christianity is based on the life and teachings of Jesus Christ, who was born in about 4 BC in Palestine and crucified by the Roman governor of Palestine in about AD 30. Jesus' teachings were spread by his followers or disciples, who established the first Christian churches. Christianity was spread to every continent by European explorers. There are Christians across the world today and most belong to Roman Catholic, Protestant or Eastern Orthodox churches.

Why do pilgrims travel to Mecca?

The most sacred place for Muslims is Mecca, in Saudi Arabia, because this was the birthplace of the Prophet Muhammad, who founded Islam in 622. It was from Mecca that Muhammad began his journey to Medina. Millions of Muslims travel to Mecca every year, as they are expected to make a pilgrimage, or *hajj*, once in their lifetime, if they are able.

⊙ *Muslims are called to prayer from the mosque five times a day and turn to face towards Mecca as they pray.*

Which was the first religion to teach about one God ?

The first main religion to teach that there was only one supreme God was Judaism, the religion of the Jews. Christianity and Islam are also 'monotheistic' or 'One God' faiths. Early religious beliefs were based on the worship of many nature-gods, such as the Sun, Moon, trees, rocks, and animals. The ancient Greeks had a large family of gods, headed by Zeus the King of the Gods. Hinduism too has many gods.

⬆ *Angkor Wat has five central towers within a moated enclosure. The tallest tower is 70 m high.*

Who was the Buddha?

The Buddha was a prince in Nepal around 500 BC, called Siddhartha Gautama. When he was about 30 years old, the prince became disillusioned with the material world and sought spiritual enlightenment through meditation. He travelled through India for about six years and finally attained 'enlightenment' and became known as 'Buddha', meaning 'enlightened one'. Buddha taught that by detachment from the material world and possessions, humans could achieve *nirvana*, a state of eternal peace.

What is Angkor Wat?

Angkor Wat is a Hindu temple built by the Khmer people, in what is now Cambodia. Built in the early 1100s, in honour of the Hindu god Vishnu, it is the largest religious building in the world. It was also used as an observatory and later housed the tomb of the Cambodian king who commissioned the building. Though Angkor Wat was later abandoned, it was rediscovered in the 1860s by a Frenchman named Henri Mouhot and was restored by archaeologists.

➡ *Statues representing Buddha are found all over parts of Asia. These Buddha statues in Japan are made from gold-leaf.*

There are at least 4,000 languages in the world. People who speak the same languages may also share the same customs, but other customs (such as New Year or birthday celebrations) are common to people all over the world. In all human societies, people mark the seasons, growing up, and events, such as marriages and deaths, in certain ways. Each culture or group has its own festivals.

❶ *Hieroglyphs are picture symbols that represent ideas and sounds. The Egyptians used hieroglyphics for more than 3,000 years for inscriptions on temple walls.*

How can customs change?

Some customs and festivals are very ancient and their original meaning has sometimes been forgotten. Hallowe'en was an ancient festival associated with the onset of winter and darkness. Medieval Christians turned it into a religious festival called All Saints' Day (November 1) and this is still celebrated by Christians in the USA and UK today. However, Hallowe'en has also become a night for young people to dress up as ghosts and play 'trick or treat'. However, in Catholic Mexico, Hallowe'en is still a religious day.`

❷ *The Chinese celebrate New Year in January and February with fireworks and parades by people carrying colourful dragon models. Dragons in China are associated with good luck. The Chinese calendar, used for more than 4,000 years, has years named after animals: rat, ox, tiger, rabbit/hare, dragon, snake, horse, sheep/goat, monkey, rooster, dog and boar/pig.*

Which is the most spoken language?

More people speak Standard Chinese or Mandarin than any other language, though the language spoken in the most countries is English. English has spread to every continent. Languages change and grow as they are spoken and new words are added. If a language is no longer spoken, it is extinct. Latin, the language of the ancient Romans, is rarely spoken though people still study and read books that were written in it. Language originally developed very slowly from basic sounds. Grammar, vocabulary and sound-patterns all change with the structure of languages. Different languages evolve with common usage and local dialects.

When did people first write down words?

The earliest known writing is Sumerian cuneiform, which dates from about 6,000 years ago. The oldest known alphabet comes from the ancient city of Ugarit, Palestine, and dates from 1450 BC. An alphabet is a collection of letter-signs standing for the sounds we make when we speak.

Do customs vary across the world?

Customs vary from one country or culture to another. In some parts of the world, such as Thailand, crossing your legs in someone's house is considered insulting. In Brazil, it is offensive to local people to make an 'o' with your thumb and forefinger – elsewhere this is a sign of satisfaction.

Where is tea drinking a polite ceremony?

Tea drinking is an important ceremony in Japan that is taken very seriously. Known as 'cha-no-yu', it is a formal occasion with strict rules, often taking place in a special room. The tea is prepared using special utensils and is served in a bowl from which each guest drinks in turn. Everyone keeps very calm and still, the aim being to find beauty and meaning in simple, ordinary acts, like drinking tea.

➔ *A tea ceremony in Japan, can often be a formal occasion, such as a state banquet for an important foreign visitor, or even part of a wedding feast. People wear their best clothes, and after the eating and drinking, speeches may be made.*

Are languages related?

Most languages belong to families, but there are exceptions, such as Basque, which is spoken in a northern region of Spain. Korean was once thought to be unrelated to any other language but it is often argued that it falls within the Altaic family. English evolved from the Indo-European 'parent' language and belongs to the Germanic branch of the family, along with German, Dutch and Swedish. Welsh belongs to the Celtic branch, and French and Spanish belong to the Romance branch.

1 Which continent has more people: South America or Africa?

2 Which sea separates Europe from North Africa?

3 Is there more land or more water making up the Earth's surface?

4 Where in China is the Forbidden City?

5 In which Asian country would you find Mount Fiji?

6 Which of these countries is not in Africa: Afghanistan, Benin or Sudan?

7 Which European country does this flag represent?

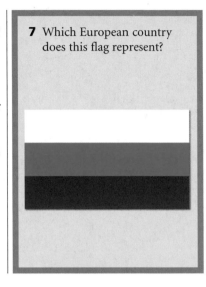

8 What is the modern name of Constantinople?

9 What city houses the Temple of the Emerald Buddha?

10 What is Sri Lanka's currency: the dollar, the pound or the rupee?

11 In which country would you find the Ural Mountains?

12 Which is South Africa's largest city?

13 Apart from Egypt, name one of the other two countries the river Nile flows through?

FACTFILE

Earth **statistics**

Population	More than 6 billion
Largest continent	Asia 17,400,000 sq km
Highest mountain	Mount Everest, Asia 8,863 m
Longest river	Amazon River, South America 6,750 km
Largest lake	Caspian Sea, Asia 371,000 sq km
Largest desert	Sahara Desert, Africa 9.3 million sq km

International **organizations**

Many countries have joined together to create international organizations providing law, aid and support around the world. They use resources from the member states to help those in need during periods of war or natural disasters. One such organization is the United Nations (UN), set up in 1945 to try to resolve disputes between countries.

↥ *Red Cross workers travel around the world to regions of war, drought, famine or flood, to provide shelter, food and medicine.*

14 In which ocean would you find the island of Zanzibar?

15 Kruger Park game reserve is in which African country?

16 Nairobi is the capital city of which African country?

17 Which city is the headquarters of the International Red Cross?

18 What are the names of the five Scandinavian countries?

19 Which tiny European state holds a Grand Prix, an open tennis competition and the Rose Ball?

20 Which country paid for the Statue of Liberty?

21 In which country would you find the volcano, Mount Etna?

22 What does the abbreviation EU stand for?

23 In which European river would you find the Lorelei Rocks?

24 Which waterfall is on the border between the United States and Canada?

25 Which is the highest lake in North America?

26 Alphabetically, what is the first US state?

Around the **world**

- The population of the world is estimated to increase by around 360,000 every day.

- Approximately 150,000 people die every day.

- There are about 1,000 minor earthquakes every day, in various regions of the world.

- The Grand Canyon is the largest gorge in the world, at 349 km long.

- The highest temperature was recorded in 1922 in Libya, at 58°C in the shade.

- Sweden in Europe has at least 90,000 lakes, which were formed during the last ice age, more than 100,000 years ago.

- Maine is the first of the US states to see the sunrise each day.

- There could be as many as 30,000 islands scattered around the Pacific.

- In a region in northern Scandinavia, in Europe, it stays constantly light throughout summer, and constantly dark during winter.

- The Aral Sea, between Kazakhstan and Uzbekistan, is shrinking because its water is being used to irrigate crops. It is now only one-third of its original size.

- McMurdo is a community in Antarctica, which has cafés, a cinema and a church, for people visiting during the summer.

- The plates of the Earth's crust are moving the ocean floor at between 1.25 and 10 cm a year.

27 In which Australian city is the famous opera house?

Key dates for **government**

FACTFILE

c. 3500 BC First local governments: kings become the first rulers.

c. 400s BC Greek city-states have male-only democratic assemblies to make laws.

100 BC Roman Empire begins to expand over much of Europe, North Africa and Middle East.

AD 800s In Europe, kings are advised by assemblies of nobles.

1500 Renaissance ideas start to challenge royal power.

1649 English Parliament executes King Charles I.

1776 The American Revolution, leading to the creation of the United States of America (USA).

1789 French Revolution overthrows the monarchy.

1900s Women in most countries win the right to vote (enfranchisement).

1945 The United Nations (UN) is set up as an international governing body in an attempt to prevent further world war.

2004 Enlarged European Union (EU) of 25 members has a Parliament and Courts of Justice, which can overrule some member states' laws.

28 Which Canadian lake, originally called Emerald Lake, lies in front of the Victoria Glacier?

29 Which is the world's largest Spanish-speaking city?

30 The Pilgrim Fathers sailed to North America from which continent?

31 In which South American city would you find the statue of 'Christ The Redeemer'?

32 In which South American country is Guarani spoken: Argentina, Ecuador or Paraguay?

33 Which European country does this flag represent?

34 Valparaiso is in which South American country?

35 Is Port Moresby the capital of Fiji, Papua New Guinea or Tahiti?

36 Botany Bay is an ex-convict settlement found in which country?

37 The All Blacks is the nickname given to the rugby team of which country?

38 Which form of government is ruled by a king or queen: republic or monarchy?

⬆ *The Supreme Court, in Washington DC. Its nine judges rule on whether the federal, state or local governments of the nation are acting according to the constitution of the US.*

Amazing **facts**

• The use of the word 'parliament' in England dates from 1241.

• The European Union (EU) has its own law court, and its rulings apply to all member states.

• The first country to give women the same voting rights as men was New Zealand in 1903.

• The idea of 'one person, one vote' dates from the 1800s.

• Left-wing governments champion the good of the majority over that of the individual. At the extreme left-wing of the political spectrum is communism: shared public ownership and the means of production, distribution and exchange.

• Right-wing governments offer greater support to the individual. At the extreme right-wing of the political spectrum is fascism, which supresses democracy and promotes the supremacy of the state over the individual.

39 Which politician lives in the White House?

40 Which of these countries is led by a communist government: China, England or India?

41 Which city in Israel is held sacred by Jews, Muslims and Christians?

42 The four Vedas are the oldest sacred books of which religion: Hinduism, Judaism or Buddhism?

43 Passover is a festival in which religion?

44 What is the official language of Macao, Mozambique and Angola?

45 Italian is one of the languages of the Vatican City, can you name the other?

46 Are walloons French, Dutch or Spanish-speaking peoples?

47 Which European country does this flag represent?

FACTFILE

Alphabet **facts**

The term alphabet derives from 'alpha' and 'beta', the first two letters of the Greek alphabet. Most English-speaking people use about 5,000 words in speech, and about 10,000 words when writing. There are more than one million words in the English language and this grows each year.

➊ *Not every word or sign can be translated. The per cent sign is universal, and so are some numbers, but Arabic, Hebrew and Chinese numbering is different.*

Amazing **language**

Longest alphabet	Cambodian (74 letters)
Most common vowel	a
Most concise language	Japanese (the longest word has only 12 letters)
Most common place name	Newton ('new town') name in English
Word with most meanings	'set' (about 200)
Most languages spoken	Papua New Guinea (over 800 local languages)
Longest speech	22 hours

Answers

1 Africa	15 South Africa	28 Lake Louise	42 Hinduism
2 Mediterranean	16 Kenya	29 Mexico City	43 Judaism
3 More water	17 Geneva, Switzerland	30 Europe	44 Portuguese
4 Beijing	18 Denmark, Finland, Iceland,	31 Rio De Janeiro	45 Latin
5 Japan	Norway and Sweden	32 Paraguay	46 French-speaking
6 Afghanistan	19 Monaco	33 Switzerland	47 Portugal
7 Bulgaria	20 France	34 Chile	
8 Istanbul	21 Italy	35 Papua New Guinea	
9 Bangkok	22 European Union	36 Australia	
10 Rupee	23 Rhine	37 New Zealand's	
11 Russia	24 Niagara Falls	38 Monarchy	
12 Johannesburg	25 Yellowstone Lake	39 The president of the USA	
13 Sudan or Uganda	26 Alabama	40 China	
14 Indian Ocean	27 Sydney	41 Jerusalem	

Celebration **dates**

Date	Celebration	Date	Celebration	Date	Celebration
1 January	New Year's Day (except some Southeast Asian countries)	3 May	World Press Freedom Day	24 October	United Nations' Day
		5 June	World Environment Day	31 October	Hallowe'en
late Jan – mid Feb	Chinese New Year	20 June	World Refugee Day	11 November	Armistice Day
14 February	St Valentine's Day	4 July	Independence Day (USA)	20 November	Universal Children's Day
21 March	World Poetry Day	14 July	Bastille Day (France)	2 December	International Day for the Abolition of Slavery
22 March	World Day for Water	8 September	International Literacy Day		
1 April	April Fool's Day	21 September	International Day of Peace	3 December	International Day of Disabled Persons
7 April	World Health Day	5 October	International Teachers' Day		
1 May	May Day	16 October	World Food Day	10 December	Human Rights Day
				25 December	Christmas Day

WORLD WONDERS

The world is filled with amazing sights both natural and man-made. The wildlife havens of Africa are home to many protected animals, while in North America the course of the Colorado River carves its way through the Grand Canyon. People have been building great monuments for many centuries. Some are now lost wonders of ancient times, while others remain to inspire and enthral people today.

Which waterfall is higher than a skyscraper?

Where are the world's mightiest mountains?

Whose tomb revealed a lost treasure?

Seven stupendous structures, built between 3000 and 200 BC, became known as the Seven Wonders of the Ancient World. Tourists of old had to travel what were then vast and difficult distances – across Europe, North Africa and eastern Asia. This was the 'civilized world', as known to the Greeks and Romans, who first listed the 'Seven Wonders'.

➊ *The word 'mausoleum' came to mean a large tomb.*

What was the Mausoleum?

This was a marble tomb built about 353 BC at Halicarnassus, in what is now southwestern Turkey. It was commissioned for Mausolus, who was ruler of a province in the Persian Empire. The beautiful tomb was created by architects and sculptors from Greece. High on the roof, over 40 m from the ground, a statue was built of King Mausolus driving in his chariot.

Which god became a Wonder?

Zeus, king of the gods who the ancient Greeks believed lived on Mount Olympus. A mighty statue of Zeus at Olympia was 12 m high (six times human-size) and was made of ivory and gold. People visited the god's temple to marvel at the statue of Zeus, made about 435 BC by Phidias, the greatest sculptor of ancient Greece.

➊ *Zeus was seated on a golden throne, wearing a robe and ornaments of gold.*

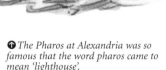

➊ *The Pharos at Alexandria was so famous that the word pharos came to mean 'lighthouse'.*

Which Wonder had a fire on top?

The Pharos or Lighthouse at Alexandria (Egypt). It was a huge tower, built on an island as a lighthouse to guide ships in and out of the harbour. The lighthouse was 122 m high, and workers kept a fire burning at the top to provide the light. The first lighthouse in history, it stood for about 1,500 years.

◑ *Water was pumped from the Euphrates River to water the flowers and trees on the Hanging Garden's terraces.*

Which Wonder was sold off for scrap?

A huge bronze statue, which stood at the harbour of Rhodes, an island in the Aegean Sea. A figure of the Sun god Helios, standing about 27 m tall, it was called the Colossus of Rhodes. The builders used stone blocks and iron bars to hold up the hollow figure. The iron was sold off as scrap metal in the AD 600s, 800 years after the Colossus was toppled by an earthquake.

◑ *The people of Rhodes made the Colossus to celebrate their victory against invaders in the 200s BC.*

Who was honoured in the Temple at Ephesus?

Artemis, a Greek goddess. In the city of Ephesus on the west coast of what is now Turkey stood a magnificent marble temple. The temple honoured Artemis, who in Greek mythology was the daughter of Zeus, king of the gods. She was the goddess of childbirth and also of wild animals and hunting.

Which is the most mysterious Wonder?

The Hanging Gardens of Babylon. The Gardens were probably near Baghdad in Iraq. Writing 400 years after the Gardens were built, a priest described them as being like a ziggurat (a pyramid) with terraces covered in trees and plants. One story says that King Nebuchadnezzar II ordered the Hanging Gardens to please one of his wives, who missed the greenery of her mountain home.

◐ *The Temple of Artemis at Ephesus was finished in about 550 BC and rebuilt after a fire in 356 BC. It had 106 columns, which were each about 12 m high.*

Of the Seven Wonders of the Ancient World, only the pyramids of Egypt remain in anything like their original splendour. The pyramids are the oldest of the Seven Wonders of the Ancient World, and the biggest.

⊕ *The royal burial chamber was reached by a passage deep inside the Great Pyramid.*

Why were the Great Pyramids built?

The pyramids were built as tombs for kings of Egypt. The Egyptians believed that their rulers would continue to live on after they had died. The pyramid tombs contained burial chambers inside which the dead king was placed, along with objects that he might need in the next world. Inside the Great Pyramid of King Khufu were sealed chambers full of treasure.

Who thought pyramids were a waste of money?

The ancient Romans. They were impressed by the size of the Egyptian pyramids, but they thought they were extravagant projects of Egyptian kings with too much wealth, too many slave-workers – and nothing better to do! The Romans spent their money on useful projects, such as the building of roads.

➲ *The three great pyramids were built about 4,500 years ago – about 2600 to 2500 BC.*

◔ *The Great Pyramids stand at Giza beside the Nile River in Egypt.*

How many pyramids are there?

The ruins of 35 large pyramids can be seen today near the Nile River in Egypt. The most famous are three enormous pyramids that stand at Giza, near the capital city of Cairo. These pyramids were built for three very powerful kings of Egypt. Their names were Khufu, Khafre and Menkaure.

⊕ *Inside the Great Pyramid, a passage led to the burial chamber. Heavy stones sealed the passage to stop robbers breaking into the tomb.*

What is a step pyramid?

The first pyramid in ancient Egypt was built for King Zoser about 2650 BC and is called the Step Pyramid, because it rises in a series of giant steps. It stands at the site of the ancient city of Memphis, near Saqqarah. Later pyramids were faced with stones, which made each side smooth, though today the sides look rough and worn.

⊕ *The Step Pyramid looked like the ziggurat-temples built in Mesopotamia (present-day Iraq). Below ground, there is a warren of tunnels, galleries and rooms.*

How were pyramids built?

The Egyptians had no machinery or iron tools and so they cut huge blocks of stone with copper chisels and saws. Most of the stones came from quarries nearby, but others were brought by boat along the Nile River. Gangs of workers dragged the stones up long ramps of earth and brick as the pyramid slowly rose higher and higher. Finally, it was coated with white stones, to gleam brilliantly in the hot desert sun.

Where else were pyramids built?

There are pyramids in America too. People of Mexico and Central America built stepped pyramids with temples on top. The Pyramid of the Sun at Teotihuacan, Mexico, is bigger (in volume) than the Great Pyramid in Egypt. This huge pyramid is more than 1,500 years old. Ancient people in Peru in South America also built pyramids.

⊕ *The Pyramid of the Sun was built by people who lived in Mexico, long before the Spanish conquerors came in the 1500s.*

The Greeks were famous for their skill at building, not only temples and palaces, but theatres and arenas too. They were also marvellous sculptors. The Romans copied Greek buildings, and made improvements – the dome, for instance. The Romans imitated the Greeks in making lifelike figures in bronze, marble, gold and ivory.

The Parthenon stands on the Acropolis. Greeks thought the goddess Athene watched over the city of Athens.

Why did the Greeks build temples?

Everywhere they settled, the Greeks built temples to honour their gods and goddesses. A temple usually had a statue of its own particular god inside. People came to the temple to bring gifts to the god and to pray for the god's help. Priests looked after the statue inside the temple.

Which Roman town disappeared under hot ash?

A Roman port called Pompeii in Italy – close to the foot of a volcano. In AD 79, the volcano, Vesuvius, suddenly erupted. Hot ashes, stones and cinders rained down on Pompeii. The layers of mud and ash preserved the Roman buildings so that today you can walk through the streets of the ruined city.

Pompeii was only rediscovered in the 1700s. Archaeologists have now uncovered about 75 per cent of the city.

Where is the Acropolis?

The Acropolis is a rocky platform on a hill in Athens, Greece. The term 'acropolis' means 'upper city'. Many of the cities of ancient Greece are built around an acropolis where the people can flee to in times of invasion, and the most sacred buildings are usually on an acropolis. Other Greek cities had an acropolis but Athens' is the most famous. The rock is about 350 m long and 150 m across. On top the Athenians built their royal palace and temples. The ruins of the most famous temple – the Parthenon – are still there.

Which Roman column tells stories?

Trajan's Column, which stands in Rome. It is a tall column of stone, erected in AD 113 to honour the Roman soldier-emperor Trajan. The column has a spiral staircase inside, and the outside is covered with carvings showing how the Roman army conquered Dacia (Romania and Hungary) under Trajan's command.

➲ *The relief carvings on Trajan's Column show us what Roman soldiers wore, and the equipment they used when going to war.*

Why did the Romans build aqueducts?

To allow towns access to fresh water. Roman engineers built pipes and arched bridges called aqueducts – raised channels that carried water from streams in mountains to cities. One of the most famous Roman aqueducts is the Pont du Gard, built in southern France about 2,000 years ago. It has three tiers, the topmost carrying water.

➲ *The Pont du Gard soars 47 m above the Gard River.*

How did the Colosseum get its name?

The Colossus of Rhodes, one of the Seven Wonders of the World, gave its name to anything gigantic. The Ancient Romans crowded the Colosseum, an oval amphitheatre seating 50,000 spectators. The huge seating area was divided into 80 sections, and had lifts and tunnels to let gladiators and wild animals into the arena. The Circus Maximus, a chariot race track in Rome, was even bigger, holding 250,000 people.

➲ *The Pantheon is a remarkable feat of engineering.*

Which Roman wonder had a hole in it?

One of the most remarkable buildings in ancient Rome was the Pantheon, a temple built during the rule of the emperor Hadrian (AD 117–138). The Pantheon was the largest circular building in the ancient world. It was topped by a dome measuring 43 m across. The dome had an opening in the top to let in light and air.

➲ *The mighty Colosseum in Rome was over 180 m long and 156 m across. It was supported by 80 arches.*

A monument is any structure built in memory of a person or an event. It can be a statue of a king, a general or an explorer, a tower or column with names and words on it, or just an ancient heap of earth grown over with grass. National monuments can include historic buildings and even natural features, such as rocks.

⊕ *Stone circles often seem to be arranged so that they correspond with ancient annual festivals, such as the Summer Solstice.*

Where is the Great Serpent Mound?

In the woodland of Ohio, USA. It looks like a giant snake coiled round upon itself, but it is actually a mound of earth. Known as the Great Serpent Mound, it was created more than 2,000 years ago, and there are hundreds of other mounds like it. The mounds were piled up by Native American people across North America. Many were burial places, but the reasons for others remain a mystery. Monks Mound in the US state of Illinois is 30 m high and covers an area the size of ten soccer pitches! All the work to make it was was done by hand.

Why did ancient peoples build circles of stone?

It was probably for religious reasons. Some structures may have been used as calendars to mark the seasons – it is thought that ancient peoples could use the positions of the stones to help them fix dates by studying the Sun and stars. They could also have been used as giant maps, to show the direction of settlements. People met at these mysterious monuments for important ceremonies.

Which Pacific island has the strangest statues?

On lonely Easter Island, in the middle of the Pacific Ocean, stand more than 600 stone statues. Most look like heads peering out of the ground. The statues were made between AD 900 and 1600. Some weigh as much as 50 tonnes. Legend tells how the heads were made by people called 'Long Ears' who came in boats from South America.

❶ The Easter Island statues are a mystery. Why were they made? And why were so many statues later pushed over?

Why does Stonehenge fascinate people?

Because no one is really certain about how it was built. Over two thousand years ago, people in Britain went to great efforts to construct a circle of stones. Stonehenge is the most famous of these strange circles. It was built in stages, from around 2800 BC, on Salisbury Plain. Using muscle power alone, the building of Stonehenge was an extremely daunting task. The stones are so heavy (some weigh as much as 50 tonnes) that dragging just one would have taken 500 men. The pairs of stones were once topped with cross-beam stones or lintels. Stonehenge was almost certainly built for the purpose of religious ceremonies, and would have been used as part of ancient rituals. The stones are one of England's most famous monuments.

❹ Local people once thought Stonehenge must have been built by the Devil.

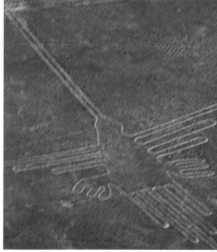

❶ The animal shapes made by the Nazca include a spider and a hummingbird. Some figures are over 120 m long.

Where are there strange pictures in a desert?

In Peru, in South America. Why the Nazca people of Peru scraped lines in the desert to make long straight lines, geometric shapes and outlines of animals and birds is a mystery. The outlines are so big that they can only be seen properly from the air, and yet they were made centuries before people had balloons or aircraft. One theory suggests the Nazca made them over 1,500 years ago to trace the movements of the Sun and stars they saw in the sky above.

For thousands of years, forts and castles have been strongholds for defence. The best place to build a fortress was usually on a hilltop, as this is the best position to see approaching attackers and because a hilltop is usually easiest to defend. Some medieval castles still tower above the surrounding landscape today.

Maiden Castle was defended by ditches and banks, and by wooden fences and gates.

Who built Britain's strongest castles?

The Normans and the medieval kings of England who followed them. After the Norman Conquest, in 1066, Norman barons built stone motte and bailey castles: the motte was an earth mound, the bailey and the enclosure around it. Later, in the Middle Ages, when Edward I, who was king of England from 1272 to 1307, conquered Wales, he built huge stone castles to subdue the Welsh. Cannons brought an end to the age of castles in the 1400s.

What was Maiden Castle?

A hillfort, built by Iron Age people in Britain. Over 2,000 years ago these people, who were Celts, lived in groups or tribes. To protect themselves, and their farm animals, they built fortified villages on hilltops. Mai Dun or Maiden Castle in Dorset was one of the biggest hillforts ('Mai Dun' is Celtic for 'great hill'). It was captured by the Romans after they invaded Britain in AD 43. Some of its ramparts rise to a height of 6 m.

Krak des Chevaliers castle in Syria. It was built by Crusaders, but Muslims added extra defences after they captured it in 1271.

What is the Krak des Chevaliers?

A mighty Crusader castle. During the Crusades, or religious wars, of the Middle Ages, both sides (Muslims and Christians) built castles. Each side did its best to capture the enemy's castles, and castles often changed hands several times. The Crusader castle that is best-preserved is Krak des Chevaliers. It has very high walls on three sides and a moat on the fourth. It has a keep that is surrounded by a precipitous slope of smooth rock, and was known to the attacking Muslims as 'the Mountain' because it was impossible to climb.

Edward I's castles, such as Conway Castle, were the wonders of their age.

Where is the Red Fort?

In the Indian city of Delhi.
The Indian name for the fort is Lal Qal'ah, and the name comes from the reddish colour of its sandstone walls, which stand over 20 m high. The building of the Red Fort was begun in 1639 at the orders of the Mogul emperor of India, Shah Jahan. Within the walls there was space for Shah Jahan's royal palaces, gardens, soldiers' barracks, as well as all the important government buildings.

⏷ *Indian castles, such as the Red Fort in Delhi, often had bigger gateways than European castles – so that elephants could get through.*

Which castle sits on a volcano?

Edinburgh Castle, in Scotland. The volcano it is perched upon, known as Castle Rock, is extinct. There has been a settlement at Edinburgh since 850 BC. The city grew in the AD 1000s when David I established his court at Edinburgh Castle. David built a tiny chapel in the castle, dedicated to the memory of his mother, Margaret. The chapel is the oldest surviving structure on Castle Rock.

⏴ *Edinburgh Castle houses Mons Meg, a massive siege gun given to James II in 1457.*

⏶ *Great Zimbabwe was a trading city. Its walls measured up to 10 m high and 240 m long. Its stone walls protected the people and cattle inside.*

Where is Great Zimbabwe?

In Zimbabwe, in Central Africa. It is a fortified settlement, and one of the most impressive and famous ancient ruins in Africa. The walls of Great Zimbabwe are made of granite rock. Historians believe that the fort was built some time after AD 1000 by the Shona people: the word 'zimbabwe' means 'house of stone' in the Shona language. It is thought to have been built over a long period, beginning in 1200 and ending in 1450.

Kings and emperors built palaces to show how rich and powerful they were. Today, some palaces are museums. Power has shifted to elected assemblies, such as parliaments, but even some presidents still live in palaces. The biggest palace in China and the most luxurious palaces of modern times were built for the homes of the rulers of oil-rich kingdoms such as Saudi Arabia and Brunei.

How old is Buckingham Palace?

The bit that most tourists see and photograph, the front, dates from 1913. So Buckingham Palace is a fairly new palace, as palaces go. It was originally Buckingham House, a mansion bought by King George III in the 1700s. From 1837 it was the London home of Queen Victoria, and ever since has been the London home of the king or queen.

Although in use for the many official events held by the Queen, areas of Buckingham Palace are open to visitors.

Which palace was built for a general?

Not all palaces were homes for kings and queens. Blenheim Palace in England was built (1705–25) for the Duke of Marlborough. He was England's most famous soldier. The huge house was a thank-you from Queen Anne and her government for Marlborough's victories against the French. It is named after one of his victories at the Battle of Blenheim. Later, Blenheim Palace was the birthplace of another famous Englishman, Winston Churchill.

China's finest artists worked to decorate the Forbidden City. Construction started in 1406 and took 14 years to complete. An estimated one million workers were involved.

Who lived in the Forbidden City?

Chinese emperors, with their families. Palaces were centres of government as well as luxurious homes. Some were cities built in miniature, like the Imperial Palace in Beijing, China. It was designed for the Ming emperors, and work on building it began in 1406. The job took a million workers ten years. The emperor and his family lived in the most secret part, known as the Forbidden City, because no foreigners were ever allowed to enter. The Forbidden City is now open to the public as a palace museum.

Who was the first president to live in the White House?

The first president to live there was John Adams. The White House, in Washington, DC, is one of the world's most recognized buildings. It is the home of the president of the United States. The original house was built in the 1790s. It was burnt down in 1814, and rebuilt. Various presidents have made changes to it over the years. The White House has 132 rooms, including the president's Oval Office.

🔽 *St Petersburg was founded by Tsar Peter the Great in 1703 to be his new capital (instead of Moscow).*

Where is the Winter Palace?

In St Petersburg, Russia. This area is so far north, close to the Baltic Sea, that in winter, days are very short. The Winter Palace was built in 1754–62 as a winter home for the royal family – another palace outside the city served as their summer home. The Russian tsars wanted the Winter Palace to rival any royal building in western Europe. Russia no longer has a tsar and the Winter Palace is now an art museum, called the Hermitage, with one of the world's great art collections – there are nearly three million works on exhibit.

Which king ordered a palace with 1,300 rooms?

King Louis XIV of France in the 1600s. Louis had big ideas and he wanted a bigger palace than any other king. In 1661 work began on his new palace at Versailles, outside Paris. It had to be big – Louis's court had 20,000 people, and Versailles became the centre of court life.

⬆ *The Palace of Versailles is now a museum.*

A wall is built to keep people in or out. Towers can be part of a wall. One of the most mysterious walls is a 160 km-long earth bank known as the Eredo in Nigeria. It is partially hidden by dense forest, and is thought to be about 1,000 years old but no one is certain why it is there.

⊕ *The Great Wall is the longest structure ever built, but in the end it did not keep out invaders.*

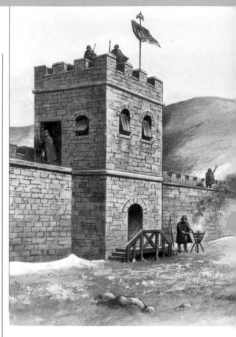

Which was the longest Roman wall?

Hadrian's Wall (named after the Emperor Hadrian) stretches for 118 km across the hills of northern England from Wallsend-on-Tyne in the east to Bowness on the Solway Firth in the west. In the AD 120s, Roman legionary soldiers built this wall to control travel between Roman Britain and the north, and to keep out northern tribes. When it was first built, the wall was 2 to 3 m thick and 117 km in length. Long stretches of the wall still wind over the hills.

Why did the Chinese build the Great Wall?

The Great Wall of China was built to protect China against 'barbarian' invaders from the north. Chinese civilization was based on farming, and the young Chinese nation was often raided by nomads from the North. In the 200s BC, the Chinese emperor Shi Huangdi ordered old frontier walls to be linked by walls and forts to keep its nusiance neighbours out. The Great Wall winds for more than 6,400 km over mountains, hills and plateaus and along the edges of deserts. The wall was 9 m high, and was originally dotted with watchtowers with a walkway along the top for patrolling guards. Some sections of the Great Wall are now in ruins or have even disappeared, but it is still one of the world's most momentous sights.

Why is the Eiffel Tower so remarkable?

People laughed when Gustave Eiffel said he planned to built a steel tower over 300 m high in Paris. But he did. The Eiffel Tower was built in two years, 1887–89, to celebrate the 100th anniversary of the French Revolution. It was assembled from 12,000 sections, held together by over two million rivets.

⬇ For 40 years, the Eiffel Tower was the tallest structure in the world. It is still the most famous landmark in France.

What made the Tower of Pisa lean?

Tall buildings are heavy, as medieval builders of Pisa, in Italy, soon discovered. In the 1150s, the city's new bell-tower began to tilt before it was half finished. The soil underneath was just too soft. Even when the tower was finished, in the 1300s, it leaned perilously. Modern engineers have worked hard to make sure that its lean does not turn into a collapse! The Leaning Tower is 56 m high and one of Italy's most popular tourist attractions.

⬆ Hadrian's wall was defended by ditches. At every Roman mile (1500 m) there was a mini fort with a tower to guard crossing points.

Where are the Petronas Towers?

In Malaysia, where they are a national symbol. The USA was the first country to build skyscrapers in the 1800s, but countries all over the world have competed to build taller skyscrapers. In 1996 the twin Petronas Towers rose high above the city of Kuala Lumpur and Malaysia was number one in the skyscraper charts. The towers are 452 m high, and house 88 storeys of offices.

Some inspiring and very large buildings have been erected for religious worship. Often, as with medieval cathedrals in Europe, construction took many years. Sometimes, the same building has served two faiths – Hagia Sophia in Constantinople (now Istanbul) was built as a Christian church, but later became a Muslim mosque. It is now a museum.

What are the world's biggest religious buildings?

The world's biggest Christian church is St Peter's in Rome (1506–1614). But bigger still is the Hindu temple-city of Angkor Wat. Built by the Khmer people of Cambodia in the 1100s, its moated enclosure measures 1,500 by 1,400 m, and it has five central towers, the tallest 70 m high. The moat around Angkor Wat measures 6 km. The temple was abandoned in the 1400s.

Where can 300,000 people pray together?

In a mosque. It is where followers of Islam (Muslims) gather for prayers. The biggest Muslim mosque is the Shah Faisal Mosque in Islamabad, Pakistan. Inside its courtyard, 40,000 people can worship. The building is named after a ruler of Saudi Arabia who helped pay for its construction. It is situated on the outskirts of Pakistan's capital city, Islamabad, which means 'place of Islam'.

Buddhism spread from India across Southeast Asia to the islands of Indonesia. Borobudur is on the island of Java.

Which temple has 500 Buddhas?

The biggest Buddhist temple is Borobudur in Java, Indonesia. Built in the AD 700s, it fell into disuse about 1000 years ago, but was restored in the early 1900s. It was built by shaping a small hill and casing it with stone blocks. The Borobudur temple has 500 images of Buddha (Siddhartha Gautama) and thousands of other sculptures. The decoration shows links with Persian, Babylonian and Greek styles. Since 1972 all of the temple's 800,000 stones have been taken away, cleaned and replaced.

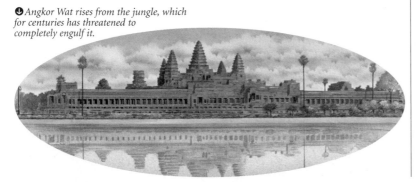

Angkor Wat rises from the jungle, which for centuries has threatened to completely engulf it.

What is the Taj Mahal?

The Taj Mahal is a tomb, built for Mumtaz Mahal, wife of the Mogul emperor of India, Shah Jahan. When she died in 1629, her husband ordered a special tomb to be built for her. It took 20,000 workers 20 years to complete the white marble building with its graceful minarets (towers). Under the white marble dome, which is 60–m–high, the emperor and his wife are buried together.

⊙ *The Taj Mahal, located near the city of Agra in India, is considered to be one of the world's greatest architectural treasures.*

⊙ *St Paul's Cathedral survived bombs during the Blitz in World War II (1939–45).*

Which is Britain's most famous cathedral?

Probably St Paul's Cathedral in London. Sir Christopher Wren's building (1675–1710) replaced a medieval cathedral burned down in the Great Fire of 1666. However, it has rivals, such as Westminster Abbey, begun by Edward the Confessor in the 1040s, and York Minster, England's biggest medieval cathedral. Many people also visit Canterbury Cathedral, which dates from the 1070s, and Salisbury Cathedral, which has the tallest spire in England at 123 m. The world's biggest cathedral (though not the biggest church) is the medieval-style Cathedral of St John the Divine, which is in New York City.

Technology – the application of science – has changed our lives amazingly. We can send space probes deep into space and take pictures with a mobile telephone. In the early 1800s, before the first steam train or camera had been invented, people would have regarded such marvels as fantasy – or magic.

↑ *Thrust SSC was designed to keep its wheels on the ground – and not become a flying car!*

What were the biggest airships of all time?

The biggest flying machines in the 1930s were two German airships. They were called the *Hindenburg* and *Graf Zeppelin*. At 245 m, they were longer than passenger jets are today. Powered by propellers, the airships cruised at around130 km/h across the oceans.The loss of the *Hindenburg*, which exploded in 1937, brought the age of passenger airships to an end.

Which car went supersonic?

In 1997 Andy Green (GB) drove the British jet Thrust SSC car across the flat sands of the Black Rock Desert in Nevada in the USA. He travelled at a speed faster than sound. His top speed of 1,227.985 km/h became a new land speed record. The car featured two Rolls-Royce Spey 205 jet engines, and it travelled faster than a jet airliner. The Thrust SSC also reached speeds more than three times faster than the fastest conventional-engined car – a 1998 McLaren F-1.

How do scientists explore distant worlds?

By studying the Universe with telescopes on the ground, and by sending telescopes into orbit around the Earth and spacecraft on journeys across the Solar System. In January 2004, scientists watched pictures of the planet Mars taken by NASA's Spirit rover. Robots make good space explorers. Astronauts need food, water and air. Robots just need energy, so they can keep sending back data. Mars Pathfinder carried a small rover called *Sojourner* to Mars in 1997. It was only about the size of a microwave oven.

⊕ *Robot explorers can trundle around millions of kilometres from Earth, beaming back pictures of Mars.*

⦿ Great Eastern *was not a success as a passenger ship, but it did lay a telegraph cable across the Atlantic Ocean.*

Which was the most wondrous ship of its day?

The *Great Eastern* was a giant in its day (1858). Over 19,000 tonnes and 211 m long, it was bigger than any ship built in the next 40 years. Designed by British engineer Isambard Kingdom Brunel, *Great Eastern* was the only ship to have screw propellers driven by its steam engines, but it also had paddle-wheels for extra power and a full set of sails.

Which is the world's fastest train?

The French TGV – a high-speed train that normally travels at around 300 km/h but in 1990 sped along at a world record speed of 515 km/h. It set the world speed record on a national rail system between Courtalain and Tours. Modern high-speed trains are five times faster than the first steam trains of the 1830s. The fastest speed reached by a steam train was 202.73 km/h by the British LNER locomotive *Mallard* in 1938. Maglev trains are exceptionally fast, as they are suspended by powerful magnets above a guide track. Early versions were built in Germany and Japan, and in 1996 a maglev train started operating at Disney World in Florida, USA. In 2002, a German-built maglev train in Shanghai, China topped 430 km/h.

Which were the biggest vehicles ever?

The biggest vehicles ever made were two Marion crawlers, giant tractors used by the US space agency NASA to move rockets and space shuttles into position for launching. The crawlers have eight caterpillar tracks and when loaded each weighs 8,000 tonnes – about 15 times heavier than the biggest dumper trucks (over 500 tonnes). They were developed to carry an assembled Saturn rocket on its 5-mile journey from the assembly building to the launching pad.

⦿ *High-speed trains run on special express routes across Europe, North America and Japan.*

Engineering puts scientific knowledge to practical use. While the construction of the Egyptian pyramids was one of the greatest engineering feats of ancient times, today there is no end to the marvels that engineering can offer – a bridge soaring high above water, a tunnel beneath the ocean and a telescope orbiting in space.

Which telescope orbits our planet?

The Space Telescope. Telescopes on the Earth get only a murky view of the stars, because the atmosphere (the air around the planet) gets in the way. The Hubble Space Telescope was launched into orbit in 1990 to give astronomers a clearer look at the Universe. It circles the Earth at a height of about 600 km, and from above the atmosphere it can observe objects 50 times fainter than Earth telescopes can see.

❶ The Space Telescope is named after the American astronomer Edwin Hubble (1889–1953) who made important discoveries about galaxies (star clusters).

❶ Suspension bridges such as the Akashi Kaikyo Bridge in Japan can carry road or rail traffic. The weight of the bridge is hung (suspended) between the tall towers.

How are very long bridges held up?

The world's longest bridges are suspension bridges, held up by wire cables slung between high towers. The Akashi Kaikyo Bridge links Japan's main island, Honshu, with the neighbouring island of Shikoku. The bridge spans 2 km of sea – the longest road bridge in the world.

❶ The white cladding on the shells of the Sydney Opera House is built from one million ceramic tiles.

Which is Australia's most famous building?

The Sydney Opera House (1973) is Australia's most famous building. Danish architect Joern Utzon designed its futuristic look – the materials needed for the roofs had not been invented when work began in 1959. The white shell roof structures are thought to echo the shape of the sails of the boats in the harbour, and beneath them are theatres and performance halls.

● *The Akosombo Dam was built in the 1960s, to supply electricity to Ghana and neighbouring countries.*

Where can you sail through a desert?

When ships use the Suez Canal, to travel between the Mediterranean and Red seas, the dry desert lands of Egypt lies on either bank. When a canal was first suggested, critics said the hot sun would dry up the water. The Suez Canal was opened in 1869, shortening the sea route between Britain and India by almost 10,000 km. The canal is about 180 km long, around 225 m wide at the surface (it gets narrower as it nears the bottom) and 20 m deep.

Where do trains travel under the sea?

Trains speed through the Channel Tunnel (Eurotunnel) under the sea between Britain and France. There are three tunnels: two rail tunnels and a smaller service tunnel, running for over 14 km under the sea and 30 km underground. The idea of a Channel tunnel was first suggested in the 1800s, but it was not until 1994 that the first high-speed trains began using Eurotunnel.

Which dam made the biggest lake?

The biggest artificial lake is Lake Volta in Ghana, west Africa. When a dam is built across a river, the water held up behind the barrier forms a lake. This water can then be used for irrigation or to drive hydro-electric turbines. Lake Volta has an area of more than 8,000 sq km, but it is still small compared to North America's biggest Great Lake, Lake Superior (82,000 sq km).

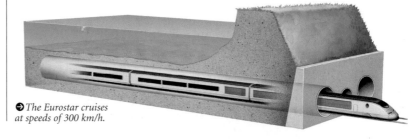

● *The Eurostar cruises at speeds of 300 km/h.*

Memorials help us remember events or people. Some memorials are so big that it's impossible to miss them. But others are hidden. Sometimes, treasures found in the ground reveal hidden stories about a long-lost past.

What was unearthed at Sutton Hoo?

A king who ruled East Anglia in England in the 600s. He was buried in a wooden ship, 27 m long. The ship had been placed in a trench, and inside lay the body of a warrior, probably a powerful local king called Raedwald of the East Angles. He had been buried with clothes, weapons and treasure. Then his ship-grave had been filled in. The ship-burial remained undiscovered until unearthed by archaeologists at Sutton Hoo in Suffolk in 1939.

⬆ *A replica of the Sutton Hoo helmet, found in the ship-burial.*

⬆ *The Gateway Arch is the tallest monument in the USA. It was completed in 1965.*

Whose journey is remembered by a giant arch?

American pioneers. The Gateway to the West in St Louis, USA is an192-m U-shaped arch that stands beside the Mississippi River. It commemorates the migration of thousands of settlers who set off in wagon trains to make new homes in the West in the 1840s–1870s.

Who was buried with an army of clay soldiers?

The Chinese emperor, Shih Huang-di, in around 210 BC. The ancient Chinese believed their dead rulers would need servants and soldiers in the after-life. So when Shi Huang-di, the first Qin emperor, died his tomb was filled with clay models of soldiers. Archaeologists were amazed to find them in 1974 when part of the huge imperial tomb complex was opened.

⬇ *The terracotta clay warriors of the Chinese emperor's immortal army.*

Whose tomb revealed a lost treasure?

Tutankhamun, who became king of Egypt about 1347 BC but died aged 18. He was buried in the Valley of the Kings. In 1922, his tomb was found by the British archaeologist Howard Carter. Inside were astonishing treasures – more than 5,000 objects including chests, necklaces, chariots, swords, ostrich feathers, models of ships, toys and jars of precious oils.

Among the finds in Tutankhamun's tomb was the gold death mask of the young king.

The Spaniards never found the Inca fortress of Machu Picchu. Today, half a million tourists visit it every year.

Which leaders stare out from a mountain?

Four US presidents, whose stone heads loom from rocky Mount Rushmore in South Dakota, USA. Carving work began in 1927. It took four years to build and cost $1 million. Each head is as big as a five-storey building and the faces tower 1,800 m above sea level. The carvings are scaled to men who would stand 141 m tall. On each carving, the president's nose is 6 m long, the mouth 5 m wide and the eyes are 3 m across. The Mount Rushmore National Memorial honours four of the most important US Presidents – these are George Washington, Thomas Jefferson, Theodore Roosevelt and Abraham Lincoln.

Where did the last Incas live in secret?

High in the Andes, at Machu Picchu and other strongholds. The Spaniards conquered the Inca civilization in the 1500s, but never managed to capture the Incas' last stronghold. The ruins of the walled Inca city of Machu Picchu lie in the mountains near Cuzco in Peru. Machu Picchu remained unknown to the world until discovered by an American explorer, Hiram Bingham, in 1911. The local people called it 'Machu Picchu', meaning 'old mountain'.

Natural landscapes are true wonders of the world. Mountains form great chains, or ranges, such as the Andes and Rocky mountains. There are great lakes, mighty rivers, grinding glaciers, seas so salty no one can sink and ice sheets so thick you could bury several office blocks beneath them!

❶ *Snow-capped Himalayan peaks in Nepal provide a dramatic view.*

Where are the world's mightiest mountains?

The highest mountains in the world are the Himalaya–Karakoram range in Asia. This great range has the world's top 20 peaks, all over 8,000 m high, and includes the world's highest peak, Mount Everest. The Himalayas are also one of the youngest mountain belts, as they were formed within the last 50 million years. The highest range of mountains in the western hemisphere is the Andes, which has more than 50 peaks that top 6,000 m.

Which is the strangest lake?

Probably the Dead Sea, which is actually a lake about nine times saltier than the oceans, such as the Pacific. The Dead Sea is in the Middle East, and is entirely surrounded by hot desert. The heat makes the seawater evaporate, leaving behind a high concentration of salt. Because of this, a bather can float in the water with no effort.

Where is the thickest ice?

In Antarctica, where the thickest ice is 4,800 m deep – more than ten times the height of the tallest building in the world. Antarctica is much bigger than Europe or Australia, but this is mainly because of the vast area of ice that covers the rock beneath. Situated at the southernmost tip of the Earth, it is large and mountainous. Antarctica is even colder than the Arctic and very dangerous. It has about 90 per cent of all the ice on the planet and is the windiest and driest of the continents. Antarctica was first explored by man less than 200 years ago, because the extremes of temperature were so great, yet millions of years ago it was ice-free and animals roamed there.

❶ *Antarctica is the only continent with no permanent human population and no trees.*

Where is Monument Valley?

In the state of Utah in the USA. Here, red sandstone rocks rise up from the desert, looking like towers and castles. The rocks are hundreds of millions of years old, and the 'monuments' have been shaped by weathering by wind, rain, frost and sun.

Where are there too many trees to count?

In the Amazon rainforest of South America, which has more trees of varying species than anywhere else. Tropical rainforests have about ten times as many tree species in a typical area than a cool-climate forest. Where you might find ten trees in a European forest, you might find 100 in the Amazon. Unfortunately the Amazon has been very badly damaged by 'deforestation' (logging) in recent years.

⊕ The lush tropical jungle of the Amazon remains one of the greatest natural wonders.

⊕ Monument Valley is a favourite location for film-makers because of its spectacular scenery.

Which is the world's biggest desert?

The Sahara in Africa, which has an area of over 9 million sq km. It covers much of northern Africa. The continent with the most deserts is Asia – it has four. Most of the Sahara is gravel, but in the sandy areas huge wave-like hummocks, or dunes, are pushed along by the wind. Cave paintings found near the region, drawn by ancient people, depict grassland animals. This shows that thousands of years ago the Sahara was wetter, with lakes and plains.

⊕ In parts of the Sahara there are sand dunes over 400 m high.

Planet Earth is the only planet in our Solar System with such a staggering variety of stupendous sights, from vast canyons to thundering waterfalls. Many of these natural wonders have been here for far longer than human-beings. Most have taken millions of years to gradually evolve to how they are today.

⊕ *The Angel Falls in South America.*

What makes the Grand Canyon so grand?

The Grand Canyon in the United States is the largest gorge in the world. The canyon is an enormous winding gash, about 446 km long and from 1.6 to 29 km wide. It is

⊕ *The rocks of the Grand Canyon change colour as the light changes during the day.*

getting deeper still, as the waters of the Colorado River continue to gradually cut away the rocks. Some rocks in the Grand Canyon are two billion years old.

Which waterfall is higher than a skyscraper?

Angel Falls in Venezuela is the highest waterfall in the world. Angel Falls has a total height of 979 m and its longest unbroken drop is 807 m. They are named after Jimmy Angel, an American pilot, who saw the spectacular Falls when he flew over them in 1935 while searching for gold.

◗ *Uluru glows orange-red with reflected light at sunrise and sunset. The rock has lots of small caves, many of which are covered with Aboriginal paintings.*

Which is America's most destructive volcano?

Mount St Helens, a volcano in the Cascade Mountains, Washington state, on the west coast. It has erupted many times in its ancient history, and in 1980 it blew its top violently. Shaken by an earthquake measuring 5.1 on the Richter scale, the north face of this tall symmetrical mountain collapsed in a massive rock debris avalanche. The explosion blew off the peak's top, and sent hot ash and smoke high into the air. The forest caught fire, melting snow caused landslides, and millions of trees were instantly flattened. Nearly 78 sq km of forest was blown over or was left dead but still standing, and 57 people were killed. The eruption lasted nine hours, but Mount St Helens and the surrounding landscape were dramatically changed within moments. Scientists expect Mount St Helens to erupt again in the future, but cannot predict exactly when it might happen.

Which is Australia's biggest pebble?

Uluru or Ayers Rock in Australia. This massive loaf-shaped block of sandstone, more than 480 million years old, lies in the Northern Territory and is 348 m high, over 2.4 km long and 1.6 km wide. The aboriginal name for the rock, now commonly used, is Uluru and means 'great pebble'. The rock is a sacred aboriginal site.

Which is the longest coral reef?

The Great Barrier Reef in Australia, which stretches for about 2,010 km along the northeast coast of Australia. A coral reef is a limestone formation made of the hardened skeletons of dead water animals called polyps. Billions of living polyps are attached to the reef. Most of the Great Barrier Reef is a national park, and an ideal environment for about 1,500 kinds of fish, crabs, giant clams, sea turtles and birds.

◗ *Scientists believe the Great Barrier Reef began to form about 30 million years ago.*

Nature's record-breakers come in all shapes and sizes, from tiny insects to enormous trees. Many animals can perform incredible feats of strength, speed and endurance. No human athlete could compete with the top animal record-breakers.

● Termites are sometimes called white ants, but they are not related to ants.

● The cheetah has long legs and at full speed its back arches for extra power.

Which is the fastest land animal?

Cheetahs are the world's fastest land animals and can move as fast as a car. Within two seconds of starting a chase a cheetah may be running at 75 km/h, and it soon reaches a top speed of about 105 km/h. Cheetahs run out of energy after only 30 seconds of sprinting, so if an antelope can keep out of the cheetah's jaws for this short time, it may escape. Cheetahs do not often climb trees as they have difficulty in getting down again. They prefer wide open spaces, where they can easily spot prey, such as gazelles and hares.

Where is the most massive tree?

The heaviest tree is a giant sequoia or 'big tree' called General Sherman, growing in Sequoia National Park, California, USA. This forest giant can reach up to 84 m high and has an average measurement of 31.4 m round its trunk. It weighs about 2,500 tonnes – as much as 350 elephants. The giant redwood is the tallest tree, growing up to 113 m tall. They can live for over a thousand years – one redwood in California is 2,200 years old.

● Giant redwood trees grow even taller than sequoias, but their trunks are not as thick.

Why are termites so astounding?

Termites are social insects – they live in colonies. Some termites are also stupendous builders, making huge mound nests. The tallest known termite mound measured almost 9 m high. Amazingly, the termite workers who build such nests are blind – as are the soldiers that protect the nest from enemies. Termite queens live up to 50 years, making them the longest-lived insects.

Which animal gives birth to the biggest baby?

The blue whale, the biggest of the great whales. The blue whale is the largest living animal in the world. Its main arteries are so large that a small person could crawl through them. At birth, a blue whale calf (baby) is already 6 to 8 m long. It has to be helped to the surface to take its first breath of air – whales are mammals, not fish. Mammals are not the biggest group of animals, but they have bigger brains in relation to their body size than other animals. The lifespan of a blue whale is estimated to be 80 years. Usually they travel alone or in small groups of two to four, although off the coast of California some groups as large as 60 have been seen.

❯ The biggest sea and land animals are mammals – the whales in the ocean and the elephants on land.

Which is the biggest of all big cats?

The Siberian tiger, from eastern Russia and China, is longer and heavier than a lion. The most northerly species of tiger, its thick fur keeps it warm in the winter snows. A tiger needs a large hunting territory and only a few hundred Siberian tigers now survive in the wild.

❶ Siberian tigers may weigh as much as 350 kg and measure 3 m in length. Tigers are only found in small regions of southern and eastern Asia. They live in a range of habitats, from tropical forests to Siberian woodlands.

How many kinds of elephant are there?

Three. Scientists used to answer 'two': the big-eared African elephant and the smaller-eared Asiatic or Indian elephant. Recent research, however, has shown that there are in fact two species of African elephant: a bigger kind that lives on the grassy plains and a smaller kind that prefers the forest. Elephants trunks are unique among living mammals – they enable elephants to manipulate tiny objects or tear down huge tree limbs. Large, flappable ears help these huge animals to cool off in hot climates.

1 Which of the Seven Wonders of the Ancient World was destroyed by an earthquake?

2 Which world wonder stood at Babylon?

3 Which world wonder was found hidden under a swamp?

4 What is the name of the ancient script used by the Egyptians?

5 The great sphinx has the head of a human and the body of what?

6 How many pharaohs had pyramids built at Giza?

7 Which German castle was the model for Walt Disney's theme park in California, USA?

8 Which G word was a fighting slave trained to entertain the citizens of ancient Rome?

9 In which mythology is Zeus the king of the Gods?

10 Which Roman arena was named after the statue Colossus?

11 What are the giant stone statues on Easter Island called?

12 How far did the makers of Stonehenge bring the bluestones?

13 Which ancient mound is situated near Avebury, UK?

14 What is the name for the ditch that is dug around castles?

FACTFILE

Gods of **Greece and Rome**

	Greek	Roman
King of the gods	Zeus	Jupiter
War	Ares	Mars
Wife of Zeus	Hera	Juno
Wisdom	Athena	Minerva
Good harvests	Demeter	Ceres
Underworld	Hades	Pluto
Love	Eros	Cupid
Music and arts	Apollo	Apollo

Up **Pompeii**

Today, visitors to Pompeii walk into houses and down lanes, just as the Pompeiians did. In museums, they can see domestic items and the remains of people killed by the volcano. Volcanic ash hardened around victims' bodies, and formed a mould. As the bodies decayed, a shell was left. By filling the shells with plaster, archaeologists have made copies of the bodies.

15 Which is the largest castle in England?

16 What is the safest part of a castle called?

17 How many rooms are there in the Forbidden City?

18 Which palace was built for the Duke of Marlborough?

19 Who the first president to live in the White House?

20 Which Roman built a wall on the border of England and Scotland?

21 Which rock is the temple of Abu Simbel carved from?

Key **dates**

509 BC	Rome set up a republic
479 BC	Greeks defeated the Persians
461–429 BC	Pericles led Athens; he ordered the Parthenon to be built
431–494 BC	Athens and Sparta at war: Sparta won
334–326 BC	Alexander the Great conquered a vast empire
140s BC	Rome conquered Greece
55–54 BC	Julius Caesar landed with an army in Britain
27 BC	Augustus became Rome's first emperor
AD 43	Romans invaded Britain
117	End of reign of Emperor Trajan, when Rome was at its peak
476	Fall of the Roman empire

Gladiator **fights**

For the ancient Romans, violence and bloodshed were used as entertainment. Gladiators were made to fight to the death to please the crowd. They fought in an arena and used lots of different weapons. Most fights took place in Rome, but cities throughout the Roman Empire had arenas for these events.

➲ *Gladiator fights were usually fights to the death.*

22 What is the name of the valley in Utah where the red sandstone rocks have been formed into dramatic shapes by the elements?

23 In which city is the Eiffel Tower?

24 What was the leaning tower of Pisa built to house?

25 Which capital city surrounds the Vatican city?

26 In which city is the Taj Mahal?

27 In which London building is the Whispering Gallery?

28 What was the name of the first space shuttle?

29 What vehicles are used to move space shuttles?

FACTFILE

Amazing **facts**

- Though no longer the tallest skyscraper, the Sears Tower in Chicago, USA (443 m) still has the most floors: 110.

- The first skyscraper was built by Le Baron Jenney in Chicago, 1885. It had just ten floors.

- The Empire State Building, New York City, is probably the world's most recognized tall building; built in 1931 it is 381 m high.

➲ *The Ananda Temple in Myanma, Burma, was completed in 1091. It rises in graduated terraces to a height of 52 m.*

30 In which year did the *Thrust SSC* break the sound barrier on land?

31 In which country is the Aswan Dam?

32 What is the closest bridge to the Houses of Parliament?

33 What is the name of the longest suspension bridge?

34 In which mountain range did the ancient Incas live?

35 Who is buried beneath the Arc de Triomphe in Paris?

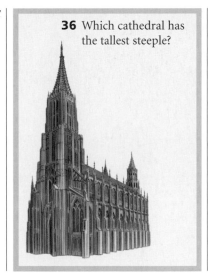

36 Which cathedral has the tallest steeple?

37 In which US state does Mount Rushmore lie?

38 Which is the longest African river?

39 Mount Snowdon is the highest peak in which European country?

40 Which is the world's largest desert?

41 What is the name of the largest canyon in North America?

42 Which waterfalls were first named 'the smoke that thunders'?

Above the clouds

In the Middle Ages, the tallest buildings were church spires and campaniles (bell-towers). Sometimes cathedral builders aimed too high and towers fell down. The main spire of Lincoln Cathedral in England was the highest in the world (160 m) until 1548, when it collapsed. Each of its three towers had spires – today there are none.

Extreme **measures**

Longest wall	The Great Wall of China
Tallest tower	CN Tower in Canada 555 m high
Most famous seaside tower	Blackpool, England
Longest Roman wall	Hadrian's Wall, northern Britain
Most topsy-turvy tower	Leaning Tower of Pisa, Italy
Biggest pagoda	Shwe Dagon pagoda, Burma
Most gloomy tower	Bloody Tower in the Tower of London
Noisiest tower	The legendary Tower of Babel

Architects have speculated as to whether the top-most storey of the Leaning Tower should be removed, in an effort to stabilize it.

43 Which natural landmark is bigger than the US state of Texas?

44 Which animal can reach speeds of over 120 km/h?

45 Which animal is 6 to 8 m long at birth?

46 What substance makes up an elephant's tusks?

47 Which wonder stretches for 6,400 km across Northern China?

FACTFILE

Ancient **treasures**

The Egyptians believed in life after death and made careful preparations for death and burial. They believed it was important to preserve the body of a dead person. The body was treated with chemicals and oils and then dried, to stop it decaying. The mummy was wrapped in linen bandages and put in a coffin, inside a tomb, along with clothes, weapons, jewels and food.

Famous **monuments**

The highest column in the world commemorates the battle of San Jacinto, fought between Texans and Mexicans in 1836. Britain's famous monuments include The Monument (a column marking the spot in London where the Great Fire of 1666 began) and Nelson's Column in Trafalgar Square in London, with a statue of Admiral Horatio Nelson on top.

◑ *When ready for burial, a mummy was placed inside a special coffin. Some of these were shaped and richly decorated.*

Answers

1 The Colossus of Rhodes	16 The Keep	31 Egypt	46 Ivory
2 The Hanging Gardens	17 9,000	32 Westminster Bridge	47 The Great Wall of China
3 The Temple of Artemis	18 Blenheim Palace	33 The Akashi Kaikyo Bridge	
4 Hieroglyphs	19 John Adams	34 The Andes	
5 A lion	20 Hadrian	35 The unknown soldier	
6 Three	21 Sandstone	36 Baum Cathedral	
7 Neuschwanstein Castle	22 Monument Valley	37 South Dakota	
8 Gladiator	23 Paris	38 Nile River	
9 Greek	24 A bell	39 Wales	
10 The Colosseum	25 Rome	40 Sahara Desert	
11 *Moai*	26 India	41 Grand Canyon	
12 385 km	27 St Paul's Cathedral	42 Victoria Falls	
13 Silbury Hill	28 Columbia	43 Great Barrier Reef	
14 Moat	29 Marion crawlers	44 Cheetah	
15 Windsor Castle	30 1997	45 Blue whale	

Treasure **hoards**

Tutankhamun's tomb – opened by Howard Carter in 1922 and found to still contain many of its fantastic treasures.

Inca loot – In 1532 the Spanish conquistador Pizarro demanded a huge ransom for the Inca leader Atahualpa – a roomful of gold, and another filled with silver. The Incas paid, but the Spaniards still killed Atahualpa. They melted down the treasures to make gold and silver bars.

Pirate treasure – Captain Kidd and other pirates may have hidden treasure on lonely islands, but wrecked ships are the best places to search!

➲ *Treasure divers still hunt for wrecks of ships lost in storms around Britain in 1588 thought to have been carrying Spanish gold.*

ARTS, SPORTS & ENTERTAINMENT

Many thousands of years ago, artists began to decorate the world in which they lived. Art can strengthen traditional values, spread new ideas, or preserve a treasured heritage from past times. It takes many forms, from words and language to dance and performance. Sport also has its roots thousands of years ago. The first Olympic Games took place in Greece in 776 BC.

Who were the first successful rock stars?

What makes a good design?

Which emperor had clay soldiers in his tomb?

People have played and listened to music ever since Stone Age cave-dwellers banged drums and shook rattles. Throughout the centuries, instruments were refined and developed, and the skills needed to play them were taught to others. Music has been written down only since about 1800 BC. A huge variety of different musical styles has been developed across the world, including classical, opera, folk, reggae, jazz, soul, rock and pop.

What are the four main groups of instruments?

The main groups of instruments are wind, stringed, percussion and brass. Wind and brass instruments are played by blowing down a hollow tube with holes in. Stringed instruments have strings stretched tight across a hollow box; the strings are vibrated with a bow (violin) plucked with the fingers or a plectrum (guitar). Percussion instruments such as drums and cymbals make sounds when struck by hammers, sticks or the hands.

French horn

Violin and bow

Guitar

Conga drums

🔼 *These are examples from three of the musical instrument groups: French horn (brass), violin and guitar (strings) and conga drums (percussion).*

Who are the greatest composers?

People may never agree on 'the greatest-ever composer', but many music-lovers place Wolfgang Amadeus Mozart (1756–91), Ludwig van Beethoven (1770–1827) and Johann Sebastian Bach (1685–1750) among their favourites. Notable works by these musical geniuses include Bach's *Brandenburg Concertos*, Beethoven's *Ode to Joy* and *5th Symphony*, and Mozart's *Eine Kleine Nachtmusik*.

J. S. Bach

Mozart

Beethoven

🔼 *All three composers wrote music for small groups of musicians as well as for full orchestras.*

Who were the first successful rock stars?

The first rock superstar was Elvis Presley, who had 94 gold singles and more than 40 gold albums. Then in the 1960s, the Beatles began their career, which made them the biggest-selling group of all time. The first solo singer to sell one million records was the opera singer Enrico Caruso. Until the 20th century, popular songs were only heard when people sang or played them 'live'. Recorded sound, which dates from the 1880s, changed the way people listened to music, and radio and the record industry combined to create the 'pop' industry, which began in the 1940s with the creation of the first popular hit charts.

⬇ *The Beatles from left to right: Paul McCartney, Ringo Starr, George Harrison and John Lennon.*

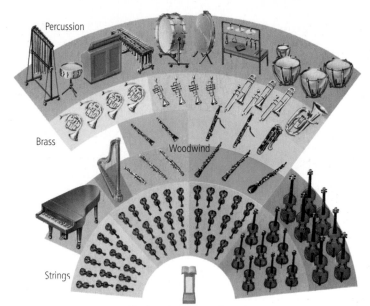

Conductor's position – the rostrum

⬆ *The instruments of the symphony orchestra are arranged in groups in an arc in front of the conductor – strings at the front, then wind, and percussion at the back.*

Percussion

Brass

Woodwind

Strings

Who wrote the longest opera?

The five longest operas (all lasting more than five hours) were written by the 19th-century German composer Richard Wagner. The longest of Wagner's operas is *The Twilight of the Gods.* An opera is a play in which the actors sing as they act, and in which music plays a much more important part than plot, dialogue or set. Operas were first staged around 1600 in Italy.

How many instruments make up an orchestra?

The modern orchestra has about 100 musicians. Orchestras have four main sections: woodwind (clarinets, flutes, oboes and bassoons), brass (horns and trumpets), percussion (drums, cymbals and bells) and strings (violins, violas, cellos and double basses). The biggest orchestra of all time had 987 instruments and was assembled in 1872 in Boston, USA.

The earliest art was made by Stone Age people, who painted pictures on walls and made figures from stone and clay. There are many kinds of art – from famous paintings sold for many millions of pounds at auction to clay pots made by children in school. Art can puzzle as well as astound. Some artists have wrapped cliffs in plastic, covered buildings in cloth, displayed a bed with dirty washing, put a dead animal in a case and cut away half a mountain in their efforts to create a unique piece.

What does a sculptor do?

Sculptors are artists who make models, such as figures carved in wood or stone, or cast in metal. The two most common techniques in sculpture are carving and moulding. Modern sculptors also create art from assembling pieces of scrap, plastic or even paper. A figure of the native Indian known as Crazy Horse being cut into the rock of Thunderhead Mountain in South Dakota, USA (still not finished after over 50 years) will be 172 m high when it is completed.

Who was Picasso?

Picasso was one of the most successful painters of the 20th century. His full name was Pablo Ruiz y Picasso; he was born in Spain in 1881 and died in 1973. He began by painting in a traditional, realistic style but then began depicting figures as fragments of geometric shapes – this style became known as Cubism. One of his most famous pictures is called *Guernica* and portrays the suffering of people during the Spanish Civil War in the 1930s.

⊘ *Picasso was a prolific artist who worked on canvas in several styles. Unlike many other artists, Picasso also earned a lot of money from his work.*

⊙ *The Venus de Milo is one of the most famous sculptures. This Roman copy of the Greek original is in The Louvre museum in Paris.*

What is ceramics?

Ceramics is the art of making fine pottery, using clay. Potters have made everyday items such as beakers and plates for more than 5,000 years. Examples of pottery are earthenware bowls, Greek and Chinese vases, and terracotta heads and figures. Painted and glazed porcelain (the most delicate form of pottery) was first made in China about 1,300 years ago.

⊘ *Porcelain vases were made in China during the period known as the Ming dynasty (1368–1644), when the arts flourished.*

⊘ Wall paintings like this are found in the tombs of Egyptian kings and queens. This picture shows a hunting scene beside the River Nile. Cave paintings depict life at the time of their creation, more than 15,000 years ago.

What is a fresco?

A fresco is a painting on a wall. In ancient Egypt, teams of master artists worked on large wall paintings. Different minerals were used to make different colours – carbon for black, ochre for red and yellow, and azurite and malachite for green and blue. During the Middle Ages and the Renaissance, frescoes were a favourite form of decoration in Europe. Fresco artists paint on fresh plaster while it is wet, so they have to work fast. They begin by drawing a sketch, from which they trace the outline on the plaster, and then brush in the colours. As the plaster dries and hardens, the colours are bonded to the wall.

What kind of paints did cave painters use?

The paints used by cave painters, more than 12,000 years ago, were made from everyday materials, such as coloured soil, clay, animal fat, soot and charcoal from their fires and the roots of plants. They painted the animals they hunted, such as ibex, wild ox and deer. The artists did not use brushes but painted with their fingers, sometimes leaving an impression of their hands, perhaps as a signature.

⊘ This drawing of a wild ox was made by one of the cave painters in Lascaux, France.

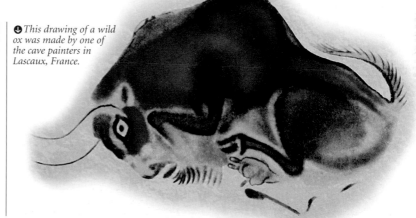

Design involves planning, and a designer's job is to create something new, either from brand new materials or by reassembling existing ones. Designers often have to be part-artist, part-engineer and part-salesperson. Some of those whose work includes design are architects, engineers, fashion designers, gardeners, graphic artists (who design books and magazines), interior decorators, stage- and movie-set designers and shop-window dressers.

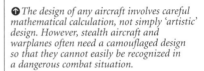

⊙ *The design of any aircraft involves careful mathematical calculation, not simply 'artistic' design. However, stealth aircraft and warplanes often need a camouflaged design so that they cannot easily be recognized in a dangerous combat situation.*

Who designed the pyramids?

The Egyptian architects who built the pyramids were scribes, astronomers and government officials, the most famous of whom was Imhotep. He lived in the 2500s BC and one of his many jobs was court physician to King Djoser. He designed the Step Pyramid at Saqqara in Egypt, as a tomb for the king. Architects design buildings by making drawings and doing calculations, but today they also use computers to picture the finished design, to see the inside, and to show how any changes will alter the product.

⊙ *The only step pyramid ever completed is situated at Saqqara. It was built by King Djoser.*

What makes a good design?

There are several principles of design, including balance, repetition, rhythm and unity (overall effect). Design is the basis of every manufacturing process, but however much fun it is to design a complex object, it will not be a success unless it can be manufactured and sold. Design involves arranging materials for a particular or desired effect – either for pleasure or to fulfil a particular function, such as a commission. If a design looks good and works efficiently, people will want to use it. The design of a warplane involves careful mathematical calculation, not simply 'artistic' design. Their strength and safety are just as important as their appearance, which is often camouflaged.

A Victorian sitting room was designed for people to sit, read, and amuse themselves in.

Who first used furniture?

The first people to use furniture were the ancient Egyptians – we know this because they put chairs, stools and tables in their tombs. Thomas Chippendale wrote the first catalogue about furniture in England in 1754. It had drawings of the pieces he offered for sale, and his designs for chairs, tables and cabinets were widely imitated. A great deal of furniture made in the late 18th century is often described as 'Chippendale', because it describes a style, even though in most cases Chippendale himself was not involved.

Furniture designers copied styles of each other, such as Chippendale, as well as from designers abroad.

What was Victorian style like?

The Victorians were the first people to have factory-made curtains, chairs, carpets and household gadgets and so the style of their homes often looks cluttered to modern eyes. People liked lots of pictures and ornaments, and filled rooms with chairs, tables, lamps, bookcases and shelves. Victorian clothes look thick and heavy to us, and sombre colours were preferred. Queen Victoria's reign lasted from 1837 to 1901, so Victorians lived during a new industrial age.

When did the fashion industry begin?

When factory-made clothes went on sale in the 19th century, poorer people were able to buy cheap copies of fashionable clothes. Previously, wealthy people had always bought elegant clothes and set styles for others to copy. In the 20th century, fashion designers such as Coco Chanel and Christian Dior set up fashion 'houses', designing exclusive designs. In the 1960s–70s, youth fashion became the rage, and today designers and super-models rival pop and movie stars as world-famous celebrities.

In the 19th century, the clothes worn by wealthy women were copied by new fashion houses, who supplied cheap clothes to poorer people.

Architecture is the art and science of designing and constructing buildings. The architect has to consider the look, the technology, the site and the cost of the building. Much of early architecture comprised monumental temples, tombs and palaces. The Greeks introduced 'classical' rules of proportion and, ever since, architectural style has reflected the tastes of the age in which it is used.

When did the Greeks build temples?

Greek architecture began to take shape about 600 BC. The beauty of the Parthenon temple on the Acropolis hill in Athens typifies Greek architecture. The Greeks loved harmonious proportions. The roofs of their graceful buildings were supported by columns built in three main styles, known as Doric, Ionic and Corinthian, which became more decorative as time passed.

Where were the first skyscrapers built?

The first skyscrapers were built in the American city of Chicago after a fire in 1871 destroyed many of its buildings. The first skyscraper was the 10-storey Home Insurance Building. Developments that made skyscrapers possible included the use of steel girders to support tall buildings internally, and the invention of the electric lift, which meant that people did not have to use stairs to reach the upper floors.

◑ *Many skyscrapers, like these in Hong Kong, China, have more than 200 storeys. Plans are continually made to build higher and higher.*

◑ *The Parthenon was built between 447 and 432 BC, using classic principles of geometry.*

What is the world's most impressive building?

Many would suggest the Taj Mahal in India. The Mogul ruler of India, Shah Jahan, built the Taj Mahal for his favourite wife, Mumtaz Mahal, when she died in childbirth in 1629. He wanted her to have the most beautiful tomb in the world. More than 20,000 labourers and artists worked on the Taj Mahal, which took 20 years to complete. The domed building is made of white marble and rests on a sandstone platform.

⊕ *Each of the Taj Mahal's four minarets is 40 m high. The top of the dome is nearly 61 m above the floor, under which is the vault where Shah Jahan is buried with his wife.*

Where is the world's most famous opera house?

Sydney Opera House in Australia has been a world-famous landmark in Sydney Harbour since it was first opened in 1973. An opera house is a theatre, usually devoted to operatic production. Sydney Opera House is used for other events, such as performance art, and has a distinctive design, with a shaped roof that makes it look as if the building is about to set sail across the water. The building was designed by Danish architect, Jorn Lutzon.

When was Stonehenge built?

Stonehenge is a group of huge stones, set in a circle on Salisbury Plain in England, built in stages between 2800 and 1500 BC. The heavy stones were dragged and positioned in alignment with the rising and setting Sun at midsummer. Stonehenge was probably a gathering point and religious centre for local tribal groups.

What is the Louvre?

The Louvre is the national museum of France. It is located in the centre of Paris, and was originally a palace, used since the 1500s by the kings of France to house their art collections. It was first opened to the public in 1793 after the French Revolution. One of the modern features of the Louvre is the steel-and-glass pyramid entrance in the central courtyard, designed by American architect I.M. Pei. It now houses some of the world's finest paintings and works.

⊕ *The glass pyramid in the courtyard of the Louvre adds a new dimension to an old building.*

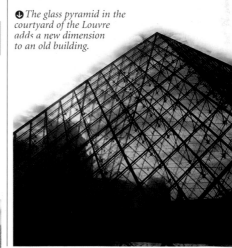

⊕ *The ancient stones of Stonehenge: some stones have fallen or been removed since the circle was first erected.*

The performing arts include performances by dancers, musicians, singers, actors and even puppets. Through these varied art forms, storytellers have long thrilled audiences, who have enjoyed the emotional experience of a 'show', whether it be comedy (humour) or tragedy (serious) or a mixture of the two.

⊙ *The modern circus clown developed from 'buffoons' who performed in Greek and Roman plays, sometimes throwing items such as nuts at the audience!*

Which country is most famous for its ballet?

Russia, as it has produced many fine dancers, including Vaslav Nijinsky, Rudolf Nureyev and Anna Pavlova, as well as famous ballet companies, who perform all over the world. However, ballet did not begin in Russia. It was first recognized as an art-form in the 1600s in France, and it was then that the five basic ballet positions were devised. Famous ballets include *Giselle, Swan Lake* and *Sleeping Beauty*.

⊙ *Steps in classical ballet use turn-out (feet pointing sideways) and pointe-work (dancing on tip-toes). Ballet dancers' must be very fit and their muscles extemely strong.*

How old are puppet performances?

Puppets are one of the earliest forms of performing entertainment. String puppets, also known as marionettes, have been popular for centuries. One of the traditions of the English seaside resort is the Punch and Judy show, performed by an entertainer who is concealed inside a cubicle using just his hands (inside glove puppets) and his voice. Other puppets have become famous as television celebrities in their own right, and some of the computer-generated figures have become almost life-like. In Indonesia people watch plays performed by 'shadow-puppets'.

When did the first circus appear?

In ancient Rome a circus was called a stadium. In the 1700s, showmen used the name 'circus' for horse shows in Europe. Philip Astley put on shows of trick-riding in the 1770s in London. Travelling circuses, which often included horses, wild animals, acrobats and clowns, became popular in the 1800s. The most famous circus is Ringling Brothers and Barnum and Bailey's (the two shows combined in 1919), which had the biggest ever Big Top (tent).

Who was the most famous silent comedian?

One of the most famous cinema stars **was Charlie Chaplin (1889–1977).** He was was also one of the first movie-stars. Chaplin learnt his craft as a comedian on the music-hall stage in London but then went to America where he made his name as a comic actor in silent movies. His success as a comedian has made him synonomous with silent movies.

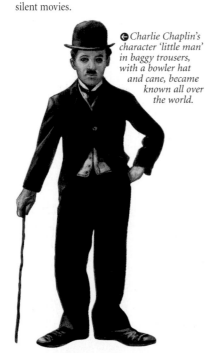

Charlie Chaplin's character 'little man' in baggy trousers, with a bowler hat and cane, became known all over the world.

Greeks sat in open-air theatres to watch one of two types of play: tragedies or comedies. Tragedies were serious plays and included a sad end, an unhappy love affair, a crime or a disaster. Comedies were humorous plays. Traditionally, tragedy and comedy were never mixed.

Fancy dress and masks are a feature of the carnival in Venice.

What is a carnival?

The original carnival was a religious holiday and feast, celebrated before the beginning of the Christian fasting period of Lent. The modern carnival is a huge outdoor theatre and parade, with dancers, decorated floats, entertainers and marching bands. Famous carnivals are held in Brazil, the USA and the UK.

Who went to the first theatres?

The first theatre-goers were the ancient Greeks, who gathered in hundreds and sat on hillsides to watch tragedies and comedies. Greek theatres were bowl-shaped arenas, surrounding a circular stage, called an orchestra. The Romans built stone theatres that could seat 40,000 to watch raucous comedies. The most successful playwright in the world is the English bard William Shakespeare (1564–1616), whose plays are staged all over the world and whose Globe Theatre has been recreated in London.

Cinema was made possible by the invention of the camera obscura and lantern slide, which projected pictures onto a screen. By the 1930s, millions of people visited the cinema every week. The advent of television in the 1950s, however, enabled more people to stay at home to watch TV and video movies on 'the box'. Now DVD (digital versatile disc) provides us with home entertainment unimagined by early pioneers of screen entertainment.

How did 'movies' develop?

Moving images, known as 'movies' developed in the early 1900s, after experiments with 'kinetoscope' peepshows. The first big movie was D. W. Griffith's epic *Birth of a Nation* in 1915. Early movies were silent and dialogue appeared as words printed on the screen. Often a pianist played appropriate music in the cinema. 'Talkies' appeared in the late 1920s.

🔼 *John Logie Baird was a pioneer of television.*

When did people first watch TV?

The first TV pictures were produced in 1924 by John Logie Baird, but a more effective electronic system was used for the first BBC TV service in 1936. When the television age began, very few people owned sets, and pictures were in flickering black-and-white. Today, satellite and cable networks provide hundreds of channels around the world, with thousands of hours of viewing.

Where is the centre of the movie industry?

Although the cinema was a French invention, thanks largely to the Lumière brothers, it was America that gave birth to the international movie industry. Movie-makers found that sunny California was an ideal place to shoot movies, and by the 1920s Hollywood had become 'the capital of the motion picture world', with large studios full of technicians, writers, make-up artists, costume designers, set-builders, producers and directors.

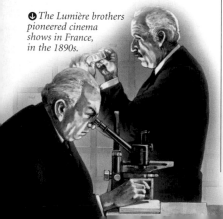

🔽 *The Lumière brothers pioneered cinema shows in France, in the 1890s.*

◀ *Modern TV cameras work in any conditions. Today, TV is the world's biggest medium for information and in-home entertainment.*

The Hollywood sign on the hill tells visitors they have reached the heart of 'movieland'.

Where would you find someone using a clapperboard?

A clapperboard is used in a movie or TV studio to mark the beginning or end of a 'take' (a short section of movie). Movies are not usually made in the order of a story. Director, scriptwriters, camera crew and actors work on the scenes in whatever order is convenient. This might be when the star is available or when the weather is right. Several takes may be needed before a scene is filmed properly. The final takes are put together in order by an editor and, if necessary, cut to create the finished movie.

Details of each take are filled in on the clapperboard, which is held up in front of the camera before filming begins.

What is the difference between a producer and a director?

In the movie industry, a producer raises money to make a new movie and organizes the financial side, while the director is in charge of filming. The director tells the camera crews how to set up their cameras, and directs the actors to act the way the script is written. In TV, however, the producer may also act as the director: the money comes from the TV company who is making the series or programme.

Alfred Hitchcock, director and master of suspense, made a cameo appearance in most of his movies.

Special effects, such as those used in the Matrix (US 2000), create excitement in a movie and allow scenes to be created that would otherwise be difficult, dangerous or impossible.

The earliest literature was oral (spoken word or song) not written. The oldest hand-printed book dates from the AD 800s, but books were not available cheaply until the invention of steam-powered printing machines in the 1800s. Paperbacks were produced from the 1930s. The most quoted writer is William Shakespeare, and the most widely read children's books of today are the adventures of Harry Potter, by British author, J. K. Rowling.

What is an illuminated manuscript?

A manuscript, or hand-written book, was either hand-printed (using a wood block) or copied by hand by monks, who decorated the pages with beautifully coloured illuminations. Often the monks began a page with a decorated letter. Before the printing press with movable type was invented in the 1440s, monks did most of the book copying in Europe. Today, ancient illuminated manuscripts, such as the *Book of Kells* and the *Lindisfarne Gospels*, are priceless treasures.

Who was the most famous fictional detective?

Sherlock Holmes, the pipe-smoking master-sleuth, created by British writer Sir Arthur Conan Doyle (1859–1930). Holmes and his friend Dr Watson solved mysteries involving mysterious dogs (*The Hound of the Baskervilles*), venomous snakes (*The Speckled Band*) and numerous robberies and murders. He was eventually 'killed off' in a final contest with his arch-enemy, the criminal genius Professor Moriarty, but was then 'reborn' by popular demand.

❷ *In* The Hound of the Baskervilles, *Sherlock Holmes investigates the mystery of the legendary hellhound of Dartmoor.*

❷ *Medieval illuminated manuscripts took such a long time to make, because they were hand-written, that they had to be treated with great care.*

Which famous novelist gave public readings of his work?

Charles Dickens (1812–70), a talented amateur actor, gave public performances of scenes from his best-selling novels. Dickens is considered one of the greatest British novelists, writing a succession of masterpieces including *Oliver Twist* (1838), *Nicholas Nickleby* (1839), *David Copperfield* (1850) and *Great Expectations* (1861).

❶ *Dickens endured hard times as a child, which he never forgot, even when he became a successful author.*

⊙ *In Lewis' imaginative story-telling, Alice meets the Mad Hatter, the March Hare and the Dormouse at a very strange tea party.*

What was Lewis Carroll's most famous work?

Alice in Wonderland. Lewis Carroll (Charles Lutwidge Dodgson 1832–98) had a shy exterior, but this English mathematician at Oxford University had a wild imagination and delighted in word play. He enjoyed telling stories to friends' children, and wrote two classic children's books: *Alice in Wonderland* (1865) and *Alice Through the Looking Glass* (1872).

➲ *Anne Frank died in a concentration camp in 1945. Her father, who survived the death camps, published her diary after the war.*

Which teenage girl kept a wartime diary?

Anne Frank, a German teenager living in hiding and in fear of her life, wrote a diary that is regarded as a moving testament to those who died in the Holocaust during World War II (1939–45). Anne's family were Jews who fled Germany to escape persecution by the Nazis. They moved to the Netherlands, but after the Germans invaded in 1940 found themselves in peril once more.

Anne, her sister, parents and four friends hid in a secret annexe at the back of an office building. She kept a diary, recording her thoughts until 1944, when the Franks and their friends were discovered and arrested.

Who were Britain's most famous literary sisters?

The Brontës were three sisters who grew up in the village of Haworth, in Yorkshire, with their brother and father, a clergyman. All three became novelists, at first sending in their work under men's names. Charlotte Brontë (1816–55) wrote *Jane Eyre*, about a governess; Emily Brontë (1818–48) wrote a passionate romance, *Wuthering Heights*, while the youngest sister Anne (1820–49) was the author of *The Tenant of Wildfell Hall*.

⊙ *The Brontë sisters (left to right): Anne, Emily and Charlotte.*

Myths are stories about gods, supernatural beings and the origins of the world. Legends are stories about heroes, strange animals and adventures, which, while not perhaps true in every detail, may be based on real events. Such stories, some very old, are told all over the world.

Who hid inside a wooden horse?

Greek warriors. The story of the wooden horse is found in *The Iliad*, a long poem by Greek poet, Homer. It tells how the Greeks and the Trojans went to war following the abduction of Helen, the wife of a Greek king, by Paris, Prince of Troy. Troy was besieged for ten years, until the Greeks brought about its downfall by a trick. They built a gigantic wooden horse, inside which warriors were concealed. They left the horse outside Troy, and the unknowing Trojans dragged it into their city. At night, the Greek warriors climbed out, opened the city gates and led the invasion on Troy.

◯ *Greek soldiers hid inside a wooden horse as a deception to overthrow the Trojans.*

◯ *According to legend, Romulus and Remus were cared for and fed by a female wolf.*

Who were Romulus and Remus?

Roman legend tells of twins named Romulus and Remus, who founded Rome in 753 BC. As babies, they were thrown into the River Tiber by a wicked uncle, but they were rescued by a she-wolf. Later, a shepherd brought them up. Remus was killed but Romulus became the first king of Rome. The Romans liked legendary explanations; the historical truth is that Rome grew from several village settlements on the seven hills upon which the city stands.

Which people told stories about Ragnarok?

The Vikings and other Norse peoples of Europe. Ragnarok, according to Norse mythology, was a battle between gods, giants and monsters who brought the end of the world. The leader of the gods, one-eyed Odin, led his warriors against his evil enemies from his great hall of Valhalla. In the slaughter, everyone died and the gods' realm of Asgard was destroyed by fire. Yet from this 'twilight of the gods' a new world was born. Two humans who hid in the branches of the World Tree, Yggdrasil, crept out to begin the life-cycle again.

◯ *The enemies of the gods rode in a ship with the terrible serpent to the last battle that ended the world.*

Who led the Argonauts?

The Argonauts, a band of 50 sailors and heroes from Greece, were led by Jason, son of King Aeson. Jason set sail on his ship, the *Argo*, to find the fabulous Golden Fleece – a golden ram's skin hung from a tree and guarded by a fearsome dragon. The Argonauts had many adventures before the arrival of Jason, with the aid of the witch Medea – they defeated the dragon and returned home with the Golden Fleece. The adventures of the Argonauts may have been based on tales told by Greek sailors, exploring the Mediterranean and Black Sea.

⊙ *One hazard encountered by Jason and the Argonauts on their voyage was the Symplegades – these were rocks that clashed together, crushing everything that passed between them.*

Who is Rama?

Rama is one of the gods in Hinduism, the predominent religion of India. He is the hero of an epic poem called the *Ramayana*, written about 2,300 years ago, in Sanskrit (an ancient Indian language often used to write scriptures). It tells how prince Rama wins Sita as his wife, but then has to rescue her from the demon-king, Ravanna, who has kidnapped her and taken her to Lanka (now Sri Lanka). Rama is helped by his brother Laksmana and an army of monkeys.

Why is Anansi the spider so popular?

Anansi is the cunning hero of West African folk tales. He is a 'trickster', living on his quick wits and duping his enemies. Slaves taken from Africa to the United States took Anansi with them, and the stories of the crafty spider probably inspired Brer Rabbit, the hero of the Uncle Remus stories.

⊙ *Hindus believe that the hero Rama was one of the ten human forms (avatars) of the god Vishnu.*

Culture is the way of life of a group of people who share certain customs, beliefs, technology and ideas. People who speak the same language may share the same culture (the Japanese, for example), but not necessarily – English is spoken by people from different cultural backgrounds. Every society has its own culture, and throughout history cultures have borrowed from one another and ideas have been communicated, shared and developed.

When was writing invented?

The earliest form of writing was created some 5,000 years ago in the ruins of Uruk, a city in Sumeria (modern Iraq). It was made by pressing a pointed tool into soft clay. The Sumerians wrote in pictograms (stylized drawings of objects). The ancient Chinese also developed a form of symbol writing using characters to stand for words. By the 1700s, there were over 40,000 Chinese characters! Compared to the 26 letters of the western alphabet, Chinese and its variants are extremely complex.

Which African people were sculptors?

The Nok people of Nigeria, in West Africa, created incredibly detailed and intricate terracotta figures more than 2,500 years ago. The Nok people and the sculptors of Benin (also in West Africa) used a method known as 'lost-wax' to cast bronze. During this process, a wax model is first made, then it is encased in soft clay or wet plaster, which hardens around it to form a mould. The mould is then heated, and the melted wax runs out of a hole, leaving a hollow inside that can be filled with molten bronze. When the bronze has set, the mould is taken apart to reveal the bronze sculpture.

⊖ *A carved head from West Africa, where craftworkers still make traditional items for the tourist trade.*

Which saint became Father Christmas?

St Nicholas, a 5th-century bishop, of whom very little is known except that he probably lived in the area of Asia Minor (modern Turkey). Legends about St Nicholas and tales of his miracles spread and he became a popular saint and Russia's patron saint. In Dutch, Nicholas was known as 'Sinter Claes', and Dutch migrants to America turned him into 'Santa Claus'. In Germany, he became 'Father January' or 'Father Christmas'.

⊙ *One of the most common legends tells of Father Christmas (Santa Claus) arriving by a sleigh that is drawn by reindeer.*

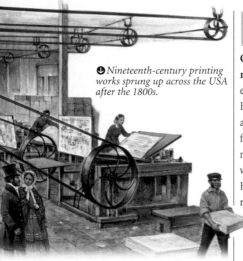

↓ *Nineteenth-century printing works sprung up across the USA after the 1800s.*

What is oral culture?

Oral culture is passed on by speech, not by being written. In this way, for example, the Celtic people of pre-Roman Britain passed on their history, folk stories and religious beliefs. There was no written form of their language. Oral cultures exist in many parts of the world, and many of the world's epic tales were told in this way. Homer's *Iliad* and *Odyssey* were told and retold by generations of Greeks before they were written down.

How did printing revolutionize culture?

In the 1440s, Johannes Gutenburg invented a screw-press that could print on paper sheets using movable pieces of type, arranged to make words. Printing made books cheaper, but it also brought in standard spellings and punctuation. Books were printed in vernacular (everyday) languages such as English, French and German, and not just in Latin. Novels, magazines and newspapers, even mail-order catalogues were all printed on machines. Knowledge was thus made more widely available to everyone.

➔ *Bards or Celtic poets sang to their lord, passing on history, and creating tales about the deeds of current heroes.*

↑ *It took 700,000 workers 40 years to build the Chinese emperor's tomb and its army of clay soldiers.*

Which emperor had clay soldiers in his tomb?

The first emperor of China, Shih Huang-di, who died in 210 BC, was buried with an army of terracotta soldiers and horses. The pharaohs of Egypt were also buried with treasures as well as everyday items. The more important the person, the more splendid the tomb. In many ancient cultures it was the custom to bury 'grave goods' with a dead person for use in the afterlife.

Snow sports originated in lands where winter snow was prevalent – skiing in Scandinavia, ice-skating on frozen canals in the Netherlands and tobogganing in the Alps. Although ancient Greeks, Romans and Polynesians swam and sailed for pleasure, organized water sports, including swimming and yacht-racing did not develop until the 19th century. Today, winter sports and water sports are included in the Olympic Games.

◐ The surf board's profile or cut determines how it surfs on the wave.

Who first stood on a surfboard?

Surfing was first enjoyed by the Polynesian islanders of the Pacific Ocean. The earliest description of someone surfing was written in Hawaii in 1779. Hawaiians used wooden boards more than 5 m long. Interest in surfing was revived in Australia and the United States, and world championships were first held in 1964.

Which is the fastest swimming stroke?

Of the four strokes in competitive swimming (breaststroke, backstroke, crawl and butterfly), the crawl is the fastest, followed by the butterfly. In competitive swimming, some races are designated 'freestyle', but all the top swimmers choose the crawl. The most widely used strokes by 19th-century swimmers were the breaststroke and sidestroke. Butterfly was officially recognized for use in racing in 1952.

What is a trimaran?

A trimaran is a sailing boat with three hulls. Trimarans and the twin-hulled catamarans were developed from the outrigger canoes used in the Pacific. Their appearance would have startled competitors in the first yacht race, between King Charles II and his brother James, Duke of York in 1661 on the River Thames. The original yachts were Dutch sailing boats.

◐ The centre hull of a trimaran has the mast and crew compartment; the two other hulls provide extra stability at high speed.

◐ All swimming strokes call for strong use of arm and leg muscles. This swimmer is using the butterfly stroke.

A waterskier can skim over the water at speeds of up to 160 km/h.

Skiers hold long sticks, called ski-poles, to help them to steer and control.

What is the difference between a kayak and a canoe?

A kayak paddler uses a two-bladed paddle, whereas a canoeist has a single-bladed paddle. Modern canoes and kayaks originated among the Native Americans and Inuit peoples of North America, who used canoes for transportation. Canoeing as a sport dates from 1866 and has been an Olympic event since 1936. In a modern canoe it is possible to turn upside down and roll upright again without coming to any harm.

The kayak paddle must hit the water at such an angle as to provide the correct stroke to propel the kayak forward.

Who was the first waterskier?

The first waterskier was an American named Ralph Samuelson who gave the first exhibition of ski jumping from a ramp in 1925. Waterskiers hold on to a tow-rope and are pulled along on water skis, which are wider than snow skis, by a motorboat. The skier does stunts, slalom turns in and out of obstacles or jumps up a sloping ramp.

When were snow skis first used?

Ancient skis over 4,000 years old have been found in Scandinavia, where people made wooden skis to get around on during the long, snowy winters. In 1843, the first skiing competition was held in Norway. Modern skis are made of plastic, metal or fibreglass, but the basic principles are unchanged: the novice skier has to learn how to start, turn, and stop. At top speed, a downhill skier can whizz along at up to over 240 km/h.

People probably first played ball games thousands of years ago. Inflated pigs' bladders were used as balls in the Middle Ages, and children used curved sticks for early versions of cricket and golf. Schools and colleges began organizing ball games as part of formal education in the 19th century, leading to the amazing growth in professional ball-sports across the world today.

➊ Baseball catchers wear protective clothing to shield against the impact of the ball.

Which team sport attracts the most spectators?

The world's most popular spectator sport is soccer, which is played and watched on every continent. Only in the USA is professional soccer not the leading team game. Soccer originated from violent medieval football games, but was organized with rules, leagues and professional teams in the 19th century. The World Cup, held every four years, is the biggest international soccer tournament. The international governing body, FIFA, was set up in 1904.

➔ Soccer is money-making entertainment, especially in Europe and South America.

How fast does a pitcher throw a baseball?

A baseball pitcher can throw the ball (which weighs 148 g) at up to 160 km/h. Baseball was first played by modern rules in New Jersey, USA in 1846, although a similar rounders-like game had been played long before this in the UK. Professional clubs first appeared in 1871 and the national league was established in 1876. The winners of the two main US leagues, the National and the American, meet every year in the seven-game World Series.

Which king played tennis?

The monarch best-known for playing tennis is England's Henry VIII who, as a young man, was an expert at real (royal) tennis, which was played on a walled court. The game later moved outside and rules for 'lawn tennis' were drawn up in the 1800s. The first Wimbledon Championship, the oldest of the 'Grand Slams', was held in 1877. The most successful men's players at Wimbledon are Bjorn Borg (five singles titles, 1976–80) and Pete Sampras (seven singles titles, 1993–2000). Martina Navratilova won her 20th Wimbledon title in 2003, equalling the women's record held by Billie-Jean King.

⬆ *Players grapple for the ball during American football, which requires them to wear padding.*

Where was golf first played?

The earliest mention of golf is in a Scottish law of 1457, banning the game. Games similar to golf were played much earlier. The oldest golf championship is Britain's 'Open', first played in 1860. The objective of golf is to get the ball into a small hole on the 'green' in as few putts as possible.

In which sport does it help to be exceptionally tall?

Basketball – very tall players can more easily send the ball into the net (basket) to score points. Basketball was invented in the USA in 1891 as an indoor winter team game. Two teams of five players try to score points by tossing the ball into the opposing team's basket. Players must not run with the ball and have time limits for passing.

Which game is played on a grid-iron?

The grid-iron is the pitch on which American football is played. Developed by university students in the 19th century, the game is a spin-off from soccer and rugby. The pitch contains lines that cross the field every 4.6 m from one sideline to the other. Two teams of 11 players compete for the Super Bowl, which is played each year by the champions of the two main leagues: the National Football Conference (NFC) and the American Football Conference (AFC).

⬇ *The ball must drop into or through basket from above to score. The ball can be bounced into the basket off the backboard.*

The first people to take running seriously and compete against one another were the ancient Greeks. Track and field athletics as we know them began in the 19th century in schools and colleges in Europe and North America. These events play a big part in the Olympic Games, and there are also regular world and regional championships. Track races and some field events can also take place indoors.

↩ *As sprinters cross the finish line, they push their heads forward so that the winner is clearly visible.*

How fast can a sprinter run?

A male sprinter can speed down the 100-m straight in about 9.8 sec – a speed of just over 40 km/h. This is slower than a horse, which can sprint at 56 km/h, or a greyhound (67 km/h), but faster than a swimmer (about 8 km/h). The 100-m sprint is the shortest outdoor race in athletics; indoor sprints are 60-m dashes.

How many hurdle races are there?

In track and field events, three races involve runners jumping over barriers called hurdles. The shortest is the 110-m hurdles race (100-m for women) in which competitors aim to stride over hurdles, which measure 107 m high for men and 84 m high for women. For both men and women, in the one-lap 400-m hurdle race the hurdles are lower. In the steeplechase, which is more than 3,000 m, athletes jump over a wooden hurdle and leap over a waterjump.

Which long jumper astonished the world?

Bob Beamon (USA) set an amazing world long jump record in 1968 at the Mexico City Olympics. The high altitude caused thin air (a lack of oxygen), making Beamon's leap of 8.9 m even more amazing. Beamon had shattered the previous world record and no jumper had ever jumped more than 8.5 m. Beamon's record lasted until 1991 when Mike Powell (USA) broke it by 5 cm.

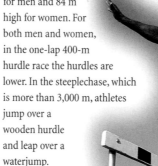

↩ *A male hurdler must jump clear of a barrier at least 1 m high.*

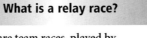

What is a relay race?

Relays are team races, played by four runners in each team. Each runner carries a baton, which must be passed to the next runner at a changeover point. The most common relays in track athletics are the 4 x 100 m and the 4 x 400 m, for both men and women. In a baton relay race, dropping the baton means the whole team is disqualified from the event.

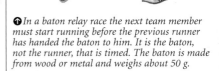

What are field events?

Field events include throwing and jumping. There are four throwing events: javelin, discus, shotput and hammer. The four jumping events are long jump, triple jump, high jump and pole vault. Pole vault athletes use a fibreglass pole to help lift themselves over a bar, which is more than 6 m high.

⊕ *A javelin thrower runs about 12 very quick strides and accelerates to 7 m/sec, gaining momentum for the throw. A throw is only valid if the javelin touches the ground with the tip first. Javelin throwing has featured in the Olympic Games since 1908.*

⊕ *In a baton relay race the next team member must start running before the previous runner has handed the baton to him. It is the baton, not the runner, that is timed. The baton is made from wood or metal and weighs about 50 g.*

⊕ *The triple jump involves three stages: a hop, a step and a two-footed jump.*

1 Gaining height

2 Gaining momentum

3 Gaining speed

4 Landing on sand with both feet as far forward as possible

The earliest sport on wheels was chariot racing, which was enjoyed by ancient Egyptians and Romans. In the 19th century, bicycles were raced, and from 1885 the motorcar and motorcycle were soon used for racing. Today, motorsport in its various forms, on purpose-built racing circuits and on roads, is followed avidly by fans across the world.

➊ *British racing champion Stirling Moss drove 84 different vehicles during his career.*

Where was the first motor race?

The first race for cars was in France in 1895. Emile Levassor won, driving his car at an average speed of just over 24 km/h. The race from Paris to Bordeaux and back covered 1,178 km. Grand Prix racing began in 1906, also in France, and is now held at circuits across the world. Today's Grand Prix cars travel more than ten times faster than in 1895.

➋ *Competitors take part in events such as indoor sprints, pursuit and time trials on steep tracks and outdoor road races.*

Which is the most famous cycle race?

The Tour de France, which was first raced in 1903. It is the biggest event for racing cyclists and takes 21 days to complete. Each stage has a separate winner but the overall winner receives the coveted yellow jersey. Cycle racing began in 1868 and the first world championships were staged in 1903. Cycling has been an Olympic sport since the first modern Olympics in 1896.

➊ *Speedway bikes have no brakes so riders must use their feet as they slide around bends, sending up showers of dirt.*

What is speedway?

Speedway, also known as dirt-track racing, is a form of motorcycle racing. Modern speedway dates from the 1920s in Australia and the first world championships were held in 1936. Unlike other forms of motorcycle racing, such as scrambling or motocross, which take place on 'natural' outdoor circuits, speedway riders compete around an oval track. During each race, which lasts for four laps, the four riders taking part slide into the tight bends.

What is the difference between a rally and a race?

During a car rally, cars set off at intervals and are timed on each section. During a race, a number of cars start in ranks from a grid and race around a circuit with bends and straights. Rallies cover several thousand kilometres and take several days to complete. They are often held across wild country: one rally is held in East Africa, another across the Sahara. The most famous rally is the Monte Carlo Rally. Car races include the Grand Prix races held in various countries, the Indianapolis 500 in the USA and the Le Mans 24-hour race in France.

Stock cars look like wrecks but keep going at full speed.

Drag racers have huge rear wheels to get them moving, and aerofoils to keep the wheels on the ground as the car accelerates.

A rally car is a modified production car, which can be driven over extremely challenging terrain, such as muddy hillsides, that tests both machine and driver.

What are stock-car and drag racing?

Stock cars are known as hot rods or old bangers, which have been modified for a crash-and-bang race around a large, speedway-sized track. Drag cars are designed to speed down a 400 m long track, at speeds of up to 500 km/h. A race lasts less than 10 sec and only two cars compete each time, until one car is left victorious. In both stock-car and drag racing, collisions are frequent and many of the cars end up looking like battered wrecks.

People have always enjoyed playing games. As town life began to develop more than 5,000 years ago, people played board games and games of chance, using dice or marked pieces, such as dominoes. The ancient Egyptians enjoyed chariot racing and wrestling, and Greek athletes took part in the Olympic Games more than 3,000 years ago. Rules for many modern games such as tennis, rugby, football and baseball were established in the 1800s. Some professional sports stars today are among the highest-paid people in the world.

Why did Romans flock to the Colosseum?

Crowds flocked to the Colosseum, a stadium in ancient Rome, to watch 'the games'. The games were not sports in the modern sense but lavish shows, during which animals and people met bloody deaths. People came to watch fights between gladiators (specially-trained fighters) or between men and wild animals. There were even mock hunts and mock sea-battles, for which the arena was flooded.

➲ Philippides ran from Marathon to Athens, then collapsed and died.

➲ In Rome's Colosseum, the spectators sat in circular tiers that rose in height around the arena, which was built like a circus ring. The structure itself was made of concrete, which was invented by the Romans.

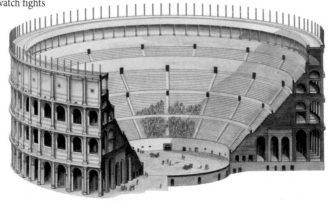

How did the Marathon race get its name?

The Marathon race takes its name from a battle in 490 BC between the Greeks and Persians on the Plain of Marathon, in Greece. After the Greek victory, a runner named Philippides ran 24 mi (38 km) to Athens, gasped 'Rejoice, we have won' and died of exhaustion. The Marathon has been set at its present distance of over 26 mi 385 yd (43 km) since 1908, and is run in various cities. Thousands of amateurs as well as top athletes take part in popular races, such as the London Marathon.

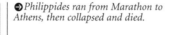

When were the first Olympic Games held?

The first Olympic Games were held in ancient Greece, in 776 BC and continued to be held there until AD 393. In 1896, the first modern Games were held in Athens, Greece, with just nine events. The Winter Olympics began in 1924. The Olympics have been held every four years since 1896, except during wartime (1916, 1940 and 1944).

Which country has the fattest wrestlers?

Japan, where sumo wrestling is practised by wrestlers of huge body weight, up to 267 kg. Sumo is at least 2,000 years old, and has strict rules and ceremonies. Being very fat is an advantage, since the object of the wrestler is to push his opponent out of the circular ring. Any hold is permitted, unlike Greco-Roman wrestling, where the wrestler cannot seize his opponent below the hips or use his legs. In freestyle wrestling, almost all moves are permitted.

⊕ *The goaltender is heavily padded during an ice-hockey game to prevent serious injury.*

⊕ *The heavier the sumo wrestler, the more strength they have to push their opponent.*

Which is the fastest team game?

In a game of ice hockey, the rubber puck can whizz over the ice at more than 160 km/h. A form of hockey on ice was played in the Netherlands in the 1500s, but modern ice hockey has its origins in 19th-century Canada. Each ice hockey team is made up of six players, and substitutes are allowed during the game, which has three periods each lasting 20 minutes.

Who first played polo?

Polo began among the horsemen of central Asia and Persia (now Iran) some 4,000 years ago. The polo 'ball' was sometimes the head of a slain enemy! Modern polo dates from the 1860s, when British army officers saw the game played in India. Polo is played on a field 274 m long by riders who wield mallets whilst mounted on ponies. The aim of the game is to score a goal by hitting a ball through the opponents' goal posts.

⊕ *Training a polo pony to twist and turn at speed takes about six months.*

1 Which trumpet-playing jazz singer was known as 'Satchmo'?

2 In which family of musical instruments are the violin, cello and guitar?

3 Which musical period came after the baroque period?

4 What kind of flowers do we associate with Claude Monet?

5 Which English artist is famed for painting swimming pools?

6 In which century was the artist Michaelangelo born?

7 Which composer began to go deaf around the year 1800, but continued writing music until his death in 1827?

FACTFILE

Piano **history**

The *pianoforte* (piano) was invented in Italy in 1709, having developed from earlier keyboard instruments such as the clavichord and the harpsicord. It inspired many great composers, including Wolfgang Amadeus Mozart, Ludwig van Beethoven and Frédéric Chopin to create some of their most beautiful compositions.

➲ *Grand pianos (such as the one shown here) are the biggest and most expensive pianos.*

Singing **sensations**

Name	Genre
James Brown (b. 1933)	Soul
Maria Callas (1923–77)	Opera
Johnny Cash (1932–2003)	Country
Ella Fitzgerald (1918–96)	Jazz
Deborah Harry (b. 1945)	Rock
Elvis Presley (1935–77)	Rock 'n' roll
Bessie Smith (1894–1937)	Blues
Britney Spears (b. 1981)	Pop

8 From which country did Charles Rennie Mackintosh originate?

9 In tailoring terms, what does 'bespoke' mean?

10 Which designer was made famous through the publication of a book entitled *The Gentleman and Cabinet Maker's Director*?

11 What name is given to the central stone of an arch?

12 What do you call the tall, decorated wooden pillars carved by Native Americans?

13 Which opera house opened in 1973 and was designed by Jørn Utzon?

14 In which Italian city did the Shakespearean merchant Antonio ply his trade?

15 Which London theatre, opened in 1871, was named after Queen Victoria's husband?

16 Is Don Alfonso a leading character in *Aida*, *Cosi Fan Tutti* or the *Barber of Seville*?

17 Which television street features the characters of Bert and Ernie?

18 Which American rock star sang "Jailhouse Rock" and "Love Me Tender"?

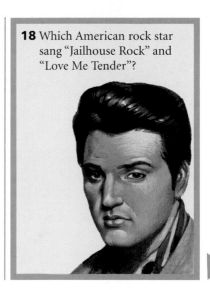

Great **composers**

Name	Date	Nationality	Name	Date	Nationality
Johann Sebastian Bach	1685–1750	German	Joseph Haydn	1732–1809	Austrian
Ludwig van Beethoven	1770–1827	German	Franz Liszt	1811–86	Hungarian
Hector Berlioz	1803–69	French	Wolfgang Amadeus Mozart	1756–91	Austrian
Johannes Brahms	1833–97	German	Alessandro Scarlatti	1660–1725	Italian
Benjamin Britten	1913–76	British	Franz Peter Schubert	1797–1828	Austrian
Frederick Chopin	1841–1904	Polish	Robert Schumann	1810–56	German
Edward Elgar	1857–1934	British	Igor Stravinsky	1882–1971	Russian
George Gershwin	1898–1937	American	Peter Ilyich Tchaikovsky	1840–93	Russian
Edvard Grieg	1843–1907	Norwegian	Giuseppe Verdi	1813–1901	Italian
George Frideric Handel	1685–1759	British	Richard Wagner	1818–83	German

19 Which play is often referred to as 'the Scottish play'?

20 What kind of animal is Disney's Dumbo?

21 What is the name of he town where Bart Simpson lives?

22 Which American author wrote the novel *The Scarlett Letter*?

23 In mythology, how many eyes did the Cyclops have?

24 Who wrote *Alice's Adventures in Wonderland* and *Alice Through the Looking Glass*?

25 In Greek mythology, Eros was the god of what?

26 Which Greek mythological hero killed the gorgon Medusa?

27 Who is the Greek goddess of love?

28 Which Italian artist painted a mural called *The Last Supper* around 1495?

29 With which art movement do you associate Salvador Dali?

30 From which art gallery was the *Mona Lisa* stolen in 1911?

31 Crouch roll and poke fall are both types of what?

FACTFILE

Key dates

Leonardo da Vinci	1452–1519	Italian painter, sculptor and architect. Famous works include the *Mona Lisa*.
El Greco	1541–1614	Spanish, painter of many religious scenes.
Rembrandt von Rijn	1606–69	Dutch master of portraits.
J M W Turner	1775–1851	English painter of mostly landscapes.
John Constable	1776–1837	English, famous for his landscapes.
Claude Monet	1840–1926	French impressionist, famous for paintings of his garden and various landscape scenes.
Vincent van Gogh	1853–90	Dutch painter of landscapes and portraits.
Pablo Picasso	1881–1973	Spanish artist whose styles included abstract Cubism.

➲ *Self-portrait by Rembrandt.*

32 Who wrote *Gulliver's Travels*?

33 Which American won seven gold medals at the 1972 Olympic Games?

34 Which of these is an alternative name for the sport of cross-country skiing: Nordic skiing or Viking skiing?

35 How often is the football World Cup held?

36 In which American sport is the Super Bowl a championship game?

37 For which national football team did Pelè play?

Modern **artists**

Alexander Calder	1898–1976	American sculptor of mobiles.
Christo	b. 1935	Bulgarian-born Belgian, famous for wrapping buildings and sections of coastline in plastic.
Salvador Dali	1904–89	Spanish Surrealist painter.
Barbara Hepworth	1903–75	British sculptor.
David Hockney	b. 1937	British painter.
Roy Lichtenstein	1923–97	American pop artist.
Henry Moore	1898–1986	British sculptor.
Piet Mondrian	1872 1944	Dutch painter of abstracts.
Andy Warhol	1928–87	American painter and graphic artist.

Salvador Dali

Andy Warhol

38 How many laps of the track are run in an outdoor 400-m race?

39 In athletics track races, what does the ringing of a bell signify?

40 Which American sprinter set a world record for the 100 m in 1999?

41 Which Frenchman was the first Formula One driver to register 50 Grand Prix wins?

42 Which Scottish driver won the Monaco Grand Prix in May 2002?

43 Irishman Stephen Roche won which sporting event in 1987?

44 Which country hosted the 2002 Winter Olympics?

45 Which martial art made its Olympic debut at the 2000 Sydney Games?

46 In 1994, which West Indian batsman scored 501 not out in one innings?

47 Which mythical bird is reborn from the ashes of its own funeral pyre?

FACTFILE

Key dates

1299 Bowling club recorded in Southampton, England.
1330 First known references to, and pictures of, hockey.
1544 Earliest mention of billiards.
1620 Mayflower pilgrims play darts.
1657 Earliest known golf match played between Scotland and England.
1744 First cricket rules were formed.

1846 First recorded baseball game under modern rules.
1860s Badminton first played.
1863 English Football Association (FA) formed.
1865 Queensberry Rules for boxing were established.
1874 Lawn tennis invented, as 'sphairistike' (Greek for 'ball').
1875 Earliest mention of snooker.
1898 First international cross-country race.

Greyhound racing is a modern version of ancient contests, such as hare-coursing, between hunting dogs. The mechanical hare was first used in 1919.

Answers

1 Louis Armstrong
2 Strings
3 Classical
4 Water Lilies
5 David Hockney
6 15th century
7 Beethoven
8 Scotland
9 Made to measure
10 Thomas Chippendale
11 Keystone
12 Totem poles
13 Sydney Opera House
14 Venice
15 The Royal Albert Hall

16 *Cosi Fan Tutti*
17 Sesame Street
18 Elvis Presley
19 *Macbeth*
20 Elephant
21 Springfield
22 Nathaniel Hawthorn
23 One
24 Lewis Carroll
25 Love
26 Perseus
27 Aphrodite
28 Leonardo da Vinci
29 Surrealism
30 The Louvre in Paris

31 Diving style
32 Jonathan Swift
33 Mark Spitz
34 Nordic
35 Every four years
36 American football
37 Brazil
38 One
39 The runners are
    on their final lap
40 Maurice Green
41 Alain Prost
42 David Coulthard
43 Tour de France
44 USA

45 Taekwando
46 Brian Lara
47 Phoenix

Amazing **olympic facts**

Record	Date	Place
First modern Olympics	1896	Athens, Greece
First women medallists	1900	Paris, France
First Winter Games	1924	Chamonix, France
First Olympic village built	1932	Los Angeles, USA
First torch-lighting ceremony	1936	Berlin, Germany
Mark Spitz wins seven gold medals	1972	Munich, Germany
Carl Lewis wins eight gold medals	1984/1992	Los Angeles, USA and Barcelona, Spain
Marion Jones wins five medals	2000	Sydney, Australia
Most events ever held (300)	2000	Sydney, Australia

An early 20th-century golf player, watched by attentive spectators in the Open Championship, which was first played in Britain in 1860.

WORLD HISTORY

History is constantly changing and being recorded, year by year, month by month, day by day. From prehistoric times to the 21st century, the written word has been one of the most important ways of passing on information. Much of what we know about ancient empires, such as Rome and Greece, is through writings people left behind.

How did the Romans come to power?

Who signed Magna Carta?

Why did the Americans declare independence?

Human beings are related to primates (monkeys and apes), and our earliest ancestors, some four million years ago, were ape-like creatures that walked upright on two legs. As these human-apes evolved, they became less like apes and more like humans. Scientists have found evidence of this from studying bones and simple stone tools that have been found. Modern humans, our direct ancestors, appeared about 100,000 years ago.

When was the earliest type of human discovered?

In 1974, the almost-complete skeleton of an *Australopithecus* female was found in Ethiopia. Scientists called the ape-like human 'Lucy'. She was no taller than a ten-year-old girl, though she was about 40 when she died three million years ago. Preserved footprints found by Mary Leakey in Tanzania proved that *Australopithecus* walked upright, like modern humans.

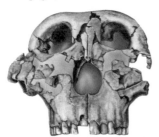

⬆ Skull of Australopithecus, *the human-like ape that walked on two legs, leaving its hands free to hold sticks or stones.*

When did people first make tools?

More than two million years ago. Remains of prehistoric people found in East Africa are accompanied by pebbles and rocks that had been flaked to make sharp cutting edges. The first tool-users have been named *Homo habilis*, which is Latin for 'handy man'. These early humans used stone tools to kill animals and to chop up meat and skins.

⬆ *Stones were flaked by chipping away the edges and were made into cutting, scraping and chopping tools.*

➲ *Stone Age people lived in caves. They used fire for warmth and cooking. The flames also gave light for artists who painted animals on the cave walls.*

How did fire change people's lives?

People began to use fire to scare away wild animals, to keep themselves warm and to cook meat. The first people to use fire were *Homo erectus*, more than 500,000 years ago. They were skilful tool-makers. They learned how to rub sticks or strike sparks from a stone to start a fire, and then how to keep the fire burning. Without fire, people could not have survived in cold lands during the ice ages.

🔊 *Hunters used fire to frighten mammoths, driving them into a pit-trap, then killing them with wooden spears tipped with stone points.*

How did people hunt mammoths?

Prehistoric people worked together to hunt animals as big as mammoths, huge relatives of the modern elephant. Groups of hunters drove the mammoths towards boggy ground, cliffs or into pits dug by the hunters, making it easier for the hunters to kill them. A mammoth provided not only meat, but also fat, skin, ivory and bones. The skins were used as clothing to keep people warm. The ivory and bones were used to make tools and framework for huts. Other animals, such as reindeer, were also hunted for their hides, bones and antlers.

What are barrows?

Barrows are ancient burial places, usually an underground chamber made of wood or stone, covered with soil and turf. The word 'barrow' comes from an old English word meaning mound or hill. Other names you might see on a map are 'tumulus', 'tump' or 'how' – these are barrows too. There are as many as 40,000 barrows in England. Most barrows are sausage-shaped, with one end higher than the other, and date from Stone Age times. The largest are over 100 m long. Later Bronze Age and Iron Age barrows were often round or cone-shaped. Barrows were made by people who believed that the dead would need their possessions with them in an afterlife. At Sutton Hoo in Suffolk, England, a king of East Anglia was buried in a wooden ship beneath a barrow mound in AD 600s. This barrow was excavated by archaeologists in 1939.

🔊 *Inside a barrow was a chamber in which the body of the dead person was placed, along with some of his belongings, such as weapons, clothing and jewellery.*

Once people started to farm and live in villages, the population in certain areas began to grow. Villages grew into towns, and towns into cities. Leaders of hunting bands became chiefs of villages and towns; the strongest chiefs became kings, ruling not just their own towns but also other settlements. These rulers created the world's first empires.

Who made the first laws?

The world's first law-making king was Hammurabi, sixth ruler of Babylon, who lived about 3,500 years ago. He drew up a set of laws to govern his citizens – for example regulating trade and taxes. Hammurabi's laws were introduced to protect the weak from being oppressed by the strong. The rulers of later empires, such as Assyria, followed his example.

○ *Ashurbanipal was king of Assyria from 668 to 627 BC. He was a cruel soldier, but a lover of the arts, who built a grand palace at Nineveh.*

Who used chariots?

Chariots were used by the first armies. A chariot was a wheeled vehicle, pulled by one or two horses. It was made of wood, with two big wheels, and was very fast. The Egyptians and the Hittites from Anatolia (present-day Turkey) fought one another on chariots. Chariots were also used by nobles for dashing around the countryside and hunting wild animals, such as antelope.

Where was Babylon?

Babylon was a great city between the rivers Tigris and Euphrates, in what is now Iraq. Civilization developed close to rivers, in fertile regions where farmers could trade with their neighbours. Two of the greatest kings of Babylon were the

○ *Egyptian war chariots were drawn by a pair of horses. One man drove the chariot, the other fired a bow and arrow or hurled spears at the enemy.*

○ *Nebuchadnezzar II added new buildings to Babylon, including the Ishtar Gate, decorated with blue tiles and named in honour of the goddess Ishtar.*

law-maker Hammurabi and the conqueror Nebuchadnezzar II, who built the Hanging Gardens of Babylon as a present for his wife, Amytis, to remind her of her mountain homeland. The gardens became one of the Seven Wonders of the World.

What were the first towns like?

The first towns were walled, and the houses were built of mud-brick. Two of the oldest towns we know about, because they were uncovered by archaeologists, are Jericho in Israel and Çatal Hüyük in southern Turkey. People lived in these towns over 10,000 years ago. All that remains of the towns now are ruins, but archaeologists have found pottery, textiles and fragments of walls, both plastered and painted.

Who made the first writing?

The earliest form of writing, dating from about 3,500 BC, comes from a region of Iraq, which in ancient times was called Sumeria. The Sumerians founded cities, such as Eridu, Uruk and Ur, all over Mesopotamia. They wrote on clay tablets with pointed tools, at first making picture-signs but then writing in symbols that represented sounds.

⬆ *Sumerian writing tools made wedge-shaped marks. The writing is called cuneiform, from the Greek word meaning 'wedge'.*

⊙ *The houses in Çatal Hüyük had no outside-facing doorways. People entered through holes in the roof – this security system kept out unwanted enemies.*

The ancient Egyptians lived beside the River Nile in Africa. In about 3100 BC, a king called Menes united two kingdoms, Upper and Lower Egypt, and established the first royal dynasty (ruling family). Later kings of Egypt were worshipped as gods. The Egyptians were great architects and artists, and developed an amazing system of picture-writing, known as hieroglyphics. Their empire lasted for almost 3,000 years.

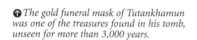

↑ The gold funeral mask of Tutankhamun was one of the treasures found in his tomb, unseen for more than 3,000 years.

Who was Tutankhamun?

Tutankhamun, pharaoh of Egypt, was only 18 when he died in 1351 BC. Later Egyptian kings were called pharaohs. His tomb, in the Valley of the Kings (not inside a pyramid) contained the most amazing treasures (because unlike other tombs it had not been robbed by thieves). Tutankhamun's tomb was opened by an archaeological team led by Howard Carter in 1922.

Why did the Egyptians build pyramids?

Pyramids were tombs built to guard the bodies of dead kings, along with their treasures. The first pyramid was built as a tomb for King Djoser of Egypt in the 2500s BC. This 'Step Pyramid', about 60 m high, was designed by Imhotep, the king's physician. Larger pyramids were built for later kings and some 80 pyramids still stand.

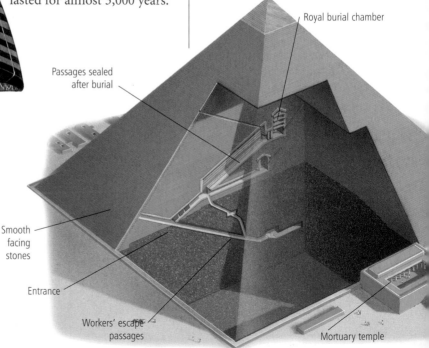

Royal burial chamber

Passages sealed after burial

Smooth facing stones

Entrance

Workers' escape passages

Mortuary temple

What gods did the Egyptians worship?

The Egyptians had many gods. People worshipped local gods in their own city or region. The greatest local god was Amun, the Sun god Ra or Re. Other gods included the cat-headed Bast, Thoth, god of learning, Osiris, god of farming and civilized life, Isis, the mother-goddess, her son Horus, god of heaven, and Anubis, god of the dead.

🔻 *The Nile was Egypt's lifeline, a green strip of civilization next to desert on either bank. People used reed boats to sail up and down the busy river.*

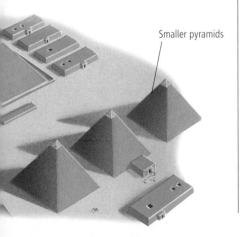

◀ *Two of the three Great Pyramids at Giza are over 130 m high. These amazing feats of engineering were built in the 2600s BC, by thousands of slaves hauling blocks of stone.*

Smaller pyramids

Why was the Nile so important to the Egyptians?

The Nile is the longest river in Africa, and its waters made farming possible for the people of hot, dry Egypt. Every year the Nile floods, as snow melts in mountains to the south, raising the level of the water. As it floods, the river spreads fertile mud over the land, which enabled Egypt's farmers to grow plentiful crops. They dug irrigation ditches to carry the Nile water to their fields. The Egyptians also used some of the world's earliest boats, called 'feluccas' to sail up and down the Nile to travel between neighbouring farms and towns.

➡ *Ramses II was a great warrior-king, whose soldiers fought to defend and enlarge Egypt's empire.*

Who was the greatest warrior-king of Egypt?

Ramses II who reigned 1289–24 BC. Ramses led the Egyptian army into battle against the warmongering Hittite people, and in 1275, fought a great battle with them at Kadesh for control of Syria. Ramses built a huge temple at Abu Simbel beside the Nile. Outside this rock temple were huge statues of the great king. His temple was moved in the 1960s when the Aswan Dam flooded its original site.

Civilizations, with towns, agriculture, laws and flourishing trade, developed in several parts of the world at roughly the same time. As well as the great cities of Egypt and Mesopotamia, other civilizations arose in the Indian subcontinent and in China. Like the earlier ones, these civilizations were first developed alongside rivers.

When did the Indus civilization flourish?

Between 2500 and 1500 BC. It emerged along the Indus River in what is now Pakistan. The Indus Valley civilization was larger than Sumer or ancient Egypt. Why this prosperous civilization came to an end is a mystery, but floods and foreign invaders may have helped bring about its downfall.

⊕ *The peoples of the Indus Valley lived as farmers and traders. Their two great cities were Harappa and Mohenjo-Daro.*

⊕ *The houses in Mohenjo-Daro were built around a central courtyard. The walls were made using mud-bricks that had been baked in a kiln. The houses all had a flat roof. The streets were straight and crossings were at a right angle, creating a grid system similar to that found in many modern cities.*

Where was Mohenjo-Daro?

This was one of the two great cities in the ancient Indus Valley. The name Mohenjo-Daro means 'Mound of the Dead'. The city was set out in a neat grid pattern with 40,000 people living in houses of mud-brick with bathrooms linked to the city drains, and a large bathhouse – which may have been used for public bathing during religious ceremonies. The other major city of the Indus region was Harappa.

The Great Wall was built mainly during the Qin dynasty (221–206 BC). Its total length was over 2,400 km.

What are Chinese junks?

Chinese sailing ships, which had sails made of woven matting, which looked like 'venetian' window blinds and were simple to operate. Some junks had five or more masts and were bigger than any western ships. For steering, Chinese sailors used the stern rudder – long before it was known in Europe. Chinese ships sailed as far as Arabia, East Africa and Indonesia, and it is likely that Chinese explorers investigated the north coast of Australia. Such voyages increased trade and made the emperor feel more powerful, but the Chinese did not set up permanent trading posts in foreign countries, as European explorers did from the late 1400s. Fleets of junks were used by pirates to ambush merchant ships in the South China Sea and the Indian Ocean.

Chinese pirates such as Ching-Chi-Ling and Shap-'ng-tsai sailed in a fleet of junks. The South China Sea was perfect for pirates with its many small islands, swamps and narrow channels, in which ships could hide.

When did people first work with iron?

About 1500 BC, when the Hittites of the Near East began smelting iron ore (heating iron-bearing rock to extract the metal). People only had stone tools until around 7000 BC, when the Hittite people in Anatolia (present-day Turkey) started using copper. Later, people invented bronze (an alloy or mixture of copper and tin), but iron was harder, sharper and long-lasting.

The Zhou rulers, who ousted the last Shang king in 1122 BC, introduced iron tools and weapons to China.

Why was the Great Wall of China built?

To protect the Chinese empire from foreign invaders. China had built a great civilization, beginning with the Shang rulers (about 1500–1027 BC). The first ruler to control all China was the emperor Shih Huang-di (221 BC). His greatest project was the Great Wall – not only did it keep out barbarians from the steppes of Central Asia. it also kept in the Chinese people.

Greek civilization grew out of the earlier cultures of Minoan Cretians and the Myceneans – a race of people who lived in what became Greece. By about 800 BC, the ideas of Greek scholars started to spread throughout the ancient world. Ancient Greece was divided into small, self-governing city-states – the most powerful of which were Athens and Sparta.

Who were the greatest Greek philosophers?

Socrates, Plato and Aristotle – their ideas have influenced people over the last 2,400 years. First came Socrates (470–399 BC), who taught the importance of truth and virtue – he was forced to kill himself by his enemies. His friend and pupil Plato (427–347 BC), founded a school, the Academy in Athens. Aristotle (384–322 BC) was a student at the Academy and later also started a school, the Lyceum in Athens.

⬅ *Aristotle came from northern Greece. He wrote about science, politics, art and religion.*

Why was Alexander so Great?

Alexander conquered a vast empire and became ruler of Macedonia, in northern Greece, in 336 BC. He founded cities such as Alexandria in Egypt. Alexander had ferocious energy: after defeating the Persians he set out to conquer India. He would have gone on marching across India had his exhausted soldiers not begged him to turn back. Alexander died in 323 BC, aged 32.

What was the Trojan War?

The Trojan War was a ten-year war and the story is told by Greek poet Homer in his poem, the *Iliad*. Mainland Greece was dominated by warriors called the Mycenaeans from 1600–1100 BC. Homer's poem tells how the Myceneans destroyed Troy, a fortress-city in the region known as Asia Minor, about 1,200 years ago. The Greek army tricked their way into Troy, pretending to give up the siege and head home. Instead they hid soldiers inside a wooden horse, which the Trojans then took into their city. The Greeks clambered out at night and opened the gates to their army, winning the war.

⬇ *Greek hoplites (foot soldiers) wore crested helmets and carried a long spear.*

⬅ *Alexander the Great on his favourite horse, Bucephalus. He led his soldiers from Greece to India, and created a vast empire in just nine years.*

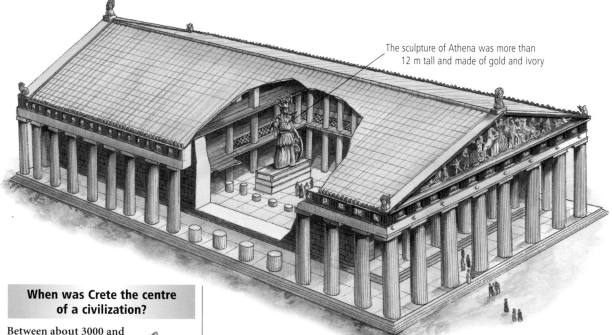

The sculpture of Athena was more than 12 m tall and made of gold and ivory

When was Crete the centre of a civilization?

Between about 3000 and 1100 BC. This period of Greek civilization is known as Minoan, after a legendary Cretian king named Minos. The remains of the royal Palace of Knossos in Crete show what a rich culture once existed there, until destroyed (perhaps by an earthquake) in the 1400s BC. The palace was rediscovered in 1899 by British archaeologist Arthur Evans in 1899.

↑ *The Parthenon was badly damaged in 1687 when in Turkish hands. The temple was once decorated with painted figures and friezes. Made from beautiful white marble, it is one of the best examples of Greek architecture.*

↩ *According to legend, the Greeks had to send seven girls and seven boys to Crete as sacrifices to a bull-headed monster called the Minotaur.*

What was the Parthenon?

The Parthenon was the most splendid temple in Athens, which was the leading city-state in ancient Greece. During the 400s BC, the Athenians built temples and shrines to the gods on a hill called the Acropolis. The Parthenon was more than 70 m long and about 18 m high, and was built to house a magnificent statue of Athena, goddess of wisdom and guardian of Athens.

The Roman Empire was the greatest the world had so far seen. By the first century AD, Roman rule extended over much of Europe, North Africa and the Near East. The Romans took their way of life and government wherever they went. They used their skills of developing central heating and running water and introduced their food and their language (Latin) to each country they conquered.

How did the Romans come to power?

The Romans were originally farmers from central Italy who rose to power by fighting their neighbours. They developed the city of Rome, erecting grand buildings and temples and eventually ruling all Italy. After conquering Greece, the Romans adopted many Greek customs and gods. Originally a republic, Rome became an empire in 27 BC, under the rule of Augustus.

⬆ *Coin of the first Christian emperor of Rome – Constantine the Great (AD 275–337).*

When was Rome founded?

According to legend, Rome was founded by Romulus and Remus in 753 BC. The Romans enjoyed the story, but actually Rome grew up from a cluster of tribal villages on seven hills beside the River Tiber. It was first ruled by kings, but became a republic in 509 BC when the last king of Rome was driven out. Roman society was divided into citizens and non-citizens, or slaves, who did all the heaviest work.

⬅ *Slaves might have been servants, miners, farmworkers, artists or even teachers.*

Why was the Roman army so powerful?

The Roman army was well trained and better disciplined than the enemies it faced. The best Roman units were the legions of about 5,000 foot-soldiers, who went into battle throwing spears and then rushed in behind their shields using short, stabbing swords. Roman soldiers were trained to march all day, build roads and forts, and swim rivers. Roman officers were usually politicians.

Armour

Kit on a pole

Curved shield

Javelin or throwing spear

Short sword

⬆ *A Roman soldier would march holding his javelin, sword and shield. His kit, tools and rations were tied to a pole over his shoulder.*

What was a villa?

The Roman villa was a country house of a farm-estate, which produced grain, wine, meat, fruit and vegetables for the local people. Some villas were grand houses, with painted walls, baths and underfloor hot-air central heating. Rich Romans built themselves country and seaside villas as holiday homes.

↑ A Roman villa was a working farm. The family lived in the main house. The farm workers lived in smaller buildings on the farm.

◗ Soldiers did the digging and stone-laying. Most Roman roads were straight, paved with stones and cambered (sloped) so that rainwater drained off.

↑ Gladiators would fight in an arena filled with thousands of spectators. The netman would try to entangle his opponent in the net.

What was a netman?

A Roman gladiator, trained to fight in the arena. Roman rulers staged lavish and often bloodthirsty entertainments to keep the people amused. Gladiators fought one another or wild animals. There were various types of gladiator – the netman wore hardly any armour, and his weapons were a net and a trident (three-pointed spear).

Why did the Romans build roads?

Roman roads were built by the army to make sure that troops on foot and supplies in wagons pulled by oxen and horses could be moved quickly around the Empire. The Romans were excellent engineers and surveyed the route for a new road with great care, ensuring that the roads they built linked all parts of their vast empire to Rome. They also developed concrete, which was used in road building. Roman roads were built to last and many can still be seen today.

The prehistory of Britain began when the British Isles were joined to the rest of Europe by land, and when the climate was very different. In warm spells, much of southern Britain enjoyed a near-tropical climate. Most of the land was covered by snow and ice during the Ice Age. As people arrived in waves, they settled and began altering the wild landscape.

⬆ *The first people to settle in the British Isles lived by hunting and fishing, and by gathering wild plants and fruits. They made tools from stone and bone.*

Who were the first Britons?

The first people to live in Britain were *Homo erectus* **people, an early type of human, who reached Britain by walking across what is now the English Channel.** After the Ice Age, a 'bridge' of dry land linked Britain to mainland Europe. People started to settle in Britain about 500,000 years ago. The first 'modern' people arrived about 30,000 years ago.

When was Stonehenge built?

Stonehenge, a group of ancient stones in Wiltshire, England, was built in three stages, beginning about 3100 BC. Some of the stones, called bluestones, were brought from Wales, a distance of 385 km. The last stages were completed about 1300 BC.

Stonehenge was almost certainly built for ceremonial reasons, where religious rituals could be held. People also used the circle of stones to help them fix dates by studying the Sun and stars.

⬇ *Building Stonehenge, using muscle power alone, was an immense undertaking. The stones form England's most famous ancient monument.*

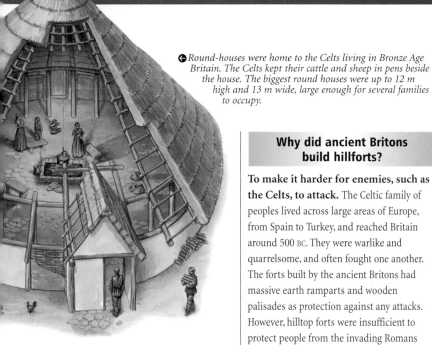

Round-houses were home to the Celts living in Bronze Age Britain. The Celts kept their cattle and sheep in pens beside the house. The biggest round houses were up to 12 m high and 13 m wide, large enough for several families to occupy.

Why did ancient Britons build hillforts?

To make it harder for enemies, such as the Celts, to attack. The Celtic family of peoples lived across large areas of Europe, from Spain to Turkey, and reached Britain around 500 BC. They were warlike and quarrelsome, and often fought one another. The forts built by the ancient Britons had massive earth ramparts and wooden palisades as protection against any attacks. However, hilltop forts were insufficient to protect people from the invading Romans in AD 43.

What was a Celtic home like?

The Celts were farmers and their homes were round houses, as big as 10 m across, with room for several families. The roof was made of timber, covered with thatch. The walls were made of woven branches (wattle) plastered with mud and animal dung. On a central hearth burnt a fire over which people cooked food in large iron pots. It was dark and smoky inside because there were no windows and no chimney to let out smoke from the fire.

How did the Celts go to war?

The Celts wore very little armour when they went to war. Some men even fought naked. Most Celtic warriors were taller than many Europeans, which helped intimidate the enemy. They dashed into battle in chariots, dismounting to fight. Warriors shouted and blew horns and trumpets as they went into battle. Afterwards, the survivors would boast of their bravery in songs and poems.

A Celtic warrior, with spiky hair and colourful trousers, armed with sword and shield was a fearsome enemy to go into battle against.

The Romans brought peace and prosperity to Britain. However, Britain was always on the fringe of the Roman Empire, and when the Romans withdrew their troops to help defend Rome itself, Britain was defenceless against attacks from across the sea. Waves of new invaders, such as Saxons and Vikings, arrived and over the years settled to become the English.

➡ *When the Roman army withdrew, many Saxons landed in Britain, seeking land to farm as well as plunder, because their own lands had become overcrowded.*

Which queen fought the Romans?

Boudicca (sometimes called Boadicea), who was queen of a tribe called the Iceni. She and her people lived in what is now East Anglia. When the Romans invaded Britain in AD 43, they quickly conquered the south of the country. In AD 60–61, however, the Iceni rose in revolt against the Romans. The Iceni destroyed London, Colchester and St. Albans, but then were defeated by the Romans. More than 80,000 Britons were killed. Rather than be captured and taken to Rome, Boudicca killed herself.

⬇ *Boudicca led a revolt following ill-treatment by Roman officials.*

What were the forts of the Saxon Shore?

The 'forts of the Saxon Shore' were built to guard the southern coast of Britain and keep out invaders. Until the early 400s when the Roman empire started to crumble, the Romans ruled Britain as far north as Hadrian's Wall. When Britain was raided by Saxons and other Germanic peoples, from mostly Denmark and northern Germany, the forts were not enough to keep out the invaders. By AD 410, the Roman army had left the Britons to defend themselves.

How did Christianity reach Britain?

The Romans brought Christianity to Britain. Celtic monks founded monasteries and took Christianity to Scotland and northern England. When Roman rule collapsed, Christian Britons in the south fled to escape the pagan (those who believed in many gods) Saxons. In AD 597, the Pope in Rome sent Augustine to teach the Saxons (the 'English') about Christianity. Augustine converted King Ethelbert of Kent, and founded a church at Canterbury.

⊕ *This mosaic of Jesus from a Roman villa in Dorset was made in the AD 300s. It shows that the people who lived there were Christians.*

Where was the Battle of Clontarf?

This was a battle fought in Ireland in 1014, between the Irish high king Brian Boru and the Vikings. Viking raiders had made Dublin one of their key bases in the British Isles. In the battle, the Irish king was killed but his army won and ended Viking power in Ireland.

Which English king led the fight against the Vikings?

Alfred, king of Wessex. Viking attacks on England began in AD 789 and by the AD 870s the raiders from Scandinavia controlled much of eastern England. Alfred won a victory at Edington in Wiltshire in AD 878, after which the Vikings made peace and agreed to stay within an area that became known as the Danelaw. Alfred was a wise ruler, and well deserved his title: Alfred the Great.

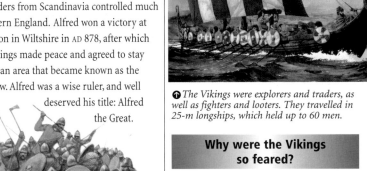

⊕ *The Vikings were explorers and traders, as well as fighters and looters. They travelled in 25-m longships, which held up to 60 men.*

Why were the Vikings so feared?

The Vikings were fierce fighters who arrived suddenly from the sea to raid towns and monasteries. They stole valuables but burnt books, for which they had no use. These bold sailors crossed the North Sea from Scandinavia to raid Britain, landing on beaches or rowing up rivers in their longships. Later, armies of Vikings ravaged the country. However, not all Vikings were bloodthirsty looters. Many brought their families to settle on farmland, or trade in towns such as Dublin and Jorvik (York).

⊙ *Irish and Viking warriors fought hand to hand at Clontarf.*

The Middle Ages are the years between the ancient world (which ends with the collapse of the Roman Empire in the AD 400s) and the start of the modern world (roughly 1500). The early centuries of the millennium were years of war and conquest across much of Europe and Asia. Only the strong countries felt safe.

The name of Mongol leader Genghis Khan (c. 1162–1227) struck terror into those who feared his army might sweep down on them.

Who was Genghis Khan?

Of all the conquerors in history, few were more feared than 13th-century Mongol leader Genghis Khan, whose name means 'lord of all'. His horsemen conquered a vast empire stretching across Asia from China as far west as the Danube river in Europe. He destroyed cities and massacred thousands, yet under his rule trade prospered and all beliefs were tolerated.

What were the Crusades?

Wars for control of Jerusalem in the Holy Land, sacred to followers of three religions: Jews, Christians and Muslims. When the Turks prevented Christian pilgrims from visiting Jerusalem, the Pope called the First Crusade in 1096. Kings, soldiers, even children from all over Europe went on Crusade. There were eight Crusades in all, but the Crusaders failed to regain control of the Holy Land.

What was feudalism?

Feudalism was a social system based on land. The king owned most of the land, though the Church was also powerful. The king let out some land (called a fief) to a lord or baron, in return for soldiers when he needed them. The barons in turn let out land to lesser lords called knights – again in exchange for service. Peasants and serfs (poor people) only lived on the land in return for the work they did for their lord.

⬆ *Medieval peasants prepared the land for the next crop. In return for their work, they were protected by their lord.*

⬇ *Muslim and Christian soldiers fought in the Holy Land. It was not all fighting – each side learned more about the other's way of life.*

Why did the Normans invade England?

Duke William of Normandy led his army to England in 1066 after King Edward the Confessor died, believing that Edward had promised him the throne. The English, however, had chosen Harold Godwinson, a soldier, to be their king. The two rivals met in battle near Hastings in 1066. William won, and so became king: 'William the Conqueror'. The Normans, who spoke French, took over lands held by English nobles, and built stone castles to defend their conquest and prevent any rebellions.

⬇ *Norman soldiers landed at Pevensey in Sussex in 1066. Knights on horseback played a key part in the Battle of Hastings.*

Who signed Magna Carta?

England's King John. Magna Carta (the Great Charter) was a list of rights requested by angry barons, who felt that John was ruling badly. In 1215, they forced the king to put his seal to (sign) the Charter and promise to obey the rules within. Ever since, Magna Carta has been seen as a landmark in the development of modern government.

⬅ *King John signed Magna Carta at Runnymede, beside the River Thames.*

People first reached North America 15,000–20,000 years ago, crossing a land bridge from Asia and travelling on foot and by boat. They gradually spread across the continent. The great civilizations of the Americas were in Central America (around Mexico) and in South America (in Peru), where people built large cities. Much of this culture was destroyed by Europeans in the 1500s.

When did 180 men conquer an empire?

When Francisco Pizarro of Spain led his men to conquer the Incas of Peru in 1532. The Spaniards found the Incas fighting a civil war. They captured the Inca ruler Atahualpa, and demanded a huge ransom in gold and silver. They then murdered Atahualpa and soon made themselves masters of the Inca empire, which stretched along most of the coast of the Pacific Ocean. The last Incas held out in the mountains in fortress towns.

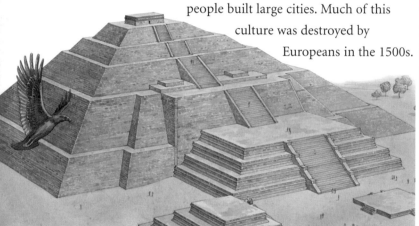

↷ The people of Ancient Mexico built temples like this one at Teotihuacan, a city at its height in about AD 500, when about 200,000 people lived there.

Who built pyramids in America?

Ancient peoples of Central America, such as the people of Teotihuacan and the Maya. The Maya were at their most powerful from about AD 200 to 900. They built cities such as Tikal (Guatemala) and huge pyramid-temples. A Maya city contained a tall pyramid-shaped temple in the centre, with special courts surrounding the temple, including ball courts for games. The Maya studied the Moon, Sun and stars, invented the first writing in America, and had a number system based on 20.

↷ Machu Picchu was the Incas' last mountain stronghold in Peru. It was unknown to outsiders until rediscovered by an American archaeologist in 1911.

Why did some Native Americans make human sacrifices?

Aztecs and some other peoples of Central America killed human victims to seek the favour of their gods. The Aztecs worshipped the Sun as the giver of life, and believed that unless they offered human victims to the Sun god their crops would fail. They thought that the hearts and blood of the victims served as food for the gods.

🡱 *A sacrificial stone knife used by Aztec priests to cut out the hearts of victims.*

What was the Aztecs' favourite game?

The Aztecs played a ball game rather like basketball. So did the Maya. The game was played in a walled court, which could be as large as 60 m long and was often next to a temple. Some historians believe the winners, not the losers, ended up being sacrificed to the gods – because they were the best!

🡲 *The object of the game was to send a ball through a stone ring in the wall. Play was very fast and players were often injured during the match.*

🡱 *The Aztec warriors' clubs and spears were no match for Spanish steel, horses and muskets.*

Who was thought of as a god by the people he attacked?

Hernán Cortés, a Spanish soldier and explorer, who landed in Mexico in 1519. The Aztecs who lived there believed that the bearded Cortés was their god Quetzalcoatl, returned to them. Their calendar told them it was a special year and so they welcomed Cortés and his small army, though they were terrified of the Spaniards' guns and horses. Within two years, Cortés had conquered Mexico.

This was an age of Renaissance – new ideas, discoveries, art and religious beliefs. European explorers set sail across the oceans, landing in America and also sailing around Africa to India and China. Art and science were changing, and so was people's approach to religion. The new ideas of the age changed the way people saw themselves and the world.

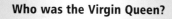

❯ Columbus had three ships – the Santa Maria, Nina and Pinta. Columbus persuaded King Ferdinand and Queen Isabella of Spain to pay for his voyage.

Who won the Battle of Agincourt?

England's King Henry V won this battle in 1415 and claimed he was the rightful King of France. Henry led his army across the English channel and defeated a larger French army at Agincourt. The French king allowed Henry to marry his daughter and made him his heir. But Henry died in 1422, and never became king of both England and France. After his death, the English lost most of their gains in France.

Why was Columbus confused?

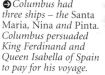

In 1492, Italian sailor Christopher Columbus believed he had reached Japan or China, when he had in fact discovered the 'New World'. Columbus had persuaded the King and Queen of Spain to finance a voyage to Asia, and his plan was to sail not east but west. Unfortunately, the map he had showed a very narrow sea, rather than the wide Atlantic Ocean, and it made no mention of America, which was unknown to geographers in Europe.

◀ French knights rode towards the small English army at Agincourt, only to be assailed by arrows from Henry V's archers.

Who was the Virgin Queen?

Elizabeth I, who became England's ruler in 1558. She was the daughter of King Henry VIII and his second wife, Anne Boleyn. Female rulers were expected to marry and many kings and princes stepped forward as potential husbands for Elizabeth. However, despite pressure from her ministers to marry and produce an heir to the throne, Elizabeth was reluctant to share her power and knew that marrying a foreign prince would make her unpopular. So she remained unmarried, and when she died in 1603, her Scottish nephew King James VI (1566–1605) became King James I of England.

Who sent the Armada to England?

King Philip of Spain, who ruled over the most powerful country in Europe in the 1500s. Catholic Philip wanted to make Protestant England Catholic, too. In 1588, he organized a huge invasion fleet, called the Armada, to overthrow England's queen, Elizabeth I. The Armada was supposed to land a Spanish army in England, but it was attacked by the English navy and then driven north by storms. The great Armada failed.

Many Armada ships were wrecked on the long voyage home around Scotland and Ireland.

Elizabeth I (1533–1603) gave her name to the Elizabethan Age.

Who destroyed England's monasteries?

King Henry VIII, who reigned from 1509–47. Henry argued with the Pope in Rome over the issue of his divorce from his first wife (he married six times). The Catholic Church was facing Protestant 'reformers' who called for 'Reformation' – changes in the Church. Henry remained Catholic, but in order to get his divorce he made himself head of the Church in England, closing down the Catholic monasteries in England. Church lands were given to the king's supporters. Even so, Henry kept his title: 'Defender of the Faith', given him earlier by the Pope.

King Henry VIII's men, sent in by the king's minister Thomas Cromwell, looted monasteries in the 1530s and seized their treasures.

Scientists used new technology to explore the wider universe and their new ideas were spread by the invention of printing. From 1700, the world entered an age of revolution, and political and economic change. By 1800, France had deposed its king, the American colonies had become the United States and the Industrial Revolution had begun.

● *Cook took with him scientists and artists to study and record the plants, animals and people of the Pacific lands.*

What caused the English Civil War?

The civil war in England was caused by a quarrel between King Charles I and his Parliament over royal power, religion and taxation. The war was fought between 1642 and 1651. The Parliamentary Army defeated the Royalists, and Charles was executed for treason in 1649. His son tried to regain the throne but was defeated in 1651, though he was eventually restored as King Charles II in 1660.

Where did Cook voyage?

James Cook (1728–79) was an English navigator who made three epic voyages to the Pacific Ocean. He explored the coasts of Australia and New Zealand, and reached the edges of Antarctica. Cook was killed by islanders in Hawaii.

When was London almost burnt down?

In 1666, when a fire in one of the city's old medieval buildings spread so rapidly that thousands of homes went up in flames. London had no proper firefighting service, so there was little people could do except run away, though attempts were made to blow-up houses to make a 'firebreak' so the fire would stop spreading.

● *In the Civil War battles, cavalry rode on horses, while foot-soldiers brandished long spear-like weapons called pikes.*

Who was Clive of India?

Robert Clive commanded the British East India Company, which fought against French rivals in India during the 1700s. From 1600, English, Dutch and French merchants competed to control trade between Asia and Europe. As a result of Clive's victories during the conflict, the Mogul emperor of India lost much of his power to the East India Company, which ruled India until 1857.

➊ *English redcoats fought Highlanders at Culloden, the last battle of the 1745–46 Jacobite rebellion.*

What was the Battle of Culloden?

Fought in April 1746, in Scotland, it was the last stand of Charles Edward Stuart or 'Bonnie Prince Charlie', to restore the Stuart monarchy in Britain. His Highland army attempted to overthrow King George II, but it was beaten by the English army, which had more men (9,000 against 5,000). Bonnie Prince Charlie fled into the hills before eventually escaping by ship to France. The Stuarts' hopes of regaining the throne had ended.

➋ *War elephants were ridden during the Battle of Plassey in 1757, won by Clive and the East India Company army.*

Why did the Americans declare independence?

The American colonists were fed up with being taxed without having a say in the British Parliament. In 1775, Britain and its American colonists went to war. In 1776, during the war, the Americans declared themselves independent, creating the United States of America. With the help of the French, the Americans won the war in 1783, under the leadership of General George Washington, who was later elected President of the USA.

➋ *The Green Mountain Boys were American soldiers of the revolution, who captured the British fort on Lake Champlain.*

The Industrial Revolution was just one of several great changes in the 1800s. This was an age of factories, railways, steamships and fast-expanding cities in Europe and North America. European powers 'scrambled' to seize colonies in Africa, and the fast-growing United States became the youthful giant on the world scene. There were amazing advances in technology too.

What was the Industrial Revolution?

The Industrial Revolution was a great change that began in Britain in the mid 1700s. People began moving to towns to work in factories, inside which were new machines driven by water and steam. By the 1830s, steam railways were carrying raw materials, coal and finished goods to the new iron steamships in the docks.

During the Victorian era in Britain, many people moved from their rural homes to work in factories and live in houses close by.

Who was Napoleon Bonaparte?

Napoleon (1769–1821) was an officer in the French army. Born on the island of Corsica, he was a supporter of the French Revolution and won many battles, though he failed to defeat the British with their strong navy. In 1799, he seized power in France, making himself emperor in 1804. He invaded Russia in 1812 but it was a disaster. Finally defeated in 1815, he died in exile six years later.

Napoleon was an infamous general, leading his army to conquer much of Europe.

Why did Napoleon fight at Waterloo?

Napoleon's enemies joined forces to meet him at Waterloo (in Belgium) on 18 June 1815 after he had given up the French throne the year before. He had left France for the island of Elba, but he was soon back, rallying his veteran soldiers for one last campaign. He was defeated by the combined armies of the English Duke of Wellington and the Prussian Marshal Blücher. He was exiled to the island of St Helena, in the Atlantic Ocean.

Which war split the United States?

The American Civil War (1861–65), which was fought over the issue of slavery. The Northern states and President Abraham Lincoln, elected in 1860, opposed slavery. The Southern states wanted to keep black slaves to work on plantations and tried to break away, splitting the nation, and so began a bitter civil war. Five days after the war ended, Lincoln was assassinated.

◉ Union (Northern) soldiers were called 'Yankees', Confederate (Southern) soldiers were known as 'Rebs'.

◉ British troops fired on the advancing French during the Battle of Waterloo.

◉ Custer and his men were outnumbered by the Native Americans, who won this battle. However, the Native Americans eventually lost the Indian Wars.

Where was Custer's last stand?

George Armstrong Custer (1839–76), made his last stand at the Battle of Little Bighorn in June 1876. From the 1840s, settlers headed west across America crossing the territories of the Plains Indians. The US Army was ordered to keep the peace and had to move tribes onto reservations. Some Native American leaders fought against this. General Custer, commander of the 7th Cavalry, split his force and led about 210 men against 2,000 Native Americans, mostly Sioux and Cheyenne, across Montana Territory. Custer and all his men were killed and the wars continued until the 1890s.

The 20th century saw two terrible world wars, an economic depression that brought unemployment to millions, and revolutions and fights for independence in countries ruled by colonial powers. It was the century of flight, of the cinema and television, of computers and traffic jams, of spaceflight and social change, equal rights and globalization – the spread of 'mass culture' to almost every country.

Why was the First World War the first modern war?

The First World War (1914–1918) was fought with new weapons that changed the nature of warfare. These weapons, such as artillery, machine guns, barbed wire, poison gas and aeroplanes meant that it was unlike any previous war. Millions of men got bogged down in trench warfare. In just one battle, the Somme (1916), more than one million soldiers were killed.

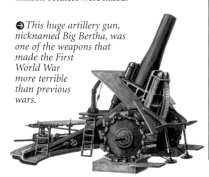

This huge artillery gun, nicknamed Big Bertha, was one of the weapons that made the First World War more terrible than previous wars.

How did warfare develop after the First World War?

The Second World War (1939–45) was more costly than the first. Few countries escaped the fighting between the Allies and the German–Japanese forces. Aircraft dropped bombs on cities. There were new weapons, such as flying bombs and rockets, and finally the atomic bombs dropped on Japan in August 1945. Later in the 20th century, smaller wars were fought in Korea (1950–53), Vietnam (1957–75), the Middle East (1948, 1956, 1967, 1973) and the Gulf (1991, 2003).

What was the Great Depression?

The Great Depression was a financial crisis that struck the developed world in the 1930s. After the New York Stock Market 'crash' of 1929, banks and businesses closed and millions of people lost their jobs. Thousands of families lost their homes because they could not afford to pay the rent, and many people lost their savings. Panic spread to Europe, where factories laid off workers. The world's economies only started to recover from the late 1930s.

Jobless men marched from Jarrow in north-east England to London, to protest at unemployment during the Depression.

Why was the United Nations set up?

The United Nations was set up in 1942 as a measure to resolve the terrible global conflict of the Second World War (1939–45). In the 1930s, a body called the League of Nations had failed to stop Germany's Adolf Hitler, and war had started. In 1945, leaders and representatives from 50 countries drew up the United Nations Charter at a meeting in San Francisco, USA. The charter was based on proposals made by China, Britain, the USA and the Soviet Union.

⊕ *Polish workers rallied behind the banner of their Solidarity trade union, which opposed the Communist government in the 1980s.*

⊕ *Fifty countries signed the charter on 26 June 1945. Poland signed it shortly after, making the first 51 Member States of the UN.*

What is Communism?

Communism is a social structure that, in theory, sets out to create a society of shared wealth and power. In 1917, a group of Communist rebels called the Bolsheviks turned imperial Russia into the Soviet Union. But by the late 1980s, Communism was failing. Factories were inefficient, people had little freedom and living standards were low. Many people wanted change, and across Eastern Europe Communist governments were removed. The Soviet Union broke up. Only China, Cuba and North Korea remain Communist.

What was the Cold War?

The Cold War was a time of suspicion between the USA and its allies, and the Soviet Union, China and other Communist countries. It began after the end of the Second World War in 1945. Each side distrusted the other, and each developed weapons of mass-destruction, such as hydrogen bombs. In the 1980s, more trade and the gradual collapse of Communism in most countries helped end the Cold War.

⊕ *During the Cold War, both sides held huge stocks of missiles and nuclear warheads, such as this US Minuteman missile.*

1 What is a long barrow?

2 What name was given to Celtic priests?

3 Odin was the chief god of which race of people?

4 What did the ancient Egyptians use to sweeten food before the discovery of sugar?

5 Was the Egyptian pharaoh Tutankhamun buried in a pyramid?

6 Which empire was conquered by Pizarro?

7 Which ancient civilization worshipped gods called Isis, Osiris and Horus?

FACTFILE

The name Homo habilis means handy man. This era of humankind was so named because of its ability to use tools.

Key **dates**

All dates are approximate and refer to the number of years ago.

4,000,000	First known hominid, *Australopithecus*, appeared.	**100,000**	A new type of *Homo sapiens* evolved. Known as *Homo sapiens sapiens*, this species is the one to which all modern humans belong.
2,000,000	*Homo habilis* evolved, and made tools.		
1,500,000	*Homo erectus* (first hominid to walk completely upright) evolves.	**33,000**	Neanderthals died out.
		13,000	Clay pottery is first made.
500,000	*Homo erectus* learned to use fire.	**10,000**	Farming began.
		7,000	First copper tools made.
120,000	Neanderthal people appeared.	**5,000**	First bronze tools made.
		3,500	First iron tools made.

8 For what is an abacus used?

9 In which year were the very first Olympic Games held: 776 BC, AD 776 or AD 1000?

10 Which material was accidentally made by ancient Egyptians when they lit a fire on a beach?

11 Of which people was Genghis Khan a war leader?

12 Where was the empire ruled by Akbar the Great?

13 The Greeks invented which type of government?

14 Who fought in the arenas of ancient Rome?

15 Which major religion was founded by Prince Gautama?

16 Which Greek philosopher founded the Academy in Athens?

17 Athena was goddess of what?

18 With which Egyptian queen did Julius Caesar and Mark Antony fall in love?

19 What name did Octavius take when he first became Roman Emperor?

20 What was the Colosseum in Rome used for?

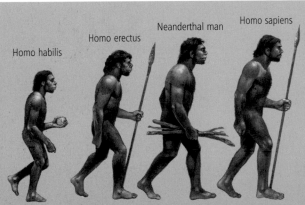

Homo habilis

Homo erectus

Neanderthal man

Homo sapiens

⊙ *Discoveries of bones have enabled scientists to name the stages of human evolution.*

⊙ *Flint was an excellent stone for making tools, and Stone Age miners dug up to 10 m deep into the ground to gather it.*

21 Fidel Castro was president of which communist country?

22 In which year did the Romans manage to successfully invade Britain?

23 About when did the Iron Age begin: 19,000 BC, 1900 BC or 190 BC?

24 Which female East Anglian leader rebelled against Roman rule in Britain in AD 122?

25 Which nation invented the wheelbarrow?

26 Which country was ruled by Kenneth MacAlpine in the AD 840s?

27 Who is the only English king called 'the Great'?

28 Which prince led the English to victory at Crécy in 1346?

29 King Richard I of England fought in which foreign wars?

30 What were the Crusades?

31 To where did a Viking named Leif Ericsson sail?

32 Which industry was revolutionized by the invention of the flying shuttle: weaving, transport or mining?

FACTFILE

Important **inventions**

The Chinese produced an amazing array of inventions in science and technology, including the abacus, acupuncture, the game of chess, the mechanical clock, eye glasses, fireworks, the flame-thrower, gunpowder, the hot-air ballon, the kite, the magnetic compass, the paddleboat, paper and paper money, porcelain and pottery, printing, the seismograph, the stern rudder, silk, the stirrup, the umbrella, the waterwheel and the wheelbarrow.

◑ The Chinese were very talented at devising water wheels turned by falling water and linked by other wheels and shafts to machinery.

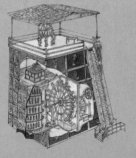

◐ The Chinese invented mechanical clocks, such the 'Cosmic Engine' – built at Khaifeng in AD 1090.

33 What was drawn up in 1806 on the orders of William the Conqueror?

34 Which explorer, who discovered America, sailed in the *Santa Maria*?

35 What sort of structures did the Incas build to worship their Gods?

36 What was the name of the first fleet sent by Spain against England in 1588?

37 A group of English Catholics conspired to blow up which London building in 1605?

38 Which English king was killed at the Battle of Bosworth in 1485?

39 Which English king did Anne Boleyn marry?

40 At which battle did the Indians defeat General Custer?

41 Which explorer was killed by islanders in Hawaii?

42 What did a man named Dunlop invent in the 1880s?

43 Who commanded the British fleet at the Battle of Trafalgar in 1805?

44 What was special about the Heinkel He-178 plane?

❶ *The 'Heaven-Rumbling Thunderclap Fierce Fire Erupter' was a gunpowder-fired device that shot out shells of poisonous gas.*

❷ *Acupuncture is a treatment still used in medicine today. It involves sticking needles into special points on the bodies of people or animals.*

❸ *In the first earthquake detector, a metal ball fell from a dragon's mouth at the top of a jar, into a toad's mouth – when even a distant quake occurred.*

45 The Battle of Hastings is recorded in which famous tapestry?

46 By what nickname was American astronaut Edwin Aldrin known?

47 With what is the inventor Charles Babbage linked: computers, medicine or balloons?

FACTFILE

Key **dates**

All dates are approximate and refer to the number of years ago.

500,000	First people settle in Britain.
230,000	Neanderthal people in Britain. First flint tools were made.
30,000	First modern humans reach Britain from mainland Europe.
15,000	Ice sheets cover much of Britain during the Ice Age.
6500 BC	Sea level rises, cutting off Britain from mainland Europe.
5000 BC	Hunters mark out tribal territories.
4000 BC	Farming people reach Britain in boats from Europe.
3100 BC	First stage of Stonehenge work.
2500 BC	'Beaker People' skilled in metalwork arrive from Europe.
750 BC	Iron Age begins in Britain.

➲ *Tin and copper were melted to make bronze, and poured into moulds to make items such as knives and mirrors.*

Answers

1 A kind of Stone Age grave
2 Druids
3 Vikings, or Norsemen
4 Honey
5 No, he was buried in a tomb
6 Inca empire
7 Egyptians
8 Mathematical calculations
9 776 BC
10 Glass
11 The Mongols
12 India
13 Democracy

14 Gladiators
15 Buddhism
16 Plato
17 Wisdom
18 Cleopatra
19 Augustus
20 Gladiator games
21 Cuba
22 AD 43
23 1900 BC
24 Boudicca
25 China
26 Scotland

27 Alfred the Great
28 The Black Prince
29 The Crusades
30 Religious wars against the Turks
31 North America
32 Weaving
33 The Domesday Book
34 Christopher Columbus
35 Pyramids or ziggurats
36 The Armada
37 Houses of Parliament
38 King Richard III

39 King Henry VIII
40 Battle of Little Bighorn
41 Captain James Cook
42 The air-filled tyre
43 Nelson
44 It was the first jet plane to fly
45 The Bayeux Tapestry
46 Buzz
47 Computers

Amazing **facts**

• Most of ancient Britain was covered with thick forest. People cut down trees to use the wood for fuel and building. Most of the ancient woodland was destroyed.

• As many as 50 people could be buried in one Stone Age tomb, called a barrow.

• A henge was a circle of posts, made from stone or wood.

• The Celts took pride in their appearance. They had tattoos, spiky hair and enjoyed wearing jewellery.

↑ *Polished metal mirrors, such as this bronze one were used before glass became widely available. Celts favoured this swirling style of decoration.*

↑ *Metal bracelets and neck ornaments, called torcs, were worn by both men and women.*

➲ *The people of ancient Britain made pots from clay, incised (cut into) with decorative patterns.*